CAMP FREE

IN THE MOUNT HOOD NATIONAL FOREST

Don Reichert

A GUIDE TO FREE CAR CAMPING AWAY FROM THE HERD

Copyright 2013 by Don Reichert
Revised edition
Cover photo from iStockphoto.com
Pictures and text by the author, except as noted
Maps by permission of National Geographic Society, Inc.
Cover and book design by Elena Cronin

All rights reserved. No part of this book may be reproduced in any form without written permission from the author.

Published by Lonesomeburger Press
PO box 83814
Portland, Oregon 97283
Lonesomeburger@gmail.com

ISBN 978-0-9889070-1-0

DISCLAIMER: This book does not claim to be an authoritative or official guide to camping in the Mount Hood National Forest. Information about camping has been gathered from many sources, including the author's own experiences and is not a substitute for the reader's judgement and common sense. Information about where to camp is as accurate as possible but is not guaranteed to be free of human error. Above all, it is the reader's responsibility to be aware of all laws and regulations governing dispersed camping, operation of motor vehicles and the harvesting of plant or animal life in the Mount Hood National Forest. The areas of cell phone receptivity listed in the book were discovered by trial and error. There is no guarantee that they will work with all cell phones.

Mt. Hood at dusk

TABLE OF CONTENTS

Acknowledgements...ii
Introduction...iii
Foreword..iv

PART I: THE "HOW TO..."

Chapter 1: Using This Book and Getting Started

- Off-season camping..2
- Rules and restrictions...2
- MVUM's and New Road Policy................................3
- Four Wheelers..4
- Recreational Vehicle Camping................................4
- Cleaning up your site – the trash plus ten percent plan..............................4
- When you witness an illegal act of dumping, 'who ya gonna call?'...................5
- Before you set up camp...5
- Disclaimer...5

Chapter 2: On Your Own in the Woods, Equipment and Practice

- Tables and Chairs..7
- Toilets..7
- Fires and Fire Rings...9
- Grates and Grills..9
- Tents...9
- Insects (and tents)...10
- Freestanding tents..11
- Sleeping bags...11
- Sleeping pads and air mattresses.........................12
- Rain shelters versus heated tents.........................13
- A word about clothing..13
- Carrying water and chopping wood (boiling water over a fire)..........................14
- Camp cookery...14
- Ice chests..14
- Five-gallon buckets (usefulness of).......................14
- Maps..15
- GPS devices..15
- Cell phones...16
- Satellite phones..16
- A list of stuff you'll need..17
- Filing a flight plan...18
- Escaping the summer heat....................................18
- Choosing a campsite..18
- More on fires...19
- Rules and guidelines..19
- Before leaving your campsite................................20

Chapter 3: Safety and Security (risk assessment)

- Are you safer in a public campground?................21
- Fire...22
- Wild Animals...22
  - Bears...22
  - Cougars...23
  - Raccoons...24
  - Mice...24
  - Insects...24
  - Ticks..24
  - Bee stings...25
- Other risk factors
  - Waterborne illness..25
  - Sanitation in camp..25
  - Drowning...26
  - Getting lost..26
  - Carelessness and lack of vigilance...................27
  - Alcohol and drug use...27
  - Random violent crime..27
  - To carry a gun or not..28
  - Exposure to toxic chemicals from a meth lab operation............................28
  - Marijuana grow operations................................28
  - Weather hazards...29
  - Lightning...29
  - Hypothermia...29
  - Dead Trees...30

PART II: THE "WHERE TO..."

HOW TO USE PART II...32

- Snagging a prime campsite near water................34
- Caveat (Inspect your site for hazards).................34
- Disclaimer...35

North Section..36
Lolo Pass Sites, FSR18, Zigzag to Lost Lake

Northeast Section..47
Barlow Pass Sites, US 26 and OR 35, from Barlow Road to Fifteenmile Campground

Central Sites...70
US 26 to FS57 and SR224, Zigzag to Ripplebrook

Clackamas West and South Sites......................111

Camp Free in the Mount Hood National Forest | i

ACKNOWLEDGMENTS

During the course of researching and writing this book, many people lent their support in the form of help, advice and encouragement.

For proofreading and editing, special thanks go to the following:

Nancy Bartholomy, Ray Cole, Louise Craft, Anke Kuindersma, Rachel Lileet-Foley, Dee Staple and Thom Rauscher.

In addition, the following deserve special mention:

- Louise Craft for the fine introduction she contributed, not to mention her assistance in editing and proofreading during the later stages of the writing.
- Ray Cole and Dee Staple for being there to bail when my boat was in danger of swamping from the pressure of deadlines.
- Gary Lofgren for his computer savvy and tolerance of my lack thereof.
- Gay Otey for giving her help in brain-storming during the concept development stage of the book, as well as her later help in proofreading and editing.
- Don Jones of High Country Explorations.com for his knowledge about cell phone reception in remote areas.
- Greg Singleton for encouraging me to think outside the glove box.
- Rick Stenson for his unfailing good humor during my two summers of field work as well as for sharing his experience and knowledge about dispersed camping, not to mention his support as a friend.
- Jeff Sullivan of Wholesale Sports for his knowledge of camp lore and the outdoors.
- Kevin Lance and others at National Geographic for technical help relating to the TOPO!©2011 Outdoor Recreation Mapping Software reproductions used in this book.
- Malcolm Hamilton, Recreational Director for the Mount Hood National Forest, not only for mucking through and treating seriously an insufferably amateurish first draft of Part I of this book, but also for his affable willingness afterwards to answer my questions relating to recreational use of the Forest, and for his guidance, which inspired me to keep to the higher ground during the book's writing.
- Andrew Coreill, Patrol Captain for the northern Oregon Law Enforcement and Investigation Section of the U.S. Forest Service for his advice on the security and safety in the Forest.
- Edwin Klaasen, USFS road engineer for helping me to understand the labyrinth of roads in the Mount Hood National Forest.

INTRODUCTION

PRIVACY, SOLITUDE, FREEDOM AT NO COST TO YOU

Are you a weekend camper, searching for respite from the heat, overcrowding, and noise of the city in summertime? Do you dream of "real camping" the old fashioned way? In this too fast-paced, helter-skelter world, do you long for the fulfillment of a true camping experience to replenish your spirit and recharge your batteries?

Have you, sadly, come to realize that using developed public campgrounds somehow defeats your purpose altogether?

Using Mt. Hood National Forest as a model, this book will serve as a treasured reference -- a Road Map -- to overcome the bottom-line-takes-all corporate management approach to our publicly-owned but privately managed National Forest campgrounds.

Whether you are a hunter, fisherman, bicyclist, RV owner, tent camper, a loner or a family unit, this book will guide you to a site where you can experience nature on your own terms, at your own pace and without the cost, constraints, rules, noise and confusion of staying in one of the tent towns that are erected every summer Friday night in public campgrounds, only to be dismantled and deserted again by Sunday night. This book will pay for itself twice over in the first weekend that you use it.

PRIVACY, SOLITUDE, FREEDOM

Let's begin our journey...

FOREWORD

It was a cool, cloudy morning in September. Coffee cup in hand, I sat under the shelter of a broad cedar tree on the shore of the Clackamas River, watching the first few drops of a light rain begin to speckle the surface of the water. The two campgrounds where I had worked all summer long as a camp host had been closed for almost a week. I had been left with the key to the gates and given permission to enjoy the place in solitude for an extra week or two as a reward for the many hours of work required of me over the summer. In a reflective mood, I began pondering the many campers I'd met throughout the summer.

Whether my campers had come for a week, a weekend, alone or in a family or other group, most had come to throw off the dreck of civilization for a time, hoping to find some solitude, solace and comfort among the ancient conifers and crystalline waters of our Mount Hood National Forest. Most had been a pleasure to meet and deal with. They understood and appreciated that I had a duty to perform, even though that duty sometimes made it necessary for me to ask them for more money for an extra car, or to interrupt their suppers to collect camping fees. Sometimes, where more people were camped in one campsite than the rules allowed, I was forced to ask families and friends to split up and rent a second campsite. There were also times when I had to remind others to observe the rules of common courtesy and respect for other campers. If there was a disturbance, it usually occurred at night in the campground across the road from where I lived in my motor home.

In the Pacific Northwest, camping is often the default vacation choice for the working class, and in the summer of 2009 it was sometimes more than evident that the camping and extra parking fees demanded by the for-profit corporation that employed me were a burden for many who in other years might not have minded. This was a summer in which many had been touched by the recession that began with the housing market collapse in 2008. Several families told me that in better times they would have taken their kids to Disneyland, but because of a lost job or an underwater mortgage, camping was now the only choice available to them.

I was also thinking of another group of people too, those who decided to go camping too late to reserve a campsite for the weekend and then arrived too late on a Friday evening to claim one of the non-reservable ones. Coming out of Portland on a Friday afternoon, they had already stopped at several of the campgrounds along the Clackamas and found them full. The disappointment and fatigue I saw in their faces when they stopped to ask me about their options were still vivid in my memory. Unfortunately, I had no immediate information about which campgrounds still had available campsites and couldn't do much more than tell them to try the next campground up the road. Sometimes I would tell them that they could camp free just off the road in many places in the National Forest, but the fact was that I couldn't really tell them specifically where to go because I was only aware of one or two nearby spots where that was possible--and those spots were usually already occupied by late Friday afternoon.

Sitting there, dry and snug under that cedar tree, sipping coffee while watching the rain writing on the surface of the water, the thought came to me that someone ought to create a guide that showed people how and where to camp free in the Mount Hood National Forest. And that, in a nutshell, is how the idea for this book was born.

Many people don't even realize that it's legal to camp outside of the developed campgrounds in our National Forests. The National Forests belong to, and are the unique birthright of, all U.S. citizens, who are free to camp in them, so long as they do so respectfully. The Forest Service term for camping outside of officially designated campgrounds is **dispersed camping**. And there are at least three very good reasons for taking advantage of your right to camp in this fashion:

1. Freedom from the many rules and regulations necessary in public campgrounds where many people are camped closely together.
2. A better night's sleep.
3. Money Saved.

During the summertime camping season, most of the corporate-managed, for-profit campgrounds anywhere near the city fill up fast and become small tent towns on summer weekends. Visit one on almost any Friday evening during the summer and you'll find people strolling, dogs barking, radios playing, diesel pickups driving through looking for a vacant spot, generators 'genning,' and kids yelling - "the whole catastrophe," to quote Zorba the Greek. Anyone who has stayed in an official campground on a busy Fourth-of-July weekend knows that getting a good night's sleep can depend on what time your neighbors decide to stop partying and go to bed, especially in those campgrounds that don't have resident camp hosts (and several of the more remote ones don't). If you have ever set up camp in the woods with the expectation of finding peace and tranquility under soaring conifer trees, only to have your heart sink at the sight of a group of summertime revelers arriving with multiple ice chests full of beer and setting up camp right next to you in preparation for partying into the night, you probably know what I'm talking about here. Consider this: when camping on your own, away from the madding crowd, only you and those in your party will be driven nuts when your dog barks incessantly into the night. You and you alone get to decide when to run your generator and your radio. When you're on your own and alone in the woods, you can pretty much do what you want, within reason. Heck, you can walk around camp in the nude if you're so inclined. The squirrels and jays in the trees aren't going to complain.

Camping in a public campground might seem cheap when compared to the cost of taking the family to Disneyland for a week, but if you look at it from the point of view of value received, you might conclude that the price is too high. And this is especially true if you are one of the many who have been forced to live on an income that has not kept pace with inflation or have lost a job or a house due to the recent financial debacle that has left our economy in such a shambles. What you can count on receiving for your hard-earned money in the majority of public campgrounds is a patch of bare ground upon which to erect your tent, the use of a pit toilet that, in spite of the best efforts of a conscientious camp host, may be contaminated with the fecal matter of some careless previous camper, a serviceable fire ring with a grate, and a picnic table. In 2010 I learned that sometimes even the picnic table part of the deal is questionable when I camped in one official campground where some of the picnic tables had been allowed to rot almost completely away before being replaced (however, to be perfectly fair, when I returned to this campground later in the season, I found that these picnic tables had been replaced with beautiful, sturdy new ones). In addition, only some of the campgrounds along the Clackamas, Collawash and Oak Grove Forks of the Clackamas River offer potable water as part of the deal. When you throw in the fees for parking an extra car and the cost of buying firewood and then pro-rate the whole thing out over a thirty-day period, the cost of camping in a public campground for a family of six would roughly equal the rental cost of a small apartment in the city. And you can probably double that for a large family, since there is usually a limit on the number people allowed per campsite.

While driving thousands of miles of Mount Hood National Forest roads during the field work phase of this book, I found that some dispersed campsites had been badly used and neglected by the public at large. This caused me to wonder whether by publishing this book, I would only be providing the feckless and irresponsible a few hundred more places in which to party down. What gave me the resolve to continue was the remembrance of the many campers I had met in the summer of 2009, in whom I had seen a great respect for and appreciation of the legacy of our National Forest. It is my hope that you, the user of this book are a kindred spirit of these good people and will proactively pay our legacy forward by leaving your campsites in better condition than you found them, if only a bit. That said, and if you are still with me, do read on….

* * *

Say it's a hot Friday afternoon in July in the Willamette Valley. The temperature hasn't been under ninety for the last week, and you begin to fantasize about how good it would feel to escape to the mountains. Overcome by that old, familiar urge for summertime adventure that awakens the child in us all, you think about gathering up your camping gear and packing it, some food, the kids and your dog Barney, into the family vehicle and taking off for the cool, tree-covered valleys of your favorite nearby national forest. But just as suddenly, you realize with a stab of disappointment that you should have thought about this a month ago because at this time of the year everybody wants to go camping, and all the non-reservable campsites within reasonable driving distance of Portland will have already been claimed by the time you get to them. Knowing that driving around aimlessly, looking for a campsite when you are tired and hungry has a way of melting morale faster than butter in a microwave, you sadly put the idea of your spontaneous summertime camping trip back in the box, close the lid and resign yourself to spending the weekend in the city.

But, hold it! With this book in your hand as plan B, you'll still be able to go camping, even if you do find all the for-profit public campgrounds full when you get to the mountains. It won't cost you a dime and you'll probably find more of the solitude and solace you seek than if you'd stuck with Plan A. And with the money you'll have saved on camping and parking fees, not to mention firewood, your investment in the book will be back in your pocket by breakfast time the next morning.

A word about those you're likely to meet while camping on your own in the Forest:
Most people who practice dispersed camping have one thing in common. Once they have discovered the freedom that they enjoy when doing so, they refuse to consider the alternative of camping in public campgrounds. If you go out of your way to meet them, you will discover that many of them not only express a respect for the beauty of the Forest that borders on reverence, but also a strong commitment to maintaining it for future generations. And if that isn't enough of an endorsement, most of the Forest Service employees with whom I talked during the course of writing this book admitted to preferring dispersed camping over camping in a public campground, as well.

Handcrafted sign at the trailhead to Buck Lake

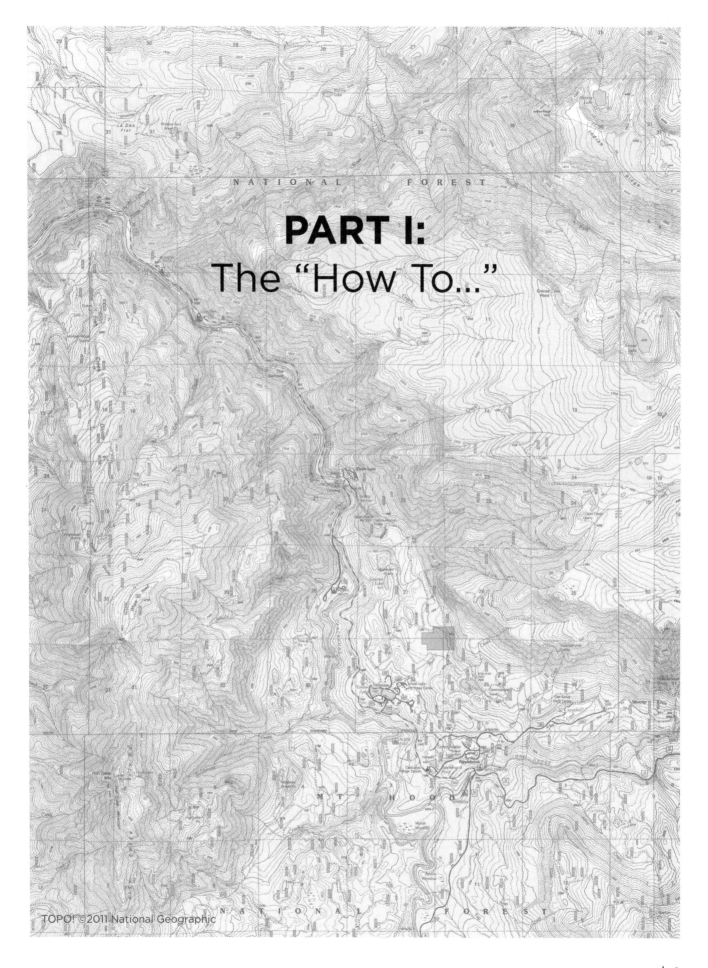

PART I:
The "How To..."

Chapter 1
Using this Book and Getting Started

Congratulations on having made the decision to camp away from the herd. Part I of this book will give you the latest information on how to do that comfortably, confidently and successfully. Part II will help you find your campsite (See "How to Use Part II" on page 32.).

Note: throughout this book, the Mount Hood National Forest will be referred to simply as "the Forest".

Off-season camping

That this book was written primarily for the summertime recreational camper does not mean that it won't be useful to those who wish to camp in the spring and fall, when there is less competition for campsites. The standard information included in every campsite in Part II, such as the altitude and whether the site is located on a gravel, dirt or paved road, will also be useful to the off-season camper.

Don't expose yourself to unnecessary risk when camping at higher altitudes in cold weather. Be aware that the Forest Service doesn't plow the majority of its roads during the winter, even the major ones. If you get caught out in the Forest by the first serious snow storm of the year you could be in deep, white trouble. Carry a weather radio and make sure you can get to a place where it will receive a strong signal. Alternatively, FM radio reception seems to be strong throughout the Forest, with Oregon Public Broadcasting, at 91.5 on the FM dial, being one of the most reliable and consistent signals to be found there.

Rules and restrictions

Dispersed camping is allowed throughout most of the Forest. Exceptions are along some sections of roads and highways that are designated "scenic" or in a few recreational areas where official campgrounds are concentrated, such as along FS57 near the end of Timothy Lake. Forest Service regulations and guidelines are subject to continual change and are kept current on its website. The Forest Service currently allows camping in dispersed sites "for a period no longer than 14 consecutive days, after which the site must be vacated. A camper may not return to the site before 30 days have passed. Campers are limited to a total of 28 camping days in a one calendar year period."

The Forest Service may close certain sensitive areas to protect wildlife habitat or watersheds, or when there is a danger to public safety posed by fire or other natural disaster, so it's always a good idea to visit or phone one of the four Forest Service district offices to find out about current guidelines, restrictions and road closures before proceeding. Here are the telephone numbers:

Barlow District at Dufur	(541) 467-2291
Clackamas River District at Estacada	(503) 630-6861
Hood River District at Parkdale	(541) 352-6002
Zigzag District at Zigzag	(503) 622-3191

Keep in mind that you can also call these numbers from any one of the cell phone hot spots in the Forest itself.

Fire season camping

During extremely dry periods, the Forest Service may prohibit open fires entirely. Those for whom a campfire is the defining experience of a camping trip are going to find their options drastically limited during these times and may be advised to either stay home or head for one of the public campgrounds, which are the only places where the no-fire rule is normally not enforced during periods of forest fire danger. A better approach would be to try doing without a campfire. Those who do usually discover that on clear, warm summer nights, the sky, which can be awe-inspiring, especially during the month of August when the Perseid meteor showers occur, rapidly becomes the focus of attention.

Roads

There are over 3,000 miles of roads in the Mount Hood National Forest. They range in driver usability from Level 5 roads to Maintenance Level 1 roads. Level 5 roads are mainly the easy-to-drive, double-lane and hard surface roads. Level 1 roads are usually closed to vehicular traffic, but are often open to other uses, such as bicycle or foot traffic.

New Road Policy

As this book was being written in 2011, the Forest Service instituted a new policy approach to roads in the National Forest. It states, "*All roads and areas on Mt Hood National Forest are closed to motor vehicles unless designated open and depicted open to motor vehicles on the Motor Vehicle Use Map (MVUM)*". The purpose of the new policy is apparently to control the impact of vehicle traffic on the Forest, especially the use of OHVs (off-highway vehicles). How this will play out in practice for the camping public, and whether it will render some or any of the campsites listed in this book inaccessible, is still to be determined.

Malcolm Hamilton, Recreational Manager for the Mount Hood National Forest, has indicated that road signage in the Forest will probably not change significantly as a result of the new policy, saying, "there will be some 'road closed' signing, however it will probably be spotty. The public should not rest assured that all roads that are closed will be signed that way" (sic). *This leaves little doubt that the responsibility to know which roads can be driven upon will rest with the person behind the wheel. There are heavy penalties for violators*. It is important to note that the new policy pertains to operating motor vehicles only, *and the fact that the road to a given campsite is closed to motor vehicles does not mean that camping is forbidden there*.

The good news is that the individual MVUMs clearly indicate which roads can be driven upon. The bad news is that it is not easy to figure out which of the 55 individual MVUMs pertain to the particular part of the Forest you are interested in exploring. To find the correct MVUM you will need to consult The "Key Locator Grid Map". But the problem with the "Key Locator Grid Map" is that it features no landmarks of any kind, not even the major ones, such as Timothy Lake and Mount Hood.

This makes the task of finding the right map a matter of trial and error. Lakes are indicated on the fifty-five individual maps, but, even here, other major landmarks, such as rivers and creeks, are left out. State and federal highways are faint and difficult to see. Main Forest Service roads are not differentiated from the secondary roads that branch off from them. And, while even the shortest of roads are labeled by their Forest Service road number on the fifty-five MVUMs, signage on the ground identifying the welter of secondary and spur roads intersecting and branching off of each other within the Forest itself is often either lacking or obscured by underbrush growing on the side of the road.

To further confuse the matter for the camper, the MVUM states that "dispersed camping (is) allowed within 125 feet of National Forest System roads as measured from the centerline of the road and indicated on map". Malcolm Hamilton, on the other hand, told me in a phone interview that this technically means that vehicles are restricted to this distance, while campers are free to camp beyond this limit, so long as they do not take their vehicles. Simply put, the fact that you can't drive there in a car doesn't mean that you can't camp there.

Motor Vehicle Use Maps (MVUMs) are available on-line and in booklet form free from the Forest Service offices in Dufur, Estacada, Parkdale and Zigzag. There are fifty-five separate MVUMs for the entire Mount Hood National Forest. In order to determine which of the fifty-five maps covers the area you are interested in, you will need to look at the "Key Locator Grid Map", which is printed on the first page of the MVUM. Having the information in the booklet format means you will have each and every MVUM that you need wherever you end up in the Forest. The Sandy office was happy to send me a copy.

To get to the MVUM online, you first have to go to the Mount Hood National Forest home page and type "MVUM" (without quotes) into the query box in the upper left hand corner and click "go". On the next page, click on the box labeled "Mount Hood National Forest – OHV riding

& camping." On the next page, click on the "Link to Key Locator Grid Map." On the Key Locator Grid Map, note the number of the map showing the area you are interested in exploring, for example, E6. Then use the back arrow at the top of your screen to take you back to the page labeled "OHV riding and camping." At the bottom of this page you will find a link to map number E6. Click on it and print the map you are interested in. Hint: it's a whole lot easier to get the hard copy booklet from the Forest Service.

Four-wheelers

This book was not written for four-wheelers. The majority of sites described in it are on established Forest Service roads below 3200 feet elevation. Most of my exploration was done in a Toyota Corolla. When the quality of a road I was driving deteriorated beyond what I judged to be the ability of the average driver, my practice was to turn around and find another road to explore. The single exception is the historic Barlow Road in the northeast section of the Forest. Much of this road is extremely challenging to drive in a passenger car, but leads to some exceptional campsites.

Recreational vehicle camping

Most of the campsites listed in Part II will accommodate some form of recreational vehicle. The decision about whether a particular campsite was suitable for a motor home, but not a travel trailer, was based on the MVUM, the terrain, the nature of the road and the placement of the trees. In short, it was fairly subjective. Since most of the campsites in the book are away from the road and under the shelter of the trees, where it can be difficult to maneuver with a travel trailer, it was usually my opinion that, where the MVUM allows vehicular traffic within 125' of the road, a smaller motor home was the better choice.

Warning: when considering camping on a particular site in your RV, always check the MVUM first.

Cleaning up your site – the "trash plus ten percent" plan

The Mount Hood National Forest's proximity to the metropolitan area of Portland, though a blessing to those who live and work there, has brought to it the twin curses of litter and pollution, especially to those areas closest to Portland. The *plain truth is that if this book contributes to the Forest's further degradation it might as well not have been written.* You and I both know that some people who use our National Forest do not feel that the world loves them, and act accordingly. And just as the Biblical declaration, "The poor we will always have with us" is true, so it is true that there will always be those among us who are immature, ignorant, disaffected and disrespectful. And, thankfully, they are in the minority. From time to time, you'll have the experience of arriving at a beautiful and otherwise pristine and desirable campsite, only to realize that the previous users did not treat the place with the respect and reverence that is its due. When this happens it is my hope you won't throw up your hands in disgust, go into a tirade about "some people's kids" and drive on, especially if you would otherwise want to use that site. I hope you will instead choose to *pay it forward*, and clean the place up.

Cleaning up a campsite doesn't have to be an all-or-nothing proposition. When breaking camp to go home it's not that hard at all to haul out *our own trash plus a little of somebody else's as well*. As a matter of fact, with the proper equipment, it is surprising how quickly a campsite can be cleaned up. Some of the sites listed in this book are popular enough to be occupied during almost every one of the twelve official weekends of summer, and if enough people commit to hauling out their own trash plus another ten percent, by the end of the summer most of even the most heavily used campsites will be ready for the next camping season. Call it the "trash plus ten percent" plan, a true boot-strap, grass roots, "Yes we can!" kind of approach to making our corner of the world a better place to live that doesn't require bi-partisan Congressional approval.

To police your camp in a quick and sanitary fashion, come equipped with a couple of sturdy 30-gallon plastic bags, some disposable gloves or heavy rubber ones, a bucket or two, and a couple of "garbage glompers" (the kind of grabbing tool used for picking up litter in parks). These devices can be purchased inexpensively from various stores around town. My favorite source is Harbor Freight Tools in Portland, Milwaukee and Vancouver. I suggest giving the devices a few test squeezes in the store before buying them, to make sure they operate smoothly. A side benefit of these handy tools is that they are good for developing hand-eye coordination. I got so good with mine by the end of a summer of using it as part of my duties as a camp host that I could pick up a cigarette butt at a fast walk without breaking stride. Setting your children about the task of picking up litter while you are busy setting up camp is a win-win situation, because it also keeps them from wandering off into the forest alone before you know what's out there.

Warning: Whatever you do, don't leave plastic bags full of garbage behind when you go home! Crows, raccoons and squirrels will smell the food odors through the plastic and get to work scattering the contents as soon as your car is out of sight. Once it's in a plastic bag, take it home with you.

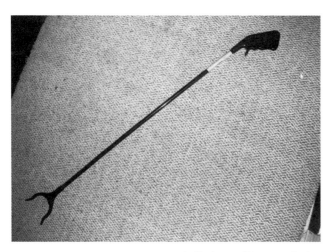

A Garbage Glomper device

When you witness an illegal act of dumping in the Forest, 'who ya gonna call?' Dump Stoppers!

Dump Stoppers is a federally-funded program devoted to reducing illegal dumping and vandalism on US Forest Service, BLM and forested Clackamas County land. It uses the Clackamas County Sheriff's Department to track down and prosecute illegal dumpers and vandals. Crews from the county jail are also used to clean up larger dumpsites. Since its inception in 2003, the program has removed 667,787 pounds of solid waste, 5,082 pounds of hazardous waste, 58,533 pounds of scrap metal, 7,342 tires, 412 vehicles, and 2 illegal structures from the forest. The official Dump Stoppers website says, "Citizens are asked to play a major role in the Dump Stoppers program. A telephone tipline is available for persons to call when they see or suspect illegal dumping on federal, county, or timber company lands. The number is (503) 650-3333. Callers are encouraged to leave their information so staff can confirm their complaint; however, callers can remain anonymous." It is also possible to report an illegal dump online at the official Dumpstoppers website, **www.clackamas.us/ dumpstoppers/**. Once there, go to the bottom of the page.

Before you set up camp

Inspect your site for hazards: During the summertime field work phase of this book, site inspections were limited to checking for the essentials necessary for camping, as well as any obvious safety concerns in the immediate area. Some of the sites in this book, though beautiful and otherwise desirable, are *not* suitable for children. Examples are those that are located on the banks of fast-moving rivers and streams that could sweep a distracted child downstream. A few might be located too close to a precipice, dead tree or other potential hazard. I cannot claim to have covered every possible risk factor and must leave it to you to make a more thorough inspection of the site and its environs when you arrive on the spot, especially if you have children or someone with special needs in your party. That said, there will be more on safety and security issues in Chapter 3.

Disclaimer

Almost without exception, the sites included in this book are those that appeared to have been used as campsites by others in the past, as evidenced by the presence of a fire ring and a bare patch of ground where a tent can be erected. This book cannot be relied upon as an authoritative guide to the ever-changing landscape of laws, policies, rules, regulations and guidelines promulgated by the US Forest Service. In deference to the Forest Service's new road policy, in Part II of this book you will find a reference to the appropriate MVUM page number for each campsite listed. Because a site is listed in this book does not mean that you are free to drive your vehicle into or onto the site. Virtually all of the campsites listed in this book were in use prior to the inception of the new MVUM guidelines, and the roads upon which they are located were, to the best of my knowledge, open to highway-legal vehicles at the time of discovery. *That said, I have made a diligent effort to exclude and delete any campsite located along roads that are closed to motor vehicles and where dispersed camping is prohibited. I have also tried to indicate which campsites are not accessible to motor vehicle traffic, but I cannot guarantee that I have been one hundred percent successful in doing so.* Because of missing or damaged road signs it was sometimes difficult to identify a location precisely. Any errors will have been inadvertent. I did find it necessary to document several sites that are not MVUM compliant along FSR46 south of milepost 50. I did this for those who might want to access them without a vehicle, and also lest they be lost in the event that the Forest Service might someday open them to vehicular traffic once again. *Therefore, to the reader falls the responsibility to be informed of all current county, state and federal laws, regulations and restrictions and guidelines that apply and are in force in the Mount Hood National Forest, including, but not limited to those pertaining to dispersed camping, fishing, hunting, the use of fire, firearms, the operation of motor vehicles and the cutting, digging or harvesting of plant or animal life of any kind.*

Furthermore, the information provided in other chapters is based on the author's opinions, insights, research, knowledge and practical experience, and is not presented as either definitive or authoritative. *The book is intended only as a guide and is not a substitute for the reader's knowledge or judgment.*

Round Lake (in the Clackamas SE section)

Chapter 2
On Your Own in the Woods, Equipment and Practice

Gear
Camping on your own doesn't mean that you'll have to buy a ton of new gear. Essentially, you need only to be concerned about replacing three things when camping away from a designated campground: the fire pit and grate, the public toilet and the picnic table. Replace those, and the experience is pretty much the same as camping anywhere else. In case you're wondering, potable water didn't make the above replacement list because it isn't part of the deal in many of the official campgrounds in the Mount Hood National Forest.

Tables and Chairs
You should be able to dispense with a table for your first dispersed camping experience, especially if you are driving a vehicle with limited cargo space. What you can do is improvise one from what you already have on hand, such as a couple of pieces of plywood and a few two-by-fours. A great chair option for those with space limitations would be one of the "Crazy Creek" brand chairs popular among backpackers and touring sea kayakers. These clever little devices fold up to a compact 1-1/2" x 20" x 20" and allow most people to sit on the ground and even recline comfortably. You can sometimes purchase off-brand ones for a little over ten dollars at discount stores. My personal preference is for the more expensive extended-back version marketed by Crazy Creek. Once you've tested the water and begin to feel comfortable camping on your own, you will find a plethora of lightweight table and chair options on the market to suit your budget, your needs and the carrying capacity of your vehicle.

Toilets
For defecation purposes, the Forest Service officially recommends digging a cathole six to eight inches deep in a location that is well away from any stream, river or lake. Unfortunately, many of the sites I have found have obviously been in continual use for many years. As a consequence, there is often not enough shrubbery left in the forest understory to provide concealment for this most private of human functions. The lack of privacy is especially common in the popular sites along the four or five major rivers that drain the Forest. Broadly speaking, too many sites close to streams and rivers have suffered the problem of too many people digging catholes too close to running water and too shallow to include toilet paper for too many years. Another problem with burying human feces and toilet paper in a shallow grave is the possibility that animals will dig it up. The Forest Service does not seem to recognize this, but most dog owners will not find it so hard to imagine.

For the above reasons, many campers are turning to the use of inexpensive *privacy shelters* in combination with some form of portable toilet. This arrangement not only allows the privacy needed for toilet functions, but makes it possible to dispose of the resultant poop by removing it from the scene and dumping it somewhere else. As a matter of fact, Mount Hood National Forest Recreational Director Malcolm Hamilton says this is actually what the Forest Service would prefer that campers do. Unfortunately, the first "somewhere else" that leaps to mind is one of the pit toilets in a nearby Forest Service campground. This may be an effective solution to the problem of reducing fecal run-off along rivers and streams, but the practice is not fair to the corporations that run these campgrounds for a profit and have to pay to keep their pit toilets pumped out throughout the summer camping season.

If you are the kind of person who doesn't want to have to haul a load of sewage in your vehicle one more mile than you absolutely have to, you will find a list of RV dump stations in the Portland area by googling for "RV dump stations around Portland, OR". Some dump stations charge a nominal fee of around five dollars, but a few are free. Don't drive too far in search of a free one.

Warning: *If you use one of the portable toilet systems that collect human waste in a plastic bag* *of any kind, NEVER, EVER DUMP THE PLASTIC BAG INTO A PIT TOILET ALONG WITH THE HUMAN WASTE IT CONTAINS!* The plastic bag will plug up the pumping equipment used to empty the pit toilets. For this reason, you should think twice about buying a portable toilet system that collects waste in a plastic bag.

A preferable, though more expensive toilet system is one that has two tanks and actually flushes. The upper tank holds clean water used for flushing and the lower tank (usually around 3.5 to 5 gallons, collects and holds the waste. These gravity flushing devices are amazingly effective and odor-free. The only problem with them is that the small volume of water released from the upper tank isn't always enough to remove every bit of fecal deposit from the inside of the bowl. A good solution to this problem is a *cheap garden weed sprayer*, which will send out a jet of water strong enough to wash down anything that doesn't disappear with the first flush.

Privacy Shelters

Privacy shelters about the size and shape of a traditional one-seat outhouse are ideal for housing your portable toilet and are available at most sporting goods stores for as little as $40. The great thing about them is that they can also be used for other things, such as changing clothes or taking a shower or sponge bath. If you intend to use your privacy shelter as a shower stall, make sure that it has a frame sturdy enough to support the weight of about five gallons of water, which is usually the minimal amount of water required for a shower. Water weighs about 8.33 pounds per gallon, or over forty pounds for five gallons. For most people, merely hoisting and securing a forty-pound bag of water high enough overhead to function as a shower will present a challenge.

Privacy Shelter

Dual tank, gravity-flush portable toilet

Of course, a privacy shelter for camping is just another name for a tent, and for the purposes of this discussion, any tent large enough to allow a camper to stand upright will probably also make a fine privacy shelter. If you have an extra tent, consider toting it along to use as a kind of multi-purpose spare room and privacy shelter. I have used tents for storage and as kitchens, rain shelters, nap rooms, conference rooms, changing rooms, bathrooms and offices, among other things. For exasperated parents they might also make a good time-out room.

Fires and Fire Rings

An out-of-control fire is a scary thing, especially if it is your out-of-control fire. Before you venture into the woods, be aware of any current Forest Service restrictions on campfires. Before you even start building a fire during the summer camping season, make sure that a shovel, bucket and a source of water are at hand. Always use an existing fire ring when available. If choosing a fresh site for your fire is your only option, make sure to choose one well away from overhanging branches, steep slopes, burnable roots or any other flammable forest material. Clear away roots, forest duff (the decaying vegetable matter on the forest floor) and top soil down to mineral earth and line the area with rocks before striking a match. Keep fires small, using material no larger in diameter than your wrist and push these larger pieces into the center of the fire. For cooking purposes, a bed of glowing coals provides a steady heat, which the rocks will absorb, hold and gradually re-radiate.

If you are planning to use alcohol or any substance which might have the effect of altering your perceptions while in the woods, anticipate this by reducing the size of your fire or putting it out entirely during the duration of this period.

If you don't like the idea of building a fire on the ground, commercial fire rings or pits are available in stores that sell camping gear, starting at around seventy dollars. It is also possible to make your own fire pit out of an old back yard barbecue, oil drum or even the insides from an old washing machine. But whether you make one or buy one, the edges should be three or more inches high all the way around. Adding legs for greater accessibility would be nice, too. Still, even when building your fire in a metal fire ring, you should clear the ground around the area of all forest debris down to mineral earth.

Grates and grills

If you're going to have a campfire anyway, it makes sense to at least put it to practical use for purifying and heating water for camp use. For this, you will want a metal grate of some kind. Again, you can buy something made for the purpose or you can improvise a grill from something you have on hand. Either way, it needs be sturdy enough to support the maximum weight you intend to put on it. The grates should be close enough together so that your hot dogs won't fall through and be incinerated. For complete control over the cooking process, look for a design that is adjustable in height. Cast iron is probably the best material for making a grill, though I have seen everything from old refrigerator grates to the tops of 55-gallon drums with holes punched in them used for this purpose.

Beyond the fire ring

The amount of satisfaction you and your family derive from your dispersed camping experience depends on how comfortable and safe the experience is *for everyone concerned*. Other than the fire ring, public toilet and picnic table, the camping equipment you already have should do just fine for dispersed camping. Nevertheless, a discussion of the basics of camping equipment is in order, starting with tents.

Tents

Your biggest expenditure in the quest for warmth and "dryth" while camping will probably be the tent you choose. Keeping people and their gear dry is a tent's *prime directive*. Since staying dry is a basic necessity for a comfortable camping experience, you'll not only need to know what features to look for in a tent, but you'll need to have some idea of the conditions under which you will be using it before you go shopping for one. I could go on and on about tents, because – okay, I'll admit it. I have a "thing" for tents that is not dissimilar to the "thing" Imelda Marcos had for shoes.

Tents are nothing but collapsible cloth shelters hanging on a frame of some kind. Most modern tents come in two parts: an inner tent that is not waterproof (but, ideally, is insect-proof) and an outer rain fly that is (supposed to be) waterproof.

The rain fly's job is to cover the parts of the tent that aren't waterproof, such as the screening, the zippers and the inner tent itself. During the night, the exhaled moisture from the occupants inside the tent passes through the permeable cloth of the inner tent and condenses on the inner side of the rain fly, where it can either evaporate or trickle down to the base of the tent. For this to work effectively, there should be a space between the fabric of the inner tent and the rain fly *all* around your tent, though normal stretching and sagging of the fabric may sometimes cause some contact between the inner tent fabric and the rain fly, especially in wet weather.

When it comes to tents, Murphy's Law applies: Whether it is due to a flaw in the tent or a mistake you made in setting it up, if there is one spot where water can come pouring through, it will only come to your attention at the worst possible time. It is not uncommon for leakage to occur in a brand-new tent because the seams of the rain fly have not been sealed with a material usually referred to as "seam seal". Many tents now come from the factory with their seams already sealed. This is a big help because it saves you from having to do a messy job that involves the handling of noxious fluids, which can leave you feeling dizzy and nauseated if applied without adequate ventilation. When buying a new tent you will immediately want to find out if you are going to have to seal the seams yourself, *especially if you are buying a large tent.* Sometimes, this is the hidden cost of a "bargain" tent.

The rain fly can be removed and set aside on clear, warm nights, allowing maximum ventilation while your inner tent continues to function as a refuge against insects. If you do remove your tent's rain fly, make sure you keep it handy, in case you wake up during the night with rain spattering your face and have to put it back on again in a hurry. To quote Dave Barry, "Rainstorms will travel thousands of miles against the prevailing winds for the opportunity to rain on a tent,...".

Another place where tents can leak is from underneath. The bottom of any tent is subject to leakage from ground that has been soaked by a hard and persistent rain, especially if it has a few tiny punctures or tears. You will almost always want to place a *water-proof ground cloth* underneath your tent to keep water from seeping in through the floor while you are sleeping. A piece of sturdy blue tarp material will do the trick. *Be careful to cut or fold it so that it is a few inches smaller than the dimensions of the inner part of your tent all the way around and doesn't extend beyond the edge of the rain fly at any point.*

I learned my lesson about the importance of ground cloths the hard way while kayak touring in British Columbia's Inland Passage. We had pulled into one of the Broken Group Islands under threatening skies late one afternoon. In anticipation of the rain, I placed a ground cloth beneath the tent when I erected it, but I was tired from paddling all day and failed to notice that the ground cloth extended beyond the edge of the tent's rain fly in just a few critical spots. The rain came with a vengeance just after we went to bed, drumming on the tent fly and draining onto the ground cloth on the uphill side of the tent. Soon it was soaking through the floor of the tent, forming little puddles wherever the ground dipped slightly. I had to go outside in a driving rain, tuck the exposed edges of the ground cloth under the tent and then sop up the puddles forming on the floor inside the tent with a sponge and a bucket.

A lesson like that sticks with you for a long time.

Protection from insects

I don't know which is more miserable: trying to sleep in a leaky tent on a stormy night or having to share one with a cloud of hungry, whining mosquitoes. Thankfully, the relatively fast-moving water coursing through most of the creek and river valleys of the Mount Hood National Forest usually doesn't allow for the accumulation of the kind of stagnant water that mosquitoes favor for breeding purposes. Consequently, you should find few of them at most of the campsites listed here.

Still, even one mosquito inside a tent is one too many for most people, including me. Let me hear the foreboding whine of a mosquito next to my ear when I'm drifting off to sleep, and I'm suddenly on high alert and won't be able to rest until I have dealt with the little bloodsucker.

Unfortunately, mosquitoes are just one of the bothersome insects that can rob you of a good night's sleep in the woods. Most tents come with some kind of netting that will keep out mosquitoes, but gnats and no-see-ums are equally bloodthirsty, and so tiny that they can pass through the wider mesh netting used in many bargain-priced tents. Face it, when you crawl into your sleeping bag at night, you are going to want to know that, no matter how persistently that cloud of mosquitoes and all of their miniscule, biting and bloodsucking brethren may beat their wings against the screening of your tent, they can't get at you. And for that, you may have to pay a little bit more for a tent with screening that is fine enough to do the job. One possible downside of the finer mesh is that it will restrict the flow of air through your tent to some degree. Usually this is an acceptable trade-off, however, since summer nights in the mountains are normally cool anyway. Also, once you are confident that your tent is a reliable barrier to the smallest of biting insects, you should be able to throw back the covers and sleep in your pajamas on the hottest of nights.

Freestanding tents

Most of the tents on the market today are freestanding. The big advantage of freestanding tents, in my opinion, is that, unlike the tents of generations past which had to be staked down, these do not, and once erected, can simply be picked up and moved to another location if the need arises. You will appreciate this feature the first morning you wake up with a raging backache from sleeping on an intolerable bump or rise that you hadn't noticed the night before. Rather than having to collapse and re-erect your tent, all you will have to do is pick it up and move it to a spot that is more suitable to your body, though you will probably find it expedient to remove your gear first.

But don't think for a minute that because a tent will stand up by itself you can leave the tent stakes at home. Winds capable of carrying your freestanding tent and all the gear inside it off into oblivion can arise suddenly and violently in the mountains. Consequently, you need to make sure that your tent is secured to the ground well enough so that it doesn't go cartwheeling over a bluff into the river while you are off fishing, especially if it is pitched out in the open, away from the shelter of trees. Imagine your dismay at seeing your tent and sleeping bags floating by on the current while you stand on the bank watching helplessly!

Whatever tent you choose needs to be strong enough not to collapse under either wind or a layer of the kind of heavy snow that can fall overnight in these mountains at either end of the summertime camping season.

Sleeping bags

Once you've got the tent that's going to take whatever nature is likely to throw at it and still keep you and yours dry and unmolested by pests, you're going to have to think about choosing a sleeping bag. Again, you're going to face a plethora of choices of designs, materials and fillings from which to choose.

Most sleeping bags are rated according to the lowest outside temperature that can be comfortably tolerated in them. Generally speaking, lighter bags are rated for summer use, mid-weight bags for three-season use and the heaviest and thickest (and, of course, most expensive), for winter use. But when it comes to choosing the bag that will work best for you, it's kind of a shot in the dark and depends a great deal on your own metabolism. Some people become little furnaces at night and throw off covers when sleeping in unheated rooms in the middle of winter. Others enjoy being completely snuggled down under heavy blankets at night, even in the middle of summer. I know someone like that, actually.

The efficiency of fillings used in sleeping bags also varies considerably. Goose down, at the top of the list, is considered to be the lightest and most efficient insulator on the planet. I'm not going to argue with that, but there are downsides to the use of this substance. For one, it does not insulate well when wet or damp (Remember the leaky tent scenario?). Also, it is expensive and is not hypo-allergenic.

A bag with synthetic insulation is a good choice for car camping, where considerations of weight and space are not as critical as when backpacking or sea kayak touring. A synthetic bag will still keep you warm even when slightly damp. And it probably won't provoke any allergic reactions from anyone in your party.

Sleeping bags come mainly in two different designs: rectangular and "mummy" style bags. The rectangular bags are larger and allow more room to move. Mummy-style bags, on the other hand, are thought to be more efficient because they conform more closely to the contours of the body and reduce the amount of air space to be warmed inside the bag. Some people, however, feel claustrophobic in mummy-style sleeping bags.

A good sleeping bag of whatever weight and for whatever season will show its quality: Look for overlapping tubes of insulation running the length of the bag and sewn in such a way that there are no cold spots, such as will occur when the tubes of insulation are created by sewing the inside lining of the bag directly to the outside lining. Look for baffles of insulation along the complete length of the zipper to prevent cold air from getting in. Zippers should be large, sturdy and function smoothly, with pulls that are easy to find and grab in the dark. You really don't want to experience waking up from a sound sleep with an urgent need to visit the bathroom only to find yourself struggling with a stuck zipper in the pitch dark. Even worse, you don't want to experience the unforgettable claustrophobic panic of feeling trapped in your sleeping bag when something goes bump in the night and wakes you up in a confused state of fight or flight. To avoid this problem, some people choose to sleep under their sleeping bags rather than inside of them, or even dispense with them altogether in favor of blankets from home. This allows them to quickly throw off their covers and be at the ready at a moment's notice. Naturally, using a sleeping bag like a blanket reduces its ability to hold in the warmth of the body. If you intend to buy a sleeping bag to use as a blanket, make sure it has a zipper that will completely unzip the bag and allow it to lie flat.

A sleeping bag's lining and outer fabric are important considerations, as well. Sleeping bags with nylon outer shells tend to slide around if the ground is anything but level. Sleeping bags that are lined with flannel can restrict movement inside the bag for anyone who is either not wearing satin or sleeping in the nude.

Make sure that the bag you buy will accommodate the length and width of your body. You will want one that is longer than you are tall. Don't be afraid to try it out right in the store. Imagine yourself as you will be sleeping when you are camping. If it feels short, restrictive or claustrophobic, keep looking until you find one that works for you.

Sleeping pads and air mattresses

A camping gear salesman once gave me the secret to getting the most warmth possible out of a sleeping bag. This secret, which I pass on to you here at no extra charge, is that the best sleeping bag in the world won't keep you warm if there is nothing underneath it to insulate against the cold ground. The warmth of a sleeping bag depends on the ability of its filling to expand inside the bag, called *loft*. However, the weight of a sleeping person's body compresses the filling underneath, thereby cancelling much of its ability to insulate. You can discover how true this is by sleeping on a two to three-inch thick stack of throw rugs in your back yard some cold night. When you wake up in the morning and start peeling the throw rugs back one-by-one, you will find them warm from your body heat all the way to the bottom.

The throw-rug experiment taught me that, on a cold night, the insulation *underneath* your sleeping bag is about as important as the insulation in the sleeping bag around you. This is especially true if you happen to be using a down-filled bag, since down is somewhat more compressible than other forms of sleeping bag fill, but is universally true of any sleeping bag to a greater or lesser degree.

There are some very thick and, no doubt, comfortable, air mattresses on the market that are easy to inflate with an inexpensive 12-volt electric air compressor which you can power with your car's cigarette lighter outlet. However, in light of the above, sleeping on a bed of pure air is not your best choice on a cold night. When using an air mattress, bring along some extra insulation to keep your body away from the cold air underneath you.

Self-inflating sleeping pads are excellent choices for camping. They both cushion your body from the hard ground and insulate it from the cold. They come in thicknesses of up to three inches and take up less space than a foam pad because they can be deflated and then rolled up. Basically, self-inflating sleeping pads are air mattresses that contain an inner mattress of open-cell foam. When the air valve is open, the foam inside the mattress begins to expand, drawing air into the air mattress. When the mattress expands to the desired thickness for sleeping, the user closes the air valve, trapping the air inside the mattress for the night. It is not a good idea to blow into a self-inflating sleeping pad to help inflate it. The air inside your lungs contains moisture which can cause mildew to grow inside of the mattress.

Rain shelters versus heated tents

A rain shelter of some sort can be a good investment. A simple tarp spread between trees can do the trick, but it is only slightly more difficult to string a tarp so that it won't sag under a heavy rain and then suddenly dump a torrent of cold rainwater down someone's neck than it is to find the two trees to string one from that are exactly where you need them to be. Here, technology can, once again, come to the rescue. There are several brands of freestanding rain shelters on the market that will work admirably. They usually come in two sizes: ten-feet-by-ten-feet or twelve feet-by-twelve-feet and sell for a hundred dollars or less at many stores.

Another solution would be to purchase a largish, cheap tent for use as an outdoor kitchen and dining room when it is raining. Needless to say, when the sun comes out again the tent will do double duty as a shelter from biting and stinging insects. For warmth, you might want to consider the added luxury of a propane heater rated for use in enclosed spaces to be used inside the tent. Though even these produce small amounts of carbon monoxide, most tents probably have adequate built-in ventilation to deal with this. If the device's instruction manual does not tell you how much ventilation is required to vent the emitted CO, or if it is not rated for enclosed spaces, do not buy it. Most such heaters currently on the market will operate on either a one-pound propane canister or can be connected to a 20-pound propane bottle, which is more economical. When visiting the woods in my 24-foot motor home in the fall, I use a small, single-panel "Mr. Heater" stove connected to a 20-pound, or five-gallon propane canister, which I keep outside of the motor home. In weather in which temperatures were mostly in the low to mid-thirties on a recent trip, one such propane tank lasted about four and a half days.
Warning: Children and dogs should be closely monitored when these devices are in use. And it would be a <u>really</u> dumb idea to try to use one at night while you are sleeping.

The obvious disadvantage to the heated tent approach is that it cuts you off from nature and deprives you of the primitive satisfaction of sitting "en groupe" or "en famille" by the campfire while you watch the storm raging around you. But if the storm is severe enough you may just be willing to trade the privilege of viewing it for the smoke-free comfort of a heated space.
Note: Also, see the section on lightning storms in Chapter Three.

A word about clothing

If you go camping more than a few times, you're going to get rained on. It's the law. This is especially true if you choose to go camping in months that are not named either "July" or "August". June can still be somewhat rainy in the mountains. And from Labor Day weekend on, there can be some real gully-washers, too. When it comes to the question of what kind of clothing to take on a camping trip to the mountains, ABP ("Always Be Prepared") is the watchword. ABP with rain gear that is sturdy enough to allow you to move around and do the rough chores required when camping, such as chopping wood and carrying water, not to mention walking through wet brush in search of fire wood. I'm talking raincoat, hat and pants here.

In the dead of summer you can get away with wearing whatever pleases you or nothing at all, for that matter. But if you have to cope with the unpleasant duality of wetness and coldness, you will want to avoid wearing almost any form of cotton, right down to your underwear. When damp or wet, cotton has the unfortunate tendency to conduct body heat away from the skin. Instead, go for those marvelous synthetic fabrics that are famous for wicking moisture away from the body. The combination that works best in the case of an unplanned weekend in the rain is as follows: Next to the skin, poly-propylene or woolen long johns. Next, a layer of Polar Fleece in the form of a sweater or shirt on the upper body and a pair of pants made of a quick-drying fabric that wicks moisture efficiently on the lower body. And, finally, you'll need a decent-quality outer coat and pants that are waterproof and breathable. Again, trite as it sounds, ABP. Hope for the best, but plan for the worst, and you'll never be sorry.

Carrying water and chopping wood

Water will be a constant need while you are camping. For a weekend trip it is entirely possible to carry enough in your vehicle to last for the duration, especially if you find ways to conserve it for drinking purposes only. Fortunately, water is abundant in our beautiful Mount Hood National Forest, especially on its western side, and you will no doubt seldom find yourself far from a source of it. Boil water for human consumption a full five minutes. But boiling water for drinking or cooking on a camp stove takes a lot of expensive camp fuel. My M.O. in the woods is to bring plenty of fresh drinking water from home and to use creek or river water for cooking, making coffee and anything else in which the water content is going to be sterilized by boiling during the preparation and/or cooking process. Likewise, I use heated, but not boiling, river water for washing and rinsing dishes, which I then allow to air-dry. I leave it to you to make your own decisions in this area.

As to the chopping-wood part of this section, bring a sharp axe, not a hatchet, and a saw designed to cut large branches and small, dead trees. Gather your firewood from dead and down timber only.

Camp cookery

Cooking preferences are so individual that I'm going to give this section short shrift. I've encountered purists who wouldn't consider anything but cooking over an open fire when camping. Some haul along complete and well-organized kitchens that can be either homemade or bear the logo of one of the companies that market outdoor products for the masses. If you prefer the control of gas cooking and are concerned about space limitations you can pack along one of the compact little two-burner stoves that run on one-pound propane canisters. Or you might consider one of the tiny stoves used by backpackers and touring sea kayakers. They are about the size of a quart jar, or less, and use either white gas or propane. I will admit that I haven't kept up with the market in this area, but recommend making sure that whichever kind you buy has full adjustability of the flame from low to high. One of my older white gas stoves, which I have used for backpacking for decades, only works dependably in the full 'on' position, making it extremely difficult to use for frying.

Ice chests

Make sure you have a good one and bring along plenty of ice for it. In hot weather, ice never lasts as long as you think it should. Also, ice chests make handy and fairly varmint-proof storage containers in camp, even when they're not used for cooling. And you can usually sit on them, too.

Five-gallon buckets

A few of these can be very handy, since they have a multitude of uses in camp, from camp stools to water and food storage to garbage cans. Andy 'n Bax, on Grand in Portland, and Home Depot sell a specialized lid for them called "Gamma Seal Lids", marketed by Gamma 2. The lids come in primary colors. In camp, I have found them to be watertight enough to keep the contents of the bucket dry in a pouring rain. They are great for carrying and storing creek water and can serve as hassocks for the foot-weary. The lid consists of two parts: a gasketed outer ring, which is pounded onto the rim of a standard five-gallon bucket, and a sturdy, threaded inner disk with a gasket that forms a seal when screwed down into the outer ring. Though the lids are secure enough to keep out insects and smaller vermin, such as mice, rats, snakes and squirrels, the marketing company stops short of endorsing them as bear and raccoon-proof. Bears are reputed to have a much keener sense of smell than dogs, so it won't do to assume they can't smell food through the sides of a perfectly sealed five-gallon bucket with a screw-down lid. When it comes to food, animals can be amazingly resourceful, so we can't assume that bears and raccoons can't figure out for themselves the universal law of lids, which, as we humans all know, is "righty-tighty, lefty-loosey".

Maps again

If you're going to be driving the back roads of the Mount Hood National Forest, you are going to need the best map you can find. Many of the roads were constructed for use by logging and mining interests and are more often than not poorly marked. The best maps that I've been able to find for navigating the back roads of the Forest are the district maps for the Barlow, Clackamas, Hood River and Zigzag districts. These are USGS Department of the Interior, U.S. Geological Survey contour Maps at a scale of 1:24,000 (one foot on the map is the equivalent of 24,000 linear feet – or about 4.5 miles on the ground). Contour lines indicate elevation changes of forty feet. In addition to elevation, these maps provide information about the nature of the terrain, the locations of quarries, mines, buildings, roads and other physical objects, including gates or berms which indicate blocked roads. They can be purchased for around five dollars either from the Mount Hood N.F. headquarters at 16400 Champion Way in Sandy, OR ((503) 668-1700) or from Nature of the Northwest at 800 NE Oregon St., Ste. 965; Portland, OR 97232 (phone: (971) 673-2331, email:info@naturenw.org). Incidentally, you will also find a wealth of recreational information on Nature of the Northwest's web site: www.naturenw.org/.

GPS devices
(Or: You can use technology in the woods, but you should never depend on it completely)

As I have mentioned previously, roads in the Mount Hood National Forest can be confusing and daunting, especially for the directionally challenged. There are so many intersections and forks that the casual or distracted driver who is unfamiliar with the terrain and/or without a map and compass is likely to become quickly confused. Getting around in the Forest is easier if your car is equipped with a GPS. At least I found my little Garmin Nuvi to be very helpful during my two summers of field work. As long as I stayed on one of the main Forest Service roads with at least a four-digit designation, such as FS2610, it provided a constant read-out of the name or number of the road on which I was driving, the direction I was driving and a fairly accurate depiction of the twists and turns, intersections and forks in the road ahead of me, not to mention the names or numbers of intersecting roads, which may otherwise have been difficult to identify due to lack of signage on the ground, which is common throughout the Forest. It also helped me identify nearby bodies of water and landmarks. Still, I never felt confident enough to leave my maps and compass behind. Nor should you. When in the woods, don't ask more of your GPS than whether you have gone the right distance on the right road (they also function as odometers) and whether you have arrived at the correct coordinates. *Use the directions given in Part II of this book, <u>along with a Forest Service district map</u>, to find your campsite.*

I found that programming a desired set of coordinates into my Nuvi by following the Garmin menu was actually very easy. Here's how: Touching the "Where To?" icon brings you to a screen which gives various choices of places to go. Touching the "down" arrow in the bottom right of the screen brings you to a second screen where one of the choices is "Coordinates". The "Coordinates" screen allows you to punch in the coordinates you seek, but only after formatting the device to accept the kind of coordinates you choose to work with. There are three formatting options:

- "ddd .ddddd": Measures the coordinates in degrees to the hundred-thousandth degree,
- "ddd mm.mmm": Expresses coordinates in degrees, minutes and thousandths of a minute. This is the one I find most comfortable to work with.
- "ddd mm' ss.s": Gives the coordinates in degrees, minutes, seconds and tenths of a second.

*For more on using your GPS in the Forest, refer to Chapter 3.

Cell phones

During the field work for this book, I saw a sign somewhere along one of the roads leading into the Forest that said there was no cell phone reception beyond that point. However, experience soon taught me that this was not entirely true. There are indeed pockets of cell phone receptivity within the Forest. Apparently there is a cell tower or two located at a point or points high enough to beam signals that reach limited parts of the forest. I discovered many of them by checking for bars on my cell phone as I drove through the Forest. If there is one of these areas within driving distance of your campsite, you will find it listed in the campsite data tables in Part II, along with the other information pertinent to that specific site. Areas where cell phone reception has been noted are also indicated by this symbol: on the various section maps in Part II. By monitoring your own cell phone, especially while driving on higher elevation Forest Service roads, you may discover yet others. You can find a wealth of information in an article on using cell phones in the back country on the Don F. Jones, Jr., website **www.highcountryexplorations.com**. Though written for the back country traveler, it is relevant to dispersed camping, as well.

Satellite phones

Few people have access to satellite phones because they are expensive to own and use. In spite of this, one can be rented at a price that some people might consider affordable, especially those camping with a large group. I was unable to find any reliable local source for them, but found that they are available online from a San Diego company called "All Road". The people at All Road told me that they can ship an Iridium phone to this area within two days. The rental cost is around $30/week, with an activation fee of $50 and an additional charge of two dollars per minute of use, though these prices may have increased by the time this book is published. Their toll-free telephone number is 1 (888) 884-7623. A cursory website query will produce names and phone numbers for other agencies that rent the devices. Satellite phones need to be able to "see" the sky. The people at All Road tell me that they won't work in cars and are not dependable under a canopy of trees.

Summing up

If you are trying dispersed camping for the very first time, let me remind you again to start with the equipment you already have. Your first experience will no doubt be an adventure in its own right. Later on, experience and your needs will be your best guide to improving the quality of any future camping trips. Take along pen and paper and make notes when ideas pop into your head. I can practically guarantee that you'll come home with a lot of them.

When buying gear, it goes without saying that your budget, your level of experience, where and when you will be camping, the frequency of your camping trips and the gear-carrying capacity of your vehicle will all have to be taken into account. Before you buy you might ponder the wisdom of my sea-kayaking and backpacking buddy, Mike Clough, who told me decades ago that the fact that his life could at some point depend on his outdoor gear made him buy the best he could afford.

✳ ✳ ✳

Okay, it's time to move on to the actual camping part of our discussion. I'll assume that you have your basic gear and that you're planning on driving right past all the commercial campgrounds where the rest of the herd will be bedding down, to seek out some secluded little retreat of your own. If you are an experienced camper and feel that you don't need a primer on dispersed camping, you have my permission to skip ahead to the nitty-gritty of where to camp in Part II.

A list of stuff you'll need:

- ✓ Some rough clothes and sturdy boots for foraging in the forest for dead wood
- ✓ Rain gear
- ✓ A fire grate
- ✓ First aid kit with tweezers for removing stingers, splinters and ticks
- ✓ A detailed map of the region you are heading into
- ✓ A good quality compass with instructions for its use, if you don't already know
- ✓ A charged cell or satellite phone
- ✓ A GPS, if you have one
- ✓ A hundred feet of 1/8" nylon cord for camp use
- ✓ Fifty to a hundred feet of ½" diameter rope
- ✓ A washbasin
- ✓ Hand sanitizer or soap dispenser with liquid hand soap
- ✓ A couple of sturdy 30-gallon plastic bags
- ✓ One or more "garbage glomper" devices for policing your campsite
- ✓ One or more buckets (required of back country campers - five-gallon ones will work fine)
- ✓ Rubber gloves for handling garbage and refuse
- ✓ A long-handled shovel (also required of back country campers)
- ✓ Tent(s)
- ✓ Sturdy plastic tarp to use as ground cloth under tent
- ✓ Large tarp or freestanding rain shelter to cover your cooking and eating area
- ✓ Sleeping bag(s)
- ✓ Camping mattresses
- ✓ Planned menu and food
- ✓ Ice chest and ice
- ✓ Camp stove
- ✓ Cooking utensils, place settings, table cloth
- ✓ A gallon-size coffee pot or other container for boiling large quantities of water over a fire
- ✓ A gallon and a half of potable water per person/per day
- ✓ Compact folding table and chairs
- ✓ Waterproof matches
- ✓ Portable outdoor toilet and toilet paper
- ✓ Privacy shelter
- ✓ Saw for cutting branches
- ✓ Axe for splitting wood
- ✓ Good sturdy gloves for handling wood

Filing a flight plan

Before leaving your driveway, you should let a family member, friend, neighbor, boss, or co-worker know your approximate destination and estimated time of return. Since you can't always be sure where you'll be spending the night when camping in the Forest at large, this is about the best you can do. In this aspect, dispersed camping is not that different from back country exploring and mountaineering. However, you might be able to call the information home from one of the cell phone hot spots listed in Part II after you've found your campsite.

Escaping the summer heat

If your purpose is to escape the heat of summer and you find that every campsite near water is already taken, your next best bet will be to seek a shaded campsite at an altitude high enough to make a difference. Generally speaking, the atmosphere cools 3 degrees F. for every thousand feet of ascent. If it's ninety degrees in Portland, you will gain roughly a ten degree advantage by seeking a campsite somewhere above three-thousand feet.

Choosing a campsite

Okay, someone may have had to help you close the trunk lid, but you did manage to cram all that gear, food and water into your rig after all. Everybody's in the car and eager to get the show on the road, including your dog Barney. You've stopped at a gas station to 'fill 'er up', and now you're eager to find your campsite. Bear in mind that, while you can drive to most of the campsites in Part II, in some you will have to park your vehicle and carry your gear to your campsite. Some sites will work for RV's, and some won't. A few campsites can only be reached by negotiating a rough, steep trail down to a spot by a river or creek. A smaller number still are located on lake shores at the end of a trail or road that takes off on the uphill side of a main Forest Service road. The longest hike to any site in the book is just a shade under a mile. The campsite data table descriptions provided in Part II should tell you whether you can drive to a given campsite or are faced with a park-and-carry situation. If it's a hike-in situation, look for a description of the length and difficulty of the hike in the "Getting there" part of the campsite description. For those who are physically capable, choosing one of the "hike-in" campsites will often lead to a camping experience that is memorable precisely because of its remoteness and because of the extra difficulty involved in getting to the spot. Remember that fifty-foot section of rope I asked you to bring along? This is to help you negotiate any section of trail that might otherwise be too steep for casual walking. The reward at the end of the rainbow (or rope, in this case) is often a taste of wilderness solitude and tranquility that you will be talking up around the water office water cooler for weeks to come.

Prior to making a campsite your own, you should do a quick inspection for potential safety hazards, especially if there are children in your group. Consult Chapter Three on "Safety and Security" for more information.

You will want your tent to be on level, porous ground. If the ground is not completely level, try to sleep with your head higher than your feet. Sleeping with your head downhill may cause you to wake up with a stuffy nose or, worse, a headache. A rake can be a handy tool for clearing away pine cones, rocks and any other debris that could interfere with a good night's sleep, but the job can be done by hand or foot, too. And a mattress will render them completely harmless.

I'll admit that I enjoy drifting off to sleep at night to the pleasant murmuring of a nearby creek, but I try to avoid camping near roaring rivers and waterfalls for the simple reason that they block out too much sound. Being rendered functionally deaf by a nearby waterfall or river while you sleep could mean the loss of your food supplies to a larcenous bear or raccoon.

If you have a freestanding tent, set it up and experiment by lying on the ground inside it before you move your stuff into it. If it doesn't feel comfortable at first, keep trying the tent in other locations until you find one that makes you feel like Goldilocks. If it looks like rain, avoid putting your tent directly under a tree, especially if you are a light sleeper. Trees laden with water from a constant rain are likely to splatter huge drops of water onto your tent at irregular intervals long after it stops raining. On the other hand, in hot, sunny weather you may want to be under the trees.

Most modern tents are made of nylon. This means that live sparks or glowing embers that escape from a rambunctious campfire are likely to go right through them. If you intend to have a fire, keep your tent well away from it.

More on fires

Try to choose an existing fire ring, but if you have to create your own, scrape the ground away to mineral earth, line it with rocks and scrape away all flammable debris for a radius of several feet around. Just remember that whatever you do unto the Forest, you will need to undo before you leave.

Actually, during the summertime when nights are warm anyway, my personal preference is to dispense with a campfire so that I can gape in unobstructed awe at the full panoply of stellar brilliance in the heavens above. On the other hand, a campfire is an essential part of the experience for many people. If a campfire is on the menu for your group, put somebody to work gathering wood as soon as possible after you find your campsite, preferably an adult. *Sending an unsupervised child into the woods to gather wood before you know what's out there is asking for trouble.* Do not cut any living trees. Take dead and dying wood only, and no larger than the diameter of a man's wrist. Also forage for some smaller pieces, ranging from about the diameter of a pencil up to about an inch. These should be as dry as possible. If it has been rainy and you can't find anything on the ground that is dry, try looking near the bases of trees and underneath downed trees. You can often use your saw to cut a length of wood from a large branch that is wet on the outside, and then either split off dry wood from the inside to use as kindling or peel off dry shavings for tinder with your knife. I always pack some store-bought fire starter along, but prefer to use it only as a last resort.

Usually there is at least one person in every group who has an affinity for making fires and the patience to keep at it until they get going. This person should be in charge of the fire and have the absolute authority of a dictator over it, at least until it is snapping and crackling away independently.

Rules and guidelines

Those who drive their cars into the Forest now need to comply with the Forest Service's new road policy and carry a copy of the MVUM with them (see Chapter One). The Forest Service posts its guidelines for dispersed camping on its website. Because regulations promulgated by the Forest Service are always subject to change, I will only say that it is the reader's responsibility to be aware of them before driving into the Forest and putting a tent stake into the ground. Don't depend on areas closed to public camping to be adequately posted with signage. If you are uncertain whether an area is open, please contact a Forest Service office and/or consult your MVUM. The Forest Service has already signaled its intention to consider closing down the popular camping areas on the Salmon River because of the problems of litter and human waste. The best advice I can give you is to be informed about the guidelines and to camp respectfully, walk lightly, and leave no trace. Make it your goal to be part of the solution, not part of the problem.

Salmon River warning sign

The Forest Service has closed down certain popular areas with boulders or gates to prevent people from driving cars into them, but in some cases has tolerated their use for camping by those willing to park their cars along the road and schlep their gear into the camping areas. You can see this along FS63 past the turnoff to Bagby Hot Springs. A large and formerly for-profit campground located on the Collawash River along FS63 was decommissioned and access to it was blocked with large boulders, only to have the boulders rolled aside by the public in apparent defiance of the Forest Service. Despite the fact of the removal of the boulders, many campers still choose to take the hint and leave their cars on the road. A group of people I talked to in this campground said they had camped there every summer for years. It's a lovely spot, but definitely in need of some clean-up.

Because dispersed camping is a do-it-yourself project, there will have been no camp host to carefully go over your campsite to make sure it was clean and pristine prior to your arrival. And the previous users may not have given much of a rip one way or another about leaving the site clean for the next camper. On the other hand, you may get lucky and find that the previous user or users were the kind of people who take the golden rule to heart and will have left behind a spotless campsite for your enjoyment. If so, great! It does happen, but you won't always be so lucky. Bottom line, be prepared to get out your garbage glompers, rubber gloves, and a bucket and do litter patrol before you start to set up your tent and other equipment. Better yet, use teamwork. Have someone start policing the area while others go about the tasks of setting up camp, gathering firewood, etc. Pick up any and all bits of toilet paper you find and burn them in your fire. Cans and pop bottles can be recycled, so take them home with you. In past years an organization known as "*Dumpstoppers*" has maintained dumpsters for public use at the Ripplebrook Guard Station and at the Zigzag District Forest Service office off US 26 in the town of Zigzag, but don't depend on this to continue. Times are tough.

Before leaving your campsite

1. **Pick up anything recyclable and all your garbage**, cigarette butts, food wrappers and other refuse. Imagine that the next camper will be someone you are fond of and have great respect for, such as a favorite teacher. **Don't leave anything behind.**

2. **Thoroughly douse your fire with water**, and make sure it's dead out.

3. If you have brought along a portable toilet, **pack up your poop** and load it in the car.

4. **If you've constructed your own fire ring, tear it down** and scatter the rocks around as you found them, using the earth you scraped away to cover the spot again.

5. **Replace the material you removed from where your tent was located.**

Congratulations. You've now done everything you could to return the place to nature and are entitled to indulge in at least a self-congratulatory pat on the back.

✱ ✱ ✱

Chapter 3
Safety and Security
(Risk Assessment)

Are you really safer in a public campground?

Buy almost any seasoned camp host a beer in a bar in Estacada and stories about the egregious behavior of some campers are sure to follow. One such store related to me took place in one of the Forest's more remote campgrounds a few years ago: Two men were awakened in the early hours of the morning by the sounds of an escalating argument between a man and a woman. The angry threats and accusations echoing throughout the campground soon made sleep impossible. No camp host was available to take charge of the situation, nor was there any way of calling for help. Fearing that the situation would erupt into violence, the men drove to the next campground, some six miles away, in search of help, but discovered that this campground also had no phone service and lost more precious time driving another three miles downriver to find a phone and report the incident. Fortunately, the police were able to get to the scene in time to diffuse the situation and, except for the loss of a good night's sleep, nobody was hurt.

Many people have the perception that camping in an official public campground is safe because there's a camp host present to deal with situations that arise and summon the police and emergency help, if necessary. Unfortunately, this is not always true. For one thing, as is obvious from the above anecdote, land-line phone service is not available in every National Forest campground. Heading out of the Forest on SR 224 to Lazy Bend Campground, the only *non-residential* land line phone service is at the little store at the Ripplebrook Guard Station, which is only open during business hours during the summer. Furthermore, there is little-to-no cell phone receptivity throughout much of the Mount Hood National Forest, especially along the Clackamas River.

Many National Forest Campgrounds not only don't have phone service, but also may not have a resident camp host who is dependably on-site 24 hours a day. Smaller and more remote campgrounds are usually serviced by a nonresident camp host. In this case, he or she usually has to take care of two, and sometimes three, campgrounds, typically residing in one and shuttling back and forth to collect fees and sell wood in the others. In the summer of 2009, I was responsible for two campgrounds located on opposite sides of the road. All summer long, I noticed that if there was going to be a problem that involved drinking or destructive and disrespectful behavior, eighty percent of the time it developed in the campground where I was not residing.

Camp hosts are not cops. They don't carry badges or guns, do not have the authority to arrest people and, as of 2011, were not required to be able to administer CPR. A camp host's life isn't easy. Certainly, most of them have war stories about campground behavior that ranges from the merely rude and disrespectful to the outright criminal. In remote campgrounds with no phone service or law enforcement nearby, hosts obviously have to drive miles to summon help when campground disturbances get out of hand to ensure that no one gets hurt.

In a situation in which someone was on the ground bleeding to death or suffering a heart attack, the time lost trying to get to a phone could mean the difference between life and death. In the more remote campgrounds, the only dependable and immediate phone service would be a satellite phone. However, satellite phone technology doesn't come cheap, and according to the Forest Service, the companies with the concessions to manage campgrounds are not currently required to provide them to their camp hosts. For more information about satellite and cell phone reception in the Forest, see Chapter 2.

In this chapter, we'll try to take a realistic look at some of the hazards that could await us when we choose to go off the beaten path and camp away from the herd. Bearing in mind that it's impossible to foresee every contingency, here is a list of some of them:

- Fire
- Wild animals and insects
- Waterborne illness or lack of proper sanitation practices
- Weather, including hypothermia and lightning strikes
- Random violent crime
- Organized crime (marijuana grows)
- Exposure to toxic chemicals, such as from a meth lab operation
- Carelessness and lack of vigilance
- Alcohol and drug use
- Drowning
- Dead Trees
- Getting lost

Fire

Little rain falls in the Mount Hood National Forest during the months of July and August. During this time, when the Forest can become tinder-dry and dangerously prone to forest fires, the Forest Service goes into a state of hyper-vigilance and may impose restrictions or bans on certain kinds of activity or, in extreme cases, close off access to the entire Forest. An example of the kinds of restrictions on camping activities that are liable to be imposed during the dry season might be as follows:

- Campfires are banned throughout the Forest, except in Forest Service campgrounds.
- Cooking must be done with a stove that can be turned off, as with a valve or button.
- No barbecue grills or coal or fuel-fired fires are allowed.
- Cigarette smoking may only be allowed in an enclosed building or car.

Signs are posted in the Forest to remind us that anyone traveling there is required to carry a bucket and a shovel. It is especially important to make sure that you comply with this requirement during dry, hot weather, so that if a fire gets out of hand, you can act quickly. When the Forest Service is hyper-vigilant, so should you be.

If you can't abide the thought of going camping without a campfire, even when in 90 degree heat, this may be the one time of the year when it would be better to camp in a designated campground. The problem is that there is typically more campsite demand than campsite supply at this time of year. On the other hand, there are benefits to be enjoyed if you can shift perspective and do without a fire during the hot months of summer. The spectacular Perseid meteor showers occur from late July through the month of August, and the fact that daytime temperatures during those two months can soar into the nineties means clear days, warmer nights and stunning views of the night sky.

Forest Service rules are subject to constant change. It is your job to know and observe the rules in effect at all times when you are in the woods, especially during dry, hot weather. Keep your shovel and bucket handy when building and burning campfires. Make sure your campfire is contained by a ring of rocks or metal and built on nothing other than mineral earth. Review the section on building a safe campfire in Chapter 2.

Wild animals

Camp the Mount Hood National Forest long enough and you are going to run into the creatures that live in it and take over the night while you are sleeping. They include bears, mountain lions, coyotes, skunks, bats, squirrels, mice, birds and insects too numerous to mention.

Observe wildlife from a distance. Do not attempt to approach or feed them, no matter how cute they are. The lesson that an animal takes away from being fed by a human is that humans are a source of food. Habituating wild animals to charity is likely to have the undesirable effect of disrupting their natural life cycles by contributing to overpopulation and interfering with their hibernation patterns and food-gathering activities. Your National Forest is not a city park; it is a wild ecosystem in which you have visiting privileges.

BEARS: When gathered around the campfire at night the imaginations of most people seem to embrace the scary prospect of being attacked by a large carnivore, such as a bear or a cougar. While I have seen some large bear scat in my travels through the Forest, I have the assurance from the Forest Service that these are from black bears (Ursus americanus), and not their much more frightening cousins, grizzly bears (Ursus arctos horribilis). While black bears have attacked humans, such attacks are rare to the point of being highly unlikely. Black bears that are unaccustomed to seeing humans tend to be shy around them. Throughout the summer, the prime directive of normal black bears in the Forest is to build up enough fat reserves to survive through the winter hibernation period. This causes them to be perennially hungry and turns them into relentless, clever and opportunistic scavengers who also happen to be strong and fast enough to kill or maim a human being.

Be especially vigilant if there are bears in the vicinity that don't appear to be afraid of humans. When black bears lose their fear of humans and come to see them as a source of food, they are going to develop a laser-like focus on getting at their food, and anyone standing in the way is liable to become collateral damage. If you should happen to come upon an unattended bear cub, remember that mom is probably lurking somewhere in the vicinity, and she won't be able to wrap her mind around the concept that you just think her kid is cute.

Bears have an unusually keen sense of smell and can easily detect food through layers of plastic and around the lid of your cooler. Keeping food in the trunk of your car can be risky. A large, hungry bear can peel the lid of a car's trunk back with the same ease you might rip off the lid of a sardine can. Armed with that knowledge, you have to ask yourself whether it is worth the price of a huge bill from an automotive body shop to protect your fried chicken. You can buy bear-proof food canisters from REI or another outdoor store. They are supposed to be effective, but are expensive. The best precaution when tent camping in bear country is to hang your food at least ten feet in the air and four feet away from the nearest tree trunk, especially at night, when bears are likely to be actively scavenging. Try to store your food at least one hundred yards from camp if possible. Likewise, cooking odors will be a beacon to any animal downwind of you, so cooking should be done well away from where you are sleeping. Don't dump grease on the ground. Either burn it in your campfire or collect it in airtight containers and store it with your food to take home and dispose of later.

When traveling on foot in bear country (and almost all of the Mount Hood National Forest should be considered bear country), it is desirable to announce your presence by making plenty of noise as you hike. And always be alert for any signs that there may be bears in the vicinity. Keep your dog on a leash when hiking in the deep woods. A dog, especially a larger dog, is liable to lead an enraged bear right back to its owner. This happened to me once, and I will tell you that I'm not eager to have another such close encounter of the ursine kind.

Bear poop on FS5720

COUGARS are another matter of concern. I'm beginning to think that there are far more of them in the Forest than most people think. In the summer of 2009 while working as a camp host, several campers who had been coming to the same campground for years told me of having seen them in the campground in prior years. One family reported finding a young cougar on their picnic table around dusk just after I'd come to collect their camp fees the night before. I saw two of them while out exploring the Forest during the summer of 2010. Both were fleeting sightings from a distance on hot summer days when the cougars' quick movements alerted me to their presence.

Cougars are silent and cunning hunters. They have been known to stalk children and small household pets even in urban environments that are contiguous to forested habitat. It is never a good idea to relax vigilance too much while in the forest, no matter the circumstances or the location. A camp host recently told me that he was standing at his door talking to a camper when a large cougar ambled nonchalantly past on the way to the river. Make sure that children are instructed not to wander too far from camp without the presence of an adult. Be sure to keep dogs tethered so they won't be able to run off into the woods after a tempting scent.

RACCOONS can be persistent, determined and clever little problem solvers, especially in areas where campground larceny has paid big dividends in the past. Their very cuteness often earns them an invitation to approach people. Working in groups under the cover of darkness, these masked and opportunistic little bandits will zero in on your food supplies with all the efficiency, silence and cunning of black-ops "Team Alpha". However, the concern about raccoons goes beyond merely protecting the sanctity of your cooler and your corn chips. Raccoons also can carry rabies. Estimates are that up to a third of the population carries the disease in some years. This fact should give any sensible person pause before he or she extends a hand or a tidbit to one of these appealing little guys.

When it comes to rabies, any wild animal with canine teeth should be suspect, but bats and foxes would be the next most likely carriers to be concerned about. While bats are the good guys of the Forest because they pay their ecological freight by eating thousands of mosquitoes and rarely bite people, it can happen when humans frighten them by suddenly entering an area used by bats for resting during the day.

Anyone bitten by a wild animal should receive immediate medical attention.

MICE are everywhere in the forest during the summer and will be out foraging in and around your food as soon as you settle in for the night.

Their lives are governed by biological imperatives no less demanding for the miniscule scale of their bodies than those of their larger mammal cousins. Leave a bag of corn chips or nuts out in the open and they will inevitably find it and make it theirs with their tiny, pellet-sized calling cards.

INSECTS: The fast-moving waters of the Forest's valleys aren't ideal for the development of mosquito larvae into adults. Nevertheless, they do manage to reproduce there. For the last several years, scientists and public health officials have been concerned about the inexorable northward and westward march of the West Nile virus, which is primarily carried by mosquitoes. The first cases in birds and animals began occurring in Malheur County in southeast Oregon in 2006. Of the 53 species of mosquitoes known to inhabit this part of the world, only a few are known to carry the virus. The good news is that I have been unable to find any information supporting the spread of the disease into the Mount Hood National Forest at this time.

TICKS *are of concern because of the threat of Lyme Disease.* According to the CDC website, the total number of cases of Lyme disease in the United States between 2002 and 2011 ranged from a low of 19,804 in 2004 to a high of 29,959 in 2009. Ninety-six percent of all reported cases occurred in the thirteen northeastern and upper Midwestern states of Connecticut, Delaware, Maine, Maryland, Massachusetts, Minnesota, New Hampshire, New Jersey, New York, Pennsylvania, Vermont, Virginia, and Wisconsin. The list below compares the number of cases of Lyme disease reported per 100,000 inhabitants in Oregon and the three northeastern states with the greatest number of reported cases in 2011:

- **Maine: 60.3**
- **New Hampshire: 67.3**
- **Vermont: 76**
- **Delaware: 84.6**
- **Oregon: 0.2**

The highest rate of reported cases in Oregon is in the southwestern part of the state. The lowest is in the area of the Willamette Valley.

According to the OSU Extension Service, of the twenty species of tick found in the state, the western black-legged tick is the only tick known to carry the disease. Phillippe Rossignol, a professor in the fisheries and wildlife department at OSU says on the site that although both adult and immature ticks can transmit the disease to humans, they must be attached to the host for 24 to 48 hours before they can transfer the bacterium to humans.

If you discover a tick on yourself or anyone in your party, follow the instructions below from the Oregon State University website:

- If possible, have someone else remove the tick from your body.
- Use tweezers or forceps rather than fingers.
- Grasp the mouth parts or head end of the tick as close to the skin as possible.
- Gently pull the tick straight out, steadily and firmly.
- The mouth parts are barbed like a harpoon and might break off in the skin. If so, don't be concerned. They do not carry the bacterium and are no more harmful than a sliver.
- Wash hands and the bite area with soap and water; apply an antiseptic to the bite area.
- Keep the tick for identification if disease symptoms occur later. Place the tick in a small container of alcohol labeled with the date removed and the place it was picked up.
- Use the same procedures and precautions when removing ticks from pets.

BEE STINGS are a threat only because some people's bodies are allergic enough to be sent into anaphylactic shock by them. If anyone in your party is allergic it would be a good idea to make sure that you are carrying a dose of epinephrine before you go into the woods, and also a good magnifying glass to help in removing stingers.

If a bee sting occurs, carefully remove the stinger, because it can release even more venom into the body if improperly removed. If visible to the naked eye or with a magnifying glass, carefully try to flick it out with a fingernail. If allergy symptoms are suspected, administer the epinephrine and a dose of an antihistamine such as Benadryl, which may prevent or reduce some allergic reactions, as well. Use your discretion and get the victim to a doctor or medical facility to be checked out and treated as soon as possible. If you choose to do none of these things, keep the victim under close observation for signs of a reaction.

Other risk factors

WATERBORNE ILLNESS: Cryptosporidium and giardia are just two of the protozoan, viral and microbial parasites in the cold mountain streams and lakes of the Mount Hood National Forest that are undetectable to the naked eye. Drink straight from the streams and they will take up residence in your gut and make you sick. Depend on it. To avoid this, you must first decontaminate water from streams or rivers before drinking it. This can be done either by treating it with iodine, filtering it, or boiling it. Iodine leaves an unpleasant after-taste. Filters are fine for a small number of people, but when a larger quantity of water is needed, boiling is usually the most practical method. What has worked for me is to bring my drinking water from home or fetch it from one of the few sources of potable water within the Forest itself and supplement as needed with boiled water from a stream or river. For drinking purposes, boil a full five minutes.

SANITATION IN CAMP requires planning and some forethought. From food handling and preparation to personal hygiene practices, whatever you do at home you should also do in camp, and this is especially true in the case of a group or family. Bring a spray bottle of bleach to use for sanitizing cutting boards. Take along a water container equipped with a spigot and dedicate it to hand washing. Keep a few bottles of hand sanitizer in strategic locations and encourage people to use them, especially after answering the call of nature.

If you elect to use the cat-hole method of defecation, choose a place well away from camp and at least 200' from any creek, river or lake. Dig your hole to a depth of six to eight inches, do your business, then use the material you removed from the hole to cover the spot so that it looks undisturbed again. If there isn't a fire ban in effect, you can dispose of your toilet paper by burning it. Otherwise, bury it with your excrement. Organisms in the upper layers of the soil will break the feces down in fairly short order.

However, there is another way of dealing with human excrement that will make you feel more like part of the solution than part of the problem: a portable toilet system, such as the one described in Chapter 2. These devices make it possible to completely remove your bodily waste from the Forest and deposit it in a designated sewage receptacle. According to Malcolm Hamilton, Recreational Director for the Mount Hood National Forest, the Forest Service actually prefers that campers use this kind of system instead of the cathole method. The idea begins to take on a more personal urgency, if you'll excuse the pun, when one is camped in an area that does not allow for much individual privacy. POYP (Pack out your poop).

DROWNING: Many of the campsites listed in this book are located near fast-moving streams or rivers that are easily capable of sweeping someone downstream, where they could be pinned beneath a log or other underwater obstruction and drowned. Children at play are especially vulnerable here, but so are people whose senses are dulled by too much alcohol or drugs. Even a fisherman who is intent on trying to land his fly on just the right section of a river where that trophy trout may lie in wait is liable to lose his balance and fall into the river. Disaster can materialize very quickly on the banks of a swift, powerful stream, and camping near fast water with children is something that should be avoided.

GETTING LOST in the Mount Hood National Forest is always a possibility, though it's much more likely to happen to those traveling on foot than to someone in a car. Two men and three dogs from Hillsboro were hiking in deep snow on the Bagby Hot Springs Trail in June, 2010 when the battery of their GPS device failed and they became confused and realized that they were lost. Rather than panicking, the men chose to hunker down near the trail and wait for rescue. All five, including the three dogs, were subsequently found by search and rescue personnel and returned to safety two days later.
Robert Bissell, 57, of Northeast Portland, an experienced hiker and backpacker who went missing when hiking alone to go fishing in the Rock Lakes Basin area on July 12 of the following month, was not so lucky. His brother reported his absence some twelve days later after finding both Bissell's car and camp deserted. A massive search lasting several days failed to locate Robert.

Both of these incidents should be taken as cautionary tales by anyone who leaves the road to travel on foot on the Forest's network of trails. We have no way of knowing what happened to Robert Bissel, but it is clear that the two men traveling on snow in the Bagby Hot Springs area relied too heavily on technology in the form of their GPS device.

Many of the roads in the Mount Hood National Forest are poorly marked, and it is all too easy to become confused while driving them. During two summers of driving and bicycling on Forest Service roads I continually met people who had driven into the Forest more or less innocently and without a proper map, only to find themselves quickly confused by its labyrinth of intersecting and branching roads. However, unless you're running low on gas or your car breaks down, getting lost on a Forest Service road in the summertime is probably more likely to result in being late to dinner than it is to end in disaster. Most Forest Service roads branch off from several Level 5 feeder roads and go relentlessly upward, which means that, when one is completely lost, salvation more than likely lies downhill. The Forest is large, but not immense. One is seldom more than 15 or 20 miles from a main road or a major landmark in any direction. Your map and compass are a cheap and low-tech form of insurance. *Don't go into the Forest without them. Refer to Chapter 2 for more information on maps and where to buy them.*

As the section on GPS units in Chapter 2 makes plain, these devices can be an invaluable aid in navigating the Forest, but should never be depended on entirely. I call my little Garmin Nuvi *Iris* ("she who sees all"). Almost without fail, Iris gave me a constant readout of the number (or sometimes the name) of the road upon which I was driving, as well as my direction and speed. And Iris had other features I found quite useful, as well. She showed a picture of the twists and turns of the route ahead of me as I drove, as well as some of the landmarks to the side of the road. I was often able to match the bends in the road Iris was showing me to the bends in the road on my map, which gave constant reassurance that I was on the right track.

A problem I had with her which underscores the need for a map was that, while the Forest Service maps identify all roads by their official Forest Service number, my GPS often identified them by their popular names, such as "Pipeline" or "Peavine". To further complicate things, some of the named roads are very long and made up of shorter sections of several numbered roads. When this happened it became especially difficult to figure out where I was without referring to the map, which identifies roads by number only.
*Also see the section in this chapter on "Getting Lost".

CARELESSLESSNESS AND LACK OF VIGILANCE: The importance of vigilance and awareness of one's surroundings in the woods cannot be overstressed. Neither police protection nor ambulances with EMTs are just a phone call away from most places in the Forest, which means that an extra measure of caution and forethought is required not only with alcohol and drugs, but with the common tools and equipment you will be using and operating. Carry a first-aid kit and always know where it is. Make sure that children are properly instructed and supervised when using any tool or device that could hurt them. Use common sense and don't operate power equipment of any kind when drinking. If you choose to keep a gun around for security purposes, make sure that children don't have access to it. Without being paranoid, try to stay ahead of the situation by anticipating safety issues before they can arise.

ALCOHOL AND DRUG use in the woods has the potential to result in disaster. Yet many people of good judgment feel strongly that their use adds value to their experience of nature, and so choose to embrace the extra risk. Although I would like to discourage this, I realize that people will do what people will do and prefer to take the saner route of encouraging moderation and forethought. Enough said.

RANDOM VIOLENT CRIME is one of the first things that come to mind when most people think about dispersed camping. In January of 2010 I talked to Andrew Coreill, Patrol Captain for the northern Oregon Law Enforcement and Investigation Section of the U.S. Forest Service, about the incidence of random, violent crime in the Forest. Coreill told me that assaults were not unheard of, but tended to cluster around a few areas that were popular. Bagby Hot Springs was one such area. Coreill indicated that vehicles left in the parking lot near the trailhead to the hot springs are sometimes broken into, and added that assaults have occurred in the vicinity as well. One man was assaulted on the trail leading to the hot springs by a young man wielding a bat a few years prior to 2010. In years past there have been about a dozen abductions in the northern tip of the Forest where it is contiguous to I-84 in which people have been taken at gunpoint to an ATM machine and ordered to empty their accounts. The victims in these cases were primarily individuals using the pull-outs along the freeway at night, often for the purpose of making out.

Coreill said that conflicts between campers at dispersed camping sites have been more common than assaults, and that these usually start out when a camper is behaving in a way that is inconsiderate of other campers, such as making an undue amount of noise or shooting guns. He added that, though police have on occasion been called in to resolve them, these disputes usually stay at the argument level.

Coreill said that campers in dispersed sites need to apply the rules of common sense and notify the Forest Service if they see anyone or anything suspicious. He cautioned that a vehicle becomes a target when no one is around and advises people to take their valuables with them when leaving camp for an extended period of time. Also, there is safety in numbers, so a party of four (adults) is more secure than a party of two, and so on.

Throughout the summers of 2010 and 2111 as I was doing the fieldwork for this book I took every opportunity to talk to the people I found camping in the Clackamas River District of the Forest. Most, but not all, were weekend campers who had been doing dispersed camping for years, often returning to the same spot year after year. None reported having had any serious confrontations with their fellow man while camped in the Forest. A retired man who had camped along one of the Forest's rivers every summer for years, told me that in over a decade of camping in the same spot, his most serious encounter with others occurred when he caught a group of young revelers who were camped nearby attempting to help themselves to his firewood. Fortunately, the young men responded positively to his forceful request to move on and find their own firewood.

An effective strategy for minimizing the possibility of ending up with obnoxious neighbors is to choose a campsite whose size will closely accommodate the number of people in your party. When you find such a site it is sometimes possible to effectively block the entrance to it by strategically parking a vehicle or vehicles, but reason dictates that this must be done without blocking access to a through road, violating Forest Service rules or depriving someone else of legitimate access to a campsite.

TO CARRY A GUN OR NOT TO CARRY A GUN is the question. And it's an entirely personal one. Many city dwellers have a negative opinion of guns. But when law enforcement isn't just a 911 call and a few minutes away, it is hard to deny that the advantage shifts dramatically to the side of a would-be malefactor. For this reason, many serious and sober people do carry weapons when camping in the woods.

EXPOSURE TO TOXIC CHEMICALS FROM A METH LAB OPERATION is much less a concern now than it was several years ago. According to one Forest Service employee I talked to about the problem, state efforts to control access to the cough and cold medicines made with ephedrine that are used in the illegal manufacture of methamphetamines have led to something like a seventy-percent reduction of the number of meth labs discovered in the Forest. These medications were formerly sold freely over the counter in most pharmacies and drug stores, but now require a prescription to be purchased in Oregon. In Washington, a signature and ID are required to purchase a limited quantity of them over the counter, and each sale is documented in a statewide database.

When a suspected meth site is reported, a Forest Service haz-mat team is immediately dispatched to evaluate it. If a determination is made that the site has been used for the production of methamphetamines, a private firm is contracted to decontaminate the site, at a cost of between four and ten thousand dollars.

Many substances besides ephedrine are used in the production of meth, including some toxic ones, like red phosphorous, iodine crystals and lithium battery acid. Meth manufacturers do not typically want to locate their operations near a road, where they would be more easily detected. Furthermore, all but a few of the campsites listed in this book are within sight of a road. Nevertheless, the possibility of stumbling upon a meth site while in the woods does exist, and "forewarned is forearmed", so let's take a look at some of the things you should be on the lookout for.

Meth lab operations are not confined to apartments and houses, but can be set up in campgrounds, rest areas, abandoned cars, storage sheds, barns, vacant buildings or even a suitcase.

Usually, they are a collection of chemical bottles, hoses and pressurized cylinders, which can take the form of modified propane tanks (sometimes spray-painted or burned, with bent or altered valves or blued fittings), fire extinguishers, scuba tanks and soda dispensers. The tanks contain anhydrous ammonia or hydrochloric acid, both of which are very poisonous and corrosive. Labs are frequently abandoned, leaving explosive and toxic chemicals behind and hanging taxpayers and the Forest Service with the expense of clean-up.

Some of the supplies used in a meth lab operation are plastic tubing, ammonia, funnels, rock salt, iodine, lithium batteries, camp stove fuel, glass containers, hydrogen peroxide, ephedrine or pseudoephedrine tablets and starter fluid, to name a few.

Below is a list of other things that might help you identify a possible meth site:

- Strong odors that don't belong in the woods,

such as cat urine, acetone, ammonia, ether or other chemical odor are all indicators that you should consider vacating the area. That said, the absence of any odor is not an indication that a site has not been used for meth production.

- Soft drink bottles with tubes coming out of them, plastic "Heet" bottles, Red Devil lye bottles, empty pill bottles or pill blister packs, evidence of cold medications containing ephedrine or pseudoephedrine, glass containers (jars or cookware) with a white residue, other evidence of white crystal residue, red chemically stained coffee filters, empty pill bottles, empty cans of toluene, alcohol or paint thinner, and/or iodine-stained fixtures of any kind, large numbers of antifreeze containers, lantern fuel cans, and drain cleaner containers, excessive amounts of duct tape, numerous plastic "Baggies", coffee filters, match book covers with the striker plates removed or torn lithium battery casings.

If you happen to stumble upon a suspicious site you should immediately vacate the area and report the finding as quickly as possible. If the site is currently in use, you may be in danger from those who put it there. It is dangerous to breathe the fumes or handle the substances and materials you may find there. Some of the chemicals may explode if exposed to air or water. Only trained haz-mat people should enter the site.

MARIJUANA GROW OPERATIONS: When I interviewed him in January of 2010 Andrew Coreill told me that *Marijuana grow operations financed by Mexican drug cartels* are on the increase in the Forest, but that, as of that time, there had not been any conflicts between growers and recreational users of the Forest. Coreill went on to say that grow operations are usually tended by illegal aliens and commonly located in sites that are away from roads and well hidden from the eyes of the public. Growers need a water source and have been known to pipe water through the forest from a creek or spring to the grow site. Hunters tramping about the woods during hunting season are most likely to stumble upon the marijuana grow operations. Coreill cautions anyone who happens to come upon a trail in the forest that looks suspicious, especially one near a source of water, to report the information. He maintains that car campers accessing the Forest via official Forest Service roads run little risk of stumbling upon marijuana grow operations, but warns against following any road or track leading off into the woods that is not an official Forest Service road. My own personal experience bears this out. During two subsequent summers of driving most of the 3,000 miles of Mount Hood National Forest roads in the course of writing this book, I never encountered any evidence of illegal drug activity of any kind. Many of the roads I drove were far off the beaten path and so overgrown with small trees that my poor Toyota Corolla's doors still bear scars from the experience.

WEATHER HAZARDS can range from dehydration to heat stroke, hypothermia and lightning strikes.

LIGHTNING: Lightning strikes can kill and maim. The power in a lightning bolt can exceed 100,000 volts. Lightning storms in mountainous areas are more likely to occur in the afternoon during the summer. Ridges and mountain tops are the worst places to be during a lightning storm. The thirty-second rule says if the thunder occurs less than thirty seconds after the lightning it's time to seek shelter, because the lightning is close enough to reach out and touch you. The safest shelter is a structure of some kind. A car is less safe, but still better than a tent, since the tent's metal frame can act as a conductor. If your hair wants to stand on end, you feel a tingling sensation on your skin or hear crackling sounds, a lightning strike in the area is imminent. If you're outside with a group of people and there is no other shelter possible, seek a low spot. Don't huddle together and give the current several bodies to run through, but separate yourself and assume a crouching position on the ground with your feet touching. The ground will carry the current to you from any nearby lightning strike, but with the feet touching each other, it will (hopefully) run up one foot and down the other instead of harming vital organs. Something else to remember is that lightning can reach up to ten miles from the edge of the storm as it retreats. You cannot assume you are safe from it until a full half-hour after the last lightning strike.

HYPOTHERMIA is defined in the Encarta Dictionary as a *"dangerously low body temperature caused by prolonged exposure to cold."* There are three levels of hypothermia, from mild to severe. In this book intended for the summertime camper I am going to limit myself to addressing just the first stage, mild hypothermia, which, if properly treated, usually ends with a complete recovery. As the body's core temperature drops below 98.6 degrees F, symptoms are numbness in the hands, slurring of the speech and shivering. In addition, the victim's judgment may be impaired to the point that he or she may not be capable of making rational decisions. The victim should be removed to a warm, dry environment out of the wind – a car with the heater going full blast would be fine. Any wet clothes should be removed and replaced with dry, warm ones. If a building or car is not available, get the victim into warm, dry, windproof, waterproof gear and build a fire. Or place the victim into a pre-warmed sleeping bag that is insulated from the ground by pine boughs, moss, clothes, or an insulated mattress (not an air mattress, which provides scant insulation from the ground). Ply the victim with hot drinks, followed by candy or another high-sugar food. If this protocol is followed the victim's core temperature should return to normal, though it may take some time.

In the summer of 2009 I had a personal experience with hypothermia. After a vigorous bike ride early one hot August afternoon, nothing seemed more appealing than a good, long soak in the invigorating waters of the Clackamas. I had been doing this routinely for fifteen or twenty minutes at a time all summer with no ill effects. This time it felt so good that I lengthened my stay to a full half-hour. It wasn't until I finally got out of the water and retreated to the inside of my motor home, where the temperature was around eighty degrees Fahrenheit, that I even realized I had become hypothermic. I felt cold and weak for about an hour and a half, even after putting on long johns, drinking a couple of cups of hot, instant soup and getting into the heaviest sleeping bag I had aboard. After that I learned to limit my soaks to a maximum of twenty minutes.

Learn to recognize the symptoms of mild hypothermia and stop them early. If hypothermia is allowed to progress to the second stage of severity the victim's life can be in danger.

DEAD TREES pose a silent menace to the unsuspecting camper. Inspect the area where you intend to set up your temporary living quarters in the woods. Don't camp near or under any tree that shows signs of insect damage or appears to be questionable. Make sure that children do not play on or around them.

Summing up

There is no doubt that camping away from the herd brings some measure of added risk, but probably not as much as most people might think. And most of it is the kind of risk that is manageable. Not one of the campers I met during my summertime travels throughout the Forest reported having had dangerous confrontations with either animals or people. Generally speaking, risk is inversely proportional to the amount of common sense and planning involved in any venture.

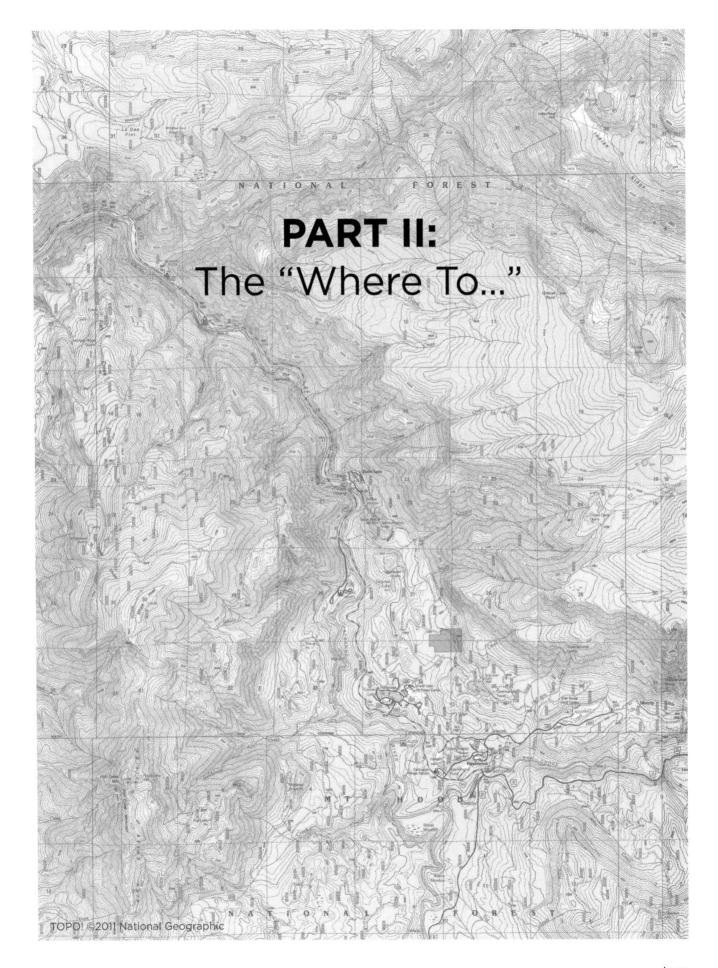

PART II:
The "Where To..."

HOW TO USE PART II

The Mount Hood National Forest is a huge place, and I do not claim to have found all its campsites, but this book will guide you to more than 200 campsites, which, combined, provide between 1400 and 1800 separate tent sites along over 2000 miles of Forest Service roads. All the campsites listed in Part II of this book are located in one of four areas of the Forest. These area maps are:

1. THE LOLO PASS or northern section of the Forest, located along Forest Service Road #18 (FS18), from Zigzag northward to Lost Lake
(Pages 36-46)

2. THE BARLOW PASS or north-east section of the Forest: The area bracketed by US 26 and SR 35 (Hood River Highway), from Barlow Road in the south to Fifteenmile Campground in the north
(Pages 47-69)

3. THE CENTRAL PART of the Forest: The area bracketed by US 26 on the east, Forest Service Road #57 on the south and SR 224 on the west
(Pages 70-110)

4. THE CLACKAMAS SOUTH AND WEST SECTION of the Forest: An area mostly comprised of Clackamas River District south of FS57 and west of OR 224 and FS46
(Pages 111-156)

To find a campsite in any one of these areas, use the map key on the inside of the front cover to find the section of the book that covers that part of the Forest. There you can scan the detailed map which shows the road numbers and the relative locations of the campsites located in each section of the Forest. The campsites are numbered within black circles. Most, but not all, of the sites you'll find here are near a source of running water or a lake. Campsites that are not close to a source of water are described as either "*dry*" or "*waterless*". It is important to remember that the locations of the campsites in the area maps are not precise because of the scale of the maps. *Likewise, the area maps are not detailed enough to be used without a Forest Service Map, since, again, due to the scale of the maps, not all roads are identified.*

You will find detailed descriptions of each campsite in the campsite description section which follows the area maps. Each campsite description uses the same format: Essential data for each campsite are given in a table format, followed by a general description as well as directions to the site.
Study the example below:

34

Loc: FS42, 0.1 mile south of FS4280, by Joe Graham Horse Camp	**Road:** Paved
L/L: N45 06 225/W121 44 607	**Access:** Drive to camp
Cell: South end Timothy Lake	**Tents:** 10-15
	El: 3420
Lndmk: Joe Graham Horse Camp	**RV:** MH OK, TT?

Description: The many tent sites here sit well away from the road among the tall conifers to provide privacy for a large party. The Oak Grove Fork of the Clackamas starts as a creek behind camp a few hundred feet from the road. This site gives access to everything Timothy Lake has to offer the recreational camper. Access to the PCT and a horse trail that goes around the lake is just south of camp.

Getting there: From US 26, go 8.1 miles south on FS42 toward Timothy Lake. Pass FS4280 on right at 8 miles and watch for the site on your left and just north of where the PCT crosses the road in the next tenth of a mile. MVUM F6-7

Here's what the campsite data table will tell you:

Loc: Location. This site is on Forest Service Road #42, one-tenth mile south of Forest Service Road #4280 and near the Joe Graham Horse Camp.

L/L: The GPS coordinates of the site.

El: The elevation above sea level, in feet.

Road: The campsite is located on a paved road (as opposed to gravel or dirt). Sometimes there will be other comments in this section concerning the quality of the road.

Tents: How many family-size tent sites are to be found at this site (admittedly, this is somewhat subjective).

Access: Whether it is possible to drive directly to the campsite or have to park some distance away and carry your gear to it. Here are the two most common designations to be found in this field and what they mean:

- Drive to site: You can drive your car all the way to your campsite, within Forest Service guidelines.
- Park and carry: You will need to park some distance away and carry your gear to your campsite.

RV: This site is okay for a motor home, but questionable for a travel trailer. Other possibilities would be: "No", meaning that no RVs of any kind should use this site, or "Road too rough".

Cell: The nearest place where you might find cell phone reception (in this case, at the south end of Timothy Lake.

 Look for this symbol on maps to indicate where cell reception can be found (though cell reception cannot be depended upon).

Lndmk: The name of a prominent landmark nearby. This campsite is located in the vicinity of the Joe Graham Horse Camp.

Following each campsite description data table you will also find the following information:

Description: A short physical description of the site as per the example above.

Getting there: Directions to the site are given from a point along either US 26 or OR 224, and sometimes both. MVUM F6-7 indicates that the site can be found somewhere on MVUM map page F6 or F7 (probably at the top of one or the bottom of the other in this case).

In addition to the abbreviations and acronyms used in the campsite data tables described above you are liable to find others, as well. Here is a list of them:

Rd.: Road
Cg.: Campground
PCT: Pacific Crest Trail
MP: Milepost
OR: Oregon Route (as in OR 224)
FS: Forest Service and short for Forest Service Road, as in FS18
FSR: Forest Service Road (as in FSR18)
MHNF: Mount Hood National Forest
W/in, w/in: within

Mileages between points may have been derived from one of three sources and may vary from the mileage indicated on your vehicle's odometer. The three sources of mileages for this book are:
- An automobile odometer
- An automobile GPS device
- By computer, using a National Geographic mapping program

The numbers assigned to campsites in Part II may appear to be somewhat arbitrary. Some campsites may have been given numbers which seem out of sequence for their location. This sometimes became unavoidable when a site was discovered after other sites in that area had already been assigned a number or when a campsite was for some reason removed from the list after having been assigned a number.

Campsites located along the major rivers, such as those along FS46 and FS57, are generally easier to get to and tend to be very appealing to the public at large, especially during the hotter months of the summer. Unfortunately, many of them are sandwiched between a road and a river, which means that the large numbers of humans drawn to them throughout the summer begin to pose serious risks to the health of the river and the nearby vegetation. The Forest Service has been trying to discourage camping in several areas along these roads, especially along FS46, by blocking vehicular access to them with heavy rocks and gates and with its new roads policy. *There are some very nice campsites located along FS46, but you should check with the Forest Service and/or refer to the MVUM before considering driving to them. There are heavy penalties attached to violations.*

Public disregard for our National Forest is a huge issue. Not only does it have an extremely negative effect on the Forest and its inhabitants, it impacts the lives of the people in and around the Forest, including the small communities nearby whose motels, restaurants, grocery stores and coffee houses depend on the annual tide of summertime visitors flowing through on their way to camp, play, hunt, fish and forage. Due to the loss of logging revenue, the Forest Service no longer has the resources it had in past decades. **It cannot afford to clean up after those who consider the Forest their back yard when it comes to recreation, but somebody else's responsibility when it comes to clean-up.** The Forest Service is already thinking of a total prohibition on dispersed camping in the popular Salmon River Canyon area due to litter and the problem of human waste.

As previously explained, not all of the campsites listed in the book are located near a river or stream. The *dry* campsites in the book are included for a particular reason. Often it's because they are located conveniently close to a popular recreation site, such as a lake or hiking trail. A few were included because of some notable feature about the site itself, such as a commanding view, exposure to a cooling breeze or the capacity to accommodate a large number of tents.

Snagging a prime campsite near water

Not all campsites are created equal. Some are definitely more appealing than others. By Friday evening during the months of July and August there's as much demand for prime dispersed campsites, or "*gems*," as I prefer to think of them, as there is for the campsites in designated Forest Service campgrounds. If you want to snag a great campsite on any weekend during these two prime camping months, be aware that you will have to be packed and out of town well before the rest of the herd charges out of the city at rush hour on Friday afternoon.

Though I have made a diligent effort to ferret out every possible campsite in my two summers of driving the roads of the Forest, there are *literally thousands of campsites still out there, waiting to be discovered.* Chances are always good that you will find a campsite near a stream or other body of water, but don't despair if you can't. There is always a shady spot up the road a ways in our welcoming National Forest that will accommodate your tent, and there is almost always a creek somewhere in the vicinity that will provide water for camp use, though some of them are so small and well-hidden that it's easy to drive by without noticing them. Experience will teach you to keep an eye peeled for potential dry campsites as well as streams that would be good sources of water as you drive through the Forest.

Caveat

Inspect your site for hazards: During the summertime field work phase of this book, the inspections of the sites noted herein were limited to checking for the essentials necessary for camping, as well as any obvious safety concerns. Some of the sites in this book, though beautiful and otherwise desirable, are not suitable for children. Examples are those that are located on the banks of fast-moving rivers and streams that could sweep a distracted child downstream. A few might be located too close to a precipice, dead tree or other potential hazard. I cannot claim to have covered every possible risk factor and must leave it to you to make a more thorough inspection of the site and its environs when you arrive on the spot, especially if you have children or someone with special needs in your party. More on safety and security issues in Chapter Three.

Disclaimer

Almost without exception, the sites included in this book are those that appeared to have been used as campsites by others in the past, as evidenced by the presence of a fire ring and a bare patch of ground where a tent can be erected. This book cannot be relied upon as an authoritative guide to the ever-changing landscape of laws, policies, rules, regulations and guidelines promulgated by the US Forest Service. In deference to the Forest Service's new road policy, in Part II of this book you will find a reference to the appropriate MVUM page number for each campsite listed. Because a site is listed in this book does not mean that you are free to drive your vehicle into or onto the site. Virtually all of the campsites listed in this book were in use prior to the inception of the new MVUM guidelines, and the roads upon which they are located were, to the best of my knowledge, open to highway-legal vehicles at the time of discovery. That said, *I have made a diligent effort to exclude and delete any campsite located along roads that are closed to motor vehicles and where dispersed camping is prohibited. I have also tried to indicate which campsites are not accessible to motor vehicle traffic, but I cannot guarantee that I have been one hundred percent successful in doing so.*

Because of missing or damaged road signs it was sometimes difficult to identify a location precisely. Any errors will have been inadvertent. I did find it necessary to document several sites that are not MVUM compliant along FSR46 south of milepost 50. I did this for those who might want to access them without a vehicle, and also lest they be lost in the event that the Forest Service might someday open them to vehicular traffic once again. *Therefore, to the reader falls the responsibility to be informed of all current county, state and federal laws, regulations and restrictions and guidelines that apply and are in force in the Mount Hood National Forest, including, but not limited to those pertaining to dispersed camping, fishing, hunting, the use of fire, firearms, the operation of motor vehicles and the cutting, digging or harvesting of plant or animal life of any kind.*

Furthermore, the practical information provided in other chapters is based on the author's opinions, insights, research, knowledge and practical experience, and is not presented as either definitive or authoritative. *The book is intended only as a guide and is not a substitute for the reader's knowledge or judgment.*

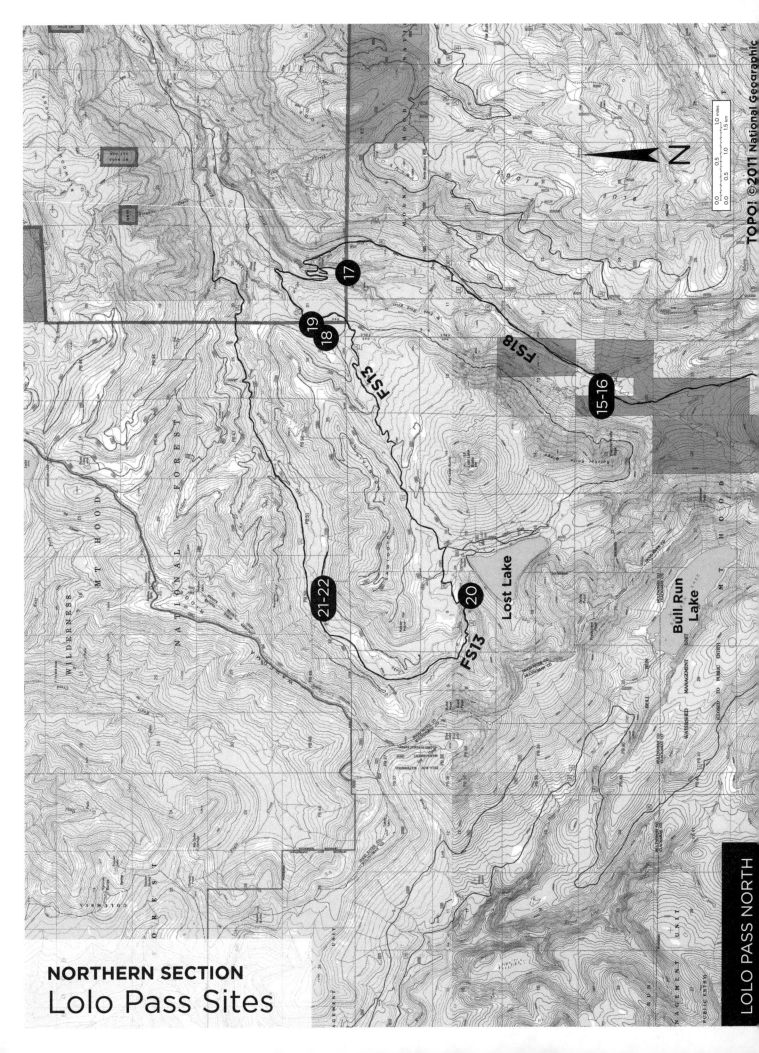

NORTHERN SECTION
Lolo Pass Sites

LOLO PASS NORTH

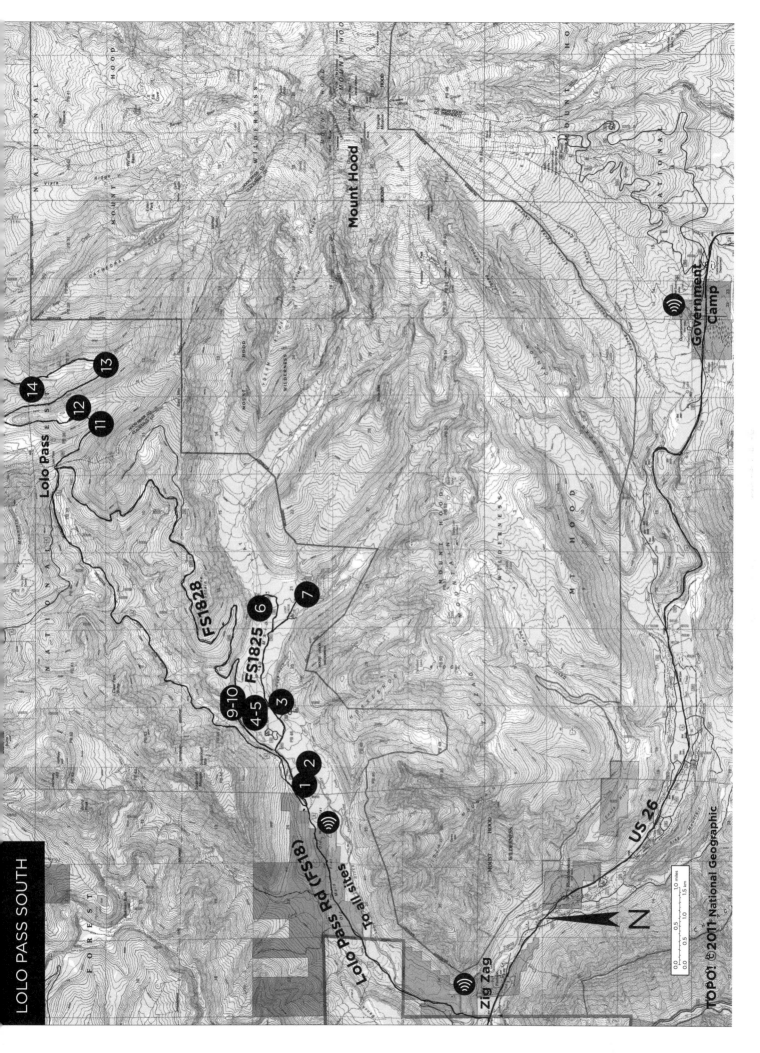

NORTHERN SECTION

Lolo Pass Sites

The Sandy River
Everywhere one looks in this drainage, there is evidence that the Sandy River is aptly named. Over the millennia it has deposited sand deeply and generously along its meandering course to the Columbia River.

Loc: FS1825, 0.2 mile from FS18/1825 junction	**Road:** Paved
L/L: N45 22 876/W121 52 768	**Access:** Can't drive to all sites
Cell: Zigzag and FS18, 2.9 to 3.1 miles SW of McNeil Cg.	**Tents:** 10-15
	El: 1990
Lndmk: Sandy River/ Muddy Fork Rd	**RV:** MH and TT

Description: This site is best described as open, flat, treed and, like a lot of sites in this part of the Forest, sandy. It is suitable for a large party camping in several family-size tents. Because the river here is a few hundred yards through the trees from the camping area, and because water from the Sandy is liable to be, well, sandy at certain times of the year, it is wise to bring a plentiful supply of water from home or from nearby Zigzag or Rhododendron. There are restaurants and a grocery store in Rhododendron and Zigzag, 4 to 6 miles distant.

Getting there: From US 26, turn onto FS18 across the road from the Forest Service offices in Zigzag. At 4.1 miles go right on FS1825 (Muddy Fork Road). After crossing the bridge, campsites are on right at 0.2 miles from the junction of FS18/1825. MVUM E4

Loc: FS1825, near Camp McNeil	**Road:** Gravel/dirt
L/L: N45 22 785/W121 52 568	**Access:** Check MVUM
Cell: Zigzag and FS18, 2.9 to 3.1 miles SW of McNeil Cg.	**Tents:** 100, or more
	El: 2000
Lndmk: Camp McNeil	**RV:** MH and TT

Description: You should almost always be able to count on finding space for a tent somewhere along the primitive but negotiable half-mile of dirt road that curves off the Muddy Fork Road to give access to these sites along the Sandy. You may have to pay for your stay by doing some clean-up here. Like many large sites where many people have camped, some of these sites have been abused by careless campers. The many trees and log jams that the Sandy has flung up on high ground during flood times offer testament to the past braiding and wandering of its streambed and often make access to the river problematic. If your object is to escape the heat of summer, this may not be the site for you. The sandy soil here seems to support mostly scrubby pine and fir trees which do not offer the dense shade of the deep forest. Another negative is that this stretch of the Sandy is both swift and noisy, so it may not appeal to those camping with children. On the other hand, this may be good news for those curmudgeons who would rather camp away from children.

Getting there: From Zigzag, go 4.1 miles on FS18, then take FS1825 (Muddy Fork Rd.) 0.8 mile. Turn right and cross the Sandy at bridge. Then proceed another 0.2 miles, where you will come to rough dirt road just past McNeil Campground. This road is rough but drivable in summer conditions, though caution is advised during periods of heavy rain. MVUM E4

3

Loc: FS 1825 across Sandy and 1.3 miles from FS18	**Road:** Gravel and dirt
L/L: N45 23 139/W121 51 580	**Access:** Park and carry
Cell: Zigzag and FS18, 2.9 to 3.1 miles SW of McNeil CG.	**Tents:** 10-15
	El: 2140
Lndmk: Lost Creek	**RV:** MH and TT

Description: This large, open area, surrounded by 40 to 50 foot-high trees at the end of the access road is an excellent site for a large party. It offers privacy and the pleasant burbling of Cast Creek, which flows by in a ravine some 200 yards to the west on its way to join Lost Creek. An easy path gives access to the creek for fishing and drawing water.

Getting there: From the Zigzag Ranger Station on US 26, drive 4.1 miles on FS18. Go right 1.3 miles on FS1825, crossing the Sandy on the Muddy Fork Road Bridge. Campsites are located about 0.1 mile to the right of FS1825 on the unmarked dirt road just past Riley Creek Horse Camp. MVUM E4

Loc: Spur Road 050 near Camp McNeil	**Road:** Dirt
L/L: N45 23 288/W121 51 767	**Access:** Park and carry
Cell: Zigzag and FS18, 2.9 to 3.1 miles SW of McNeil CG.	**Tents:** 20-30
	El: 2160
Lndmk: McNeil Campground	**RV:** No

Description: Basically, this is an open, flat, sandy area covered with grass and low-growing kinnikinnick. It features room for many tents and large groups. The lack of trees in this area makes it less than ideal for hot weather camping, but might make it a good choice for a spring or early summer trip. Be sure and bring plenty of water. Or, if you don't mind purifying and boiling your drinking water, you might consider taking it from nearby Lost or Cast Creeks instead of the Sandy, especially if there's a lot of silt and sand coming down the river.

Getting there: From Zigzag, drive 4.1 miles on FS18. Turn right on FS1825, crossing the Sandy on the Muddy Fork Road Bridge at about 0.8 miles from the junction. At 1.3 miles from FS18/1825 and a short distance after passing McNeil Campground, find spur 050, on the left. Camping areas open up a few hundred yards from the road. MVUM E4

6

Loc: Ramona Falls Trailhead	**Road:** Paved and gravel
L/L: N45 23 230/W121 49 912	**Access:** Park and carry
Cell: Zigzag and FS1825, 2.9 to 3.1 miles SW of McNeil C.G	**Tents:** 20-30
	El: 2420
Lndmk: Sandy River, Ramona Falls Trailhead	**RV:** Parking area only

Description: Located near the Ramona Falls Trail trailhead, this is a beautiful choice. Its many campsites are scattered over a large area, each offering the gift of privacy and seclusion. If budget cuts don't get it, the shiny, portable blue outhouse I found in the parking area, which is apparently intended for the use of hikers using the Ramona Falls Trail, may still be there when you arrive. You will find many level tent sites within a short distance of the parking lot. Or, if you desire to get closer to the river and enjoy a more primitive camping experience, you can carry your gear 200 to 300 yards to a bench above the river. Here you will find several campsites with fire pits scattered out under the trees.
The Ramona Falls Trail loosely follows the Sandy upstream into the wilderness area to the Falls and may provide an interesting side trip while you are camping here.

Getting there: Go 4.1 miles from Zigzag on FS18. Turn right onto 1825 at junction. Continue on 1825, crossing the Sandy at about 0.8 miles. At 2.5 miles from the FS18/1825 junction take FS100 to the left toward Ramona Falls Trail for 0.4 miles, and then take Road 024 for 0.2 miles to trailhead parking area. MVUM E4
Note: A Northwest Forest Pass is required for parking in any trailhead parking lot from May 15 through the summer.

Loc: FS1825-109, 3.3 miles east of FS18	**Road:** Gravel
L/L: N45 22 724/W121 49 794	**Access:** Park and carry
Cell: Zigzag and FS 18, 1.8 miles SW of FS18/1825 junction.	**Tents:** 1-2
	El: 2200
Lndmk: Lost Creek and Lost Creek Campground, 0.5 mile north	**RV:** No

Description: Here you'll find a delightful and secluded camp just right for a small party about a hundred yards off of FS1825-109. Lost Creek is crystal clear and pristine, so take care to leave it as you found it.

Getting there: Drive 4.1 miles NE of Zigzag on FS18. Go right on FS1825 at junction, crossing bridge at about 0.8 miles from FS18. At 2.8 miles from FS18, fork left at the Lost Creek Campground onto FS1825-109. Go another 0.5 mile and park at a wide spot in road about 100 yards north of FS1825-111. A faint trail over rough but level ground leads to a fire ring and a campsite near Lost Creek. MVUM E4

Loc: FS1828, 0.9 mile from bridge across the Sandy	**Road:** Paved
L/L: N45 23 512/W121 51 557	**Access:** Park and carry about 100 yards
Cell: Zigzag and FS18, 1.8 miles SW of FS18/1825 junction	**Tents:** 3-4
	El: 2125
Lndmk: Clear Fork of the Sandy River	**RV:** No

Description: Surrounded by a magnificent grove of conifers and within sight of a sparkling little river that to all appearances is eminently fishable, this sheltered and shady little spot is among the most appealing you're likely to stumble across in your travels through Mount Hood National Forest.

Getting there: From Zigzag, drive 4.1 miles on FS18. Turn right on FS1825. At 0.8 miles, where FS1825 crosses the Sandy, keep left on FS1828 and go 0.9 mile. Park on the right side of the road just after crossing the Clear Fork of the Sandy River. A trail on the left side of the road leads to the campsite. MVUM E4

Loc: FS1828, 1.0 mile from FS1825/1828 junction	**Road:** Paved
L/L: N45 23 533/W121 51 414	**Access:** Drive into camp
Cell: Zigzag and FS 18, 1.8 miles SW of FS18/1825 junction.	**Tents:** 2-3
	El: 2220
Lndmk: Clear Fork of the Sandy River	**RV:** MH OK, TT?

Description: Though not directly on the river, this cool, shady and sheltered camp is accessible by car from the road. A fisherman's trail leads out of camp towards the river and also gives access to a second campsite about a hundred yards closer to the river.

Getting there: Follow instructions for site 9 to the FS1825/1828 junction. Drive 1.0 miles past the junction. Site is on left, 0.1 mile past Site 9. MVUM E4

Loc: FS18-1810, 12.2 miles from US 26	Road: Gravel
L/L: N45 25 220/W121 47 016	Access: Drive to camp
Cell: Zigzag or FS 18, 1.8 miles SW of 18/1825 junction	Tents: 1
	El: 3400
Lndmk: Elk Creek	RV: Small MH

Description: Because of its proximity to where Elk Creek comes bubbling out of a mixture of second-growth fir and rhododendron bushes and crosses under FS18, this site is just right for a small, self-contained motor home. Though the deep shade of old-growth conifers is not likely to be found here during the day, the ear-pleasing sounds of this happy little mountain stream just outside your window will make it a wonderful place to wake up in the morning.

Getting there: Take FS18 from Zigzag approximately 11 miles. At Lolo Pass turn right onto FS18-1810 and go 0.9 miles to where Elk creek crosses under the road. Site is on right near a spot where the road turns north. If you pass the turn-off to Trail No. 627 you need to turn around and backtrack about a quarter-mile. MVUM F4

Loc: McGee Creek Trail Rd.	Road: Gravel
L/L: N45 25 343/W121 46 749	Access: Drive to camp
Cell: Try near camp or head back toward Zigzag	Tents: 3-4
	El: 3565
Lndmk: McGee Creek trailhead	RV: MH

Description: The road into this dry campsite is difficult, but there is beauty everywhere in this Forest, and the magical thing about this place is its ethereal quiet and a commanding view of the sky. It would be unequalled as a site for viewing the Perseid meteor showers that occur in mid-August. Mount Hood fills up the sky in one directon, while Mount Adams blocks out a good chunk of it in the other. Continue up the road a couple tenths of a mile and find what looks to be an old look-out structure. During the hot months of summer, the lack of deep forest shade here is counterbalanced by both the possibility of a cooling breeze coming directly off the mountain's remaining snow. Make sure you bring sun screen and something to provide shade.

Getting there: Take FS18 northwest from US26 at Zigzag to Lolo Pass Rd (approximately 11 miles). Turn right onto 18-1810 and go 1.3 miles to McGee Creek Trail Rd. Go right 0.6 miles to site, on right. Be aware that the road changes numbers as it curves to the left and goes uphill away from the McGee Creek Trailhead. From this point on, the going might be difficult for a large motor home. Those with travel trailers would be well-advised to stay on FS18. MVUM F3

Loc: FS18, 2.4 miles past McGee Creek Trail Rd.	**Road:** Gravel
L/L: N45 25 088/W121 46 131	**Access:** Drive to camp
Cell: McGee Creek Trail Rd., Zigzag	**Tents:** 1-2
	El: 2956
Lndmk: Clear Fork of the Sandy River	**RV:** Yes, on road

(Site 13)

Beargrass is found at higher altitudes throughout the Forest in summer months

Description: Dropping steeply through spruce and maple, McGee Creek may be too swift for fishing here. Nevertheless, it would make a comfortable overnight spot for someone with an RV. The soft forest duff near the creek almost calls the tent camper to "sleep here!" Yet it would be wise to resist the idea because of the temptation to cut trees or level vegetation to accommodate a larger tent. Minimal impact, remember?

Getting there: From US 26 at Zigzag, take FS18 to Lolo Pass (about 11 miles). Turn right on FS18-1810 at the top of the pass and continue 3.7 miles to the site, on the left side of the road and 2.4 miles past McGee Creek Rd. MVUM F4

Loc: FS18, 11.6 miles from US26	**Road:** Gravel
L/L: N45 25 930/W121 46 445	**Access:** Drive to camp.
Cell: Zig-Zag or FS18, 1.8 miles SW of FS18/1825 junction	**Tents:** 1
	El: 2600
Lndmk: McGee Creek	**RV:** MH

Description: Located on sparkling McGee Creek, this tempting site is probably too close to the road for tent camping, but would make a great overnight stay for someone with a smaller, self-contained motor home.

Getting there: From US 26 at Zigzag, turn onto FS18, heading northeast to Lolo Pass. At the top of the pass (approximately 11 miles) turn right onto FS18-1810 and drive 4.9 miles to site, located on a pull-out on the left where an unnamed Creek crosses under the road to join McGee Creek (3.6 miles past McGee Creek Trail Rd). MVUM F3

Camp Free in the Mount Hood National Forest | 43

Loc: FS18, 0.3 miles north of Spur 100	Road: Paved
L/L: N45 28 168/W121 46 605	Access: Drive to camp
Cell: Zig-Zag and FS18, 1.8 miles SW of FS18/1825 junction	Tents: 1-5
	El: 2380
Lndmk: Ladd Stump Creek	RV: MH and TT

Description: Ladd Stump Creek may flow a little too swiftly to provide good fishing, but it offers two different sites for the camper. Tent campers may prefer the more private and secluded site to be found nestled among the trees about a hundred yards from the road, which also features a fine fire ring, while those with RV's can park in the handy and level pull-out just past the creek. Access to water for camp use is to be found on the opposite side of the road.

Getting there: From Zigzag, turn onto FS18 and drive approximately 11 miles to Lolo Pass. From Lolo pass, turn right onto FS18-1810 and go 7.8 miles to site, on the left and 0.3 mile beyond spur Road 100, which takes off at an acute angle to the left to follow the overhead power lines in the vicinity. MVUM F3

Loc: FS 18, 8.0 miles from Lolo Pass	Road: Paved
L/L: N45 28 304/W121 46 509	Access: Park and carry 100'
Cell: McGee Creek Rd (See directions, site #12), Zig-zag or FS18, 1.8 miles SW of FS18/1825 junction.	Tents: 2-3
	El: 2360
Lndmk: FS18/spur100 junction	RV: MH and TT

Description: A dry but secluded site about 100 feet from FS18. Close spacing of trees prohibits the use of large tents here, but the site is entirely suitable for small ones and RV's. A serviceable outhouse is to be found hidden in trees on the east side of the road. Some cleaning may be required.

Getting there: From Zigzag, take FS18 approximately 11 miles northeast to Lolo Pass. Turn right onto FS18-1810 and go another eight miles to site, on left, approximately 0.5 mile past spur 100. MVUM F3

Loc: FS18 and the West Fork of the Hood River	Road: Dirt
L/L: N45 31 205/W121 44 681	Access: Park and carry 0.4 mi.
Cell: Zigzag, FS18, 1.8 miles SW of FS18/1825 junction	Tents: 7-8
	El: 1720
Lndmk: Dry Run Bridge	RV: No

Description: This site, located on an unnamed creek that plunges steeply to join the West Fork of the Hood River, will accommodate tents, but not recreational vehicles. Fish the Hood River or just lie around camp in your anti-gravity chair and soak up the shade on a hot summer day. The confluence of both creek and river can be glimpsed through the trees below camp. Some cleaning may be required.

Getting there: From Zigzag, take FS18 approximately 11 miles to Lolo Pass. Turn right at the pass on FS18-1810 and drive a total distance of 13.1 miles to the Dry Run Bridge across the West Fork of the Sandy River. Don't cross the bridge, but park and carry gear 0.4 mile south on the primitive road that meanders through dense brush to the campsite, just past a rock slide area. MVUM F3

Loc: Laurel Creek/ Road 1330, off Lost Creek Rd	**Road:** Gravel
L/L: N45 31 452/W121 45 632	**Access:** Drive to site
Cell: ?	**Tents:** 1-2
	El: 2100
Lndmk: Lost Lake Rd., Laurel Creek	**RV:** MH

Description: Picturesque Laurel Creek, bracketed by dense mountain foliage and cool, moss-covered boulders and bubbling happily over flat rocks as it flows under FS1330, may be fishable. Then again, it may just be beautiful. Either way, you'll want to stay a while.

Getting there: From Zigzag, drive 11 miles to Lolo Pass on FS18 and go right on FS18-1810 for another 14 miles. A little over a mile after crossing the Dry Run Bridge over the West Fork of the Hood River, turn left on Lost Lake Rd and go about one mile, then turn right onto FS1330 and go 0.2 mile to the campsite, where road widens out near Laurel Creek. FS1330 dead ends 0.3 mile beyond this point. MVUM F3

Loc: FS1330, off Lost Lake Rd	**Road:** Gravel
L/L: N45 31 797/W121 45 471	**Access:** Drive to camp
Cell: ?	**Tents:** 2-3
	El: 2150
Lndmk: Lost Lake Rd and Laurel Creek	**RV:** Small MH

Description: Set among the trees at the end of FS1330, this dry camp provides just an extra silly millimeter of seclusion compared to No. 18. The disadvantage, of course is that one will have to backtrack to Laurel Creek for water.

Getting there: Drive to site No. 18, then follow FS1330 another 0.3 mile to end of road. Just past site 18, FS1330 curves right and heads gradually downhill. MVUM F2-F3

Camp Free in the Mount Hood National Forest | 45

Loc: Lake Branch Creek, off FS 13	Road: Paved
L/L: N45 29 885/W121 49 845	Access: Drive to site
Cell: ?	Tents: 2
	El: 2845
Lndmk: Lost Lake, Lake Branch Creek	RV: MH and TT

Description: Located on Lake Branch Creek just off FS13, this site is about a half a mile as the crow flies from Lost Lake. This section of the road is paved and should be sparsely traveled, at least during the week. Summer holiday weekends are another matter throughout the forest, which seems to draw Portlanders like a magnet during those times. Though a convenient path near camp provides easy access to the creek for drawing water, thick brush along the creek near camp prevents walking along the shore to wet a line. Blueberries and mountain huckleberries abound in the area, making it an ideal late summer getaway for breakfast lovers. There also appears to be another possible campsite on the opposite side of the road. As always, pay your dues and leave it just a little cleaner than you found it.

Getting there: From Zigzag, drive 11 miles on FS18 to Lolo Pass. Go right on FS18-1810 another 13.6 miles. Hang a left on Lost Lake Road toward Lost Lake. Go right on FS13 just before entering Lost Lake Campground. Go west 1 mile to Lake Branch Creek. Camp is on left and right on the northeast side of the creek before you cross the bridge. MVUM E3

Loc: Lake Branch Creek and FS1330	Road: Gravel
L/L: N45 31 500/W121 49 883	Access: Drive to sites
Cell: ?	Tents: 5-6 each site
	El: 2205
Lndmk: FS13, FS 1330 and Lake Branch Creek	RV: MH and TT

Description: These are both prime sites!! The limpid waters of Lake Branch Creek spread out and slow down here as it glides past these two camps, tempting the angler to try for one of the fish that just have to be hiding in the shadows around dusk. Both camps offer shade and solitude and will accommodate a fair number of tents. Enjoy your stay and take care of this place for those yet to come.

Getting there: From the entrance to Lost Lake Resort, take FS13 (Lake Branch Road) 4.3 miles west to FS1330. Go right 0.1 mile to sites, on right and left sides of the road. MVUM F2-F3

✱ ✱ ✱

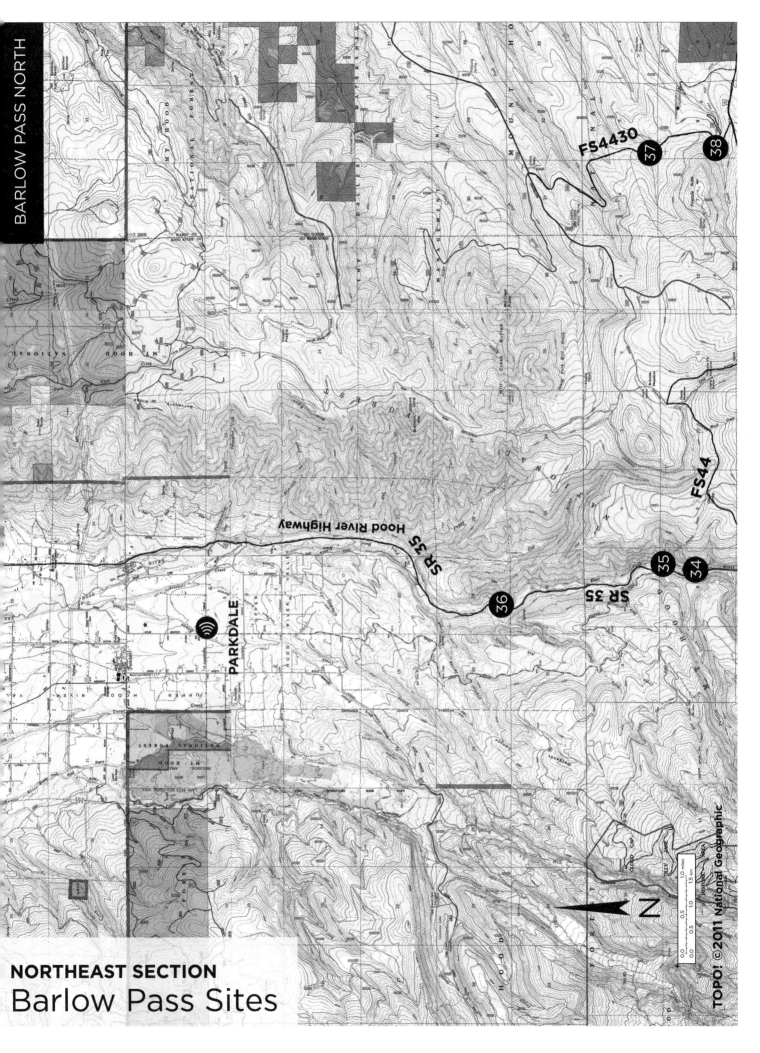

NORTHEAST SECTION
Barlow Pass Sites

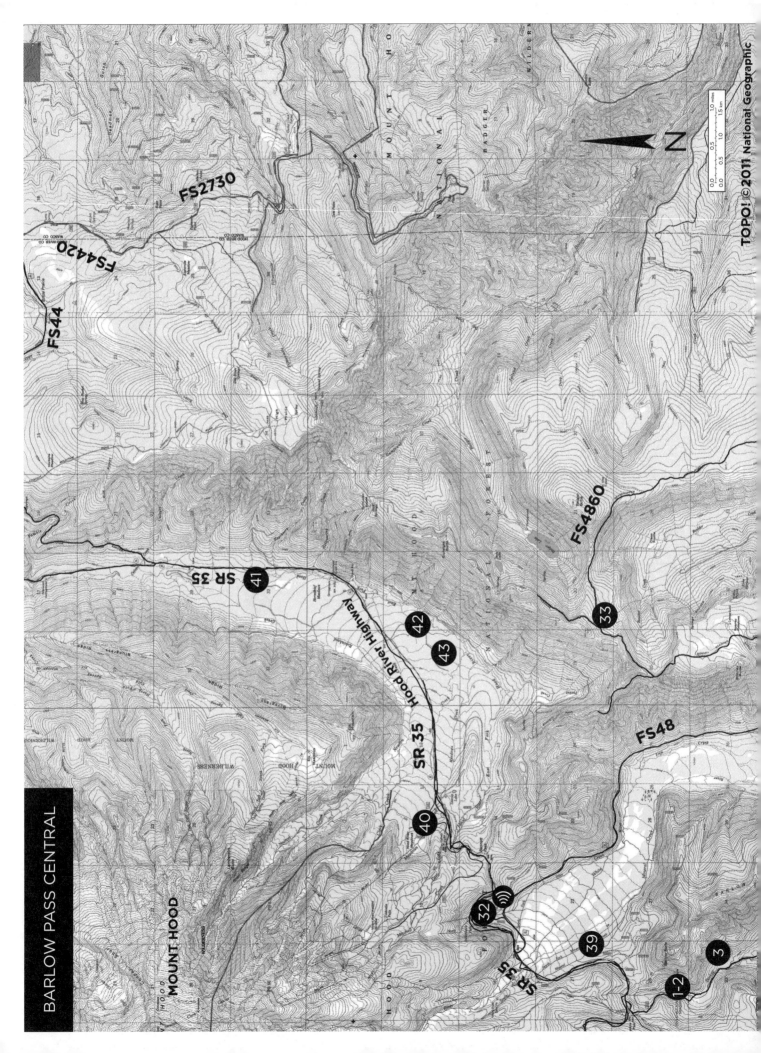

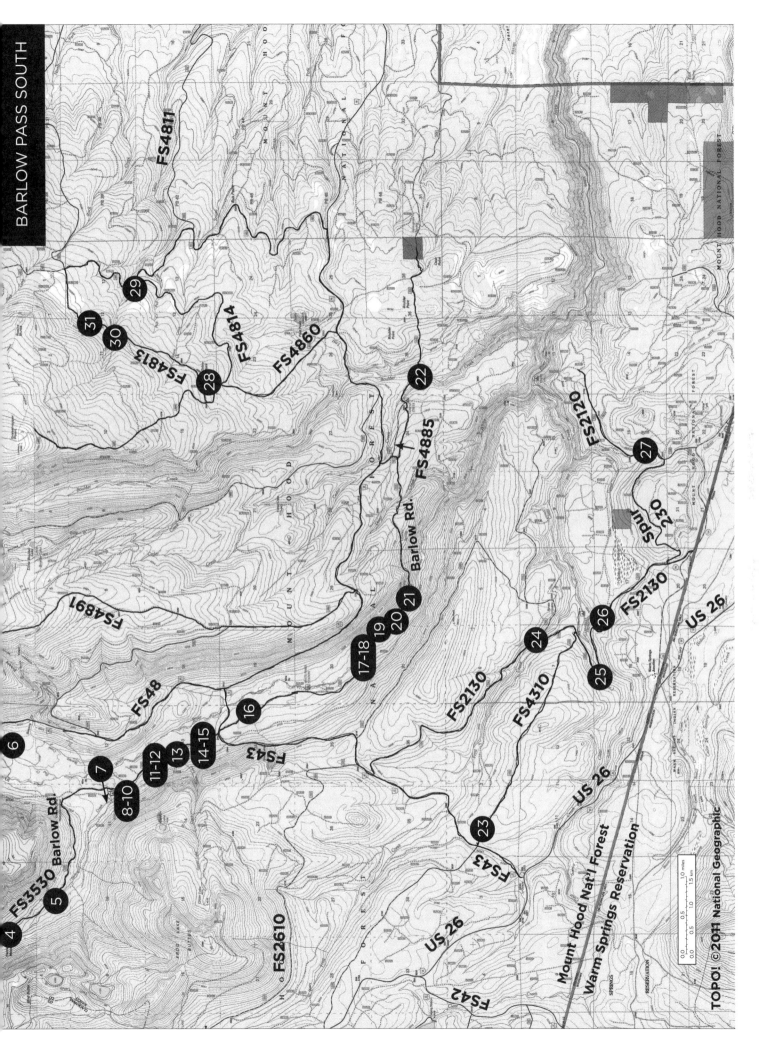

NORTHEAST SECTION
Barlow Pass Sites

US 26 and OR 35, from Barlow Road to Fifteenmile Campground

Warning: Barlow Road is not for the faint of heart!
With the exception of a few miles north and south of FS43, most of its length in this section of the Forest is tricky to drive in anything but a four-wheel drive vehicle. By driving with exceptional care, I was able to negotiate most of it in my lightly-loaded Toyota Corolla sedan, but this was in summertime when conditions were optimal. Nevertheless, almost every other vehicle I saw on this road was either a pick-up or had 4WD capability. My recommendation is to avoid Barlow Road unless you have a high-clearance vehicle and/or have had experience driving on extremely rough roads with the vehicle you have, especially if you will be loaded down with kids, dogs and camping gear. If you are not a confident driver with experience in driving on primitive roads, you should turn around the first time you encounter one of the many ditches that cut across Barlow Road every few hundred yards for most of its length through the Forest. Some of them are eighteen inches to two feet in depth and are perfectly capable of high-centering a sedan. That said, there are some really choice campsites to be found along the more vehicle-friendly sections of this road and beyond.

①

Loc: Barlow Rd.	**Road:** Dirt, poor
L/L: N45 16 419/W121 40 802	**Access:** Drive to camp, pick-up or better
Cell: Gov't camp, US 26	**Tents:** 6-7
	El: 3780
Lndmk: Devil's Half Acre Cg.	**RV:** Road too rough

Description: This camp on Barlow Creek along the historical Barlow Road is located on the Forest Service's now decommissioned Devil's Half Acre Campground. There are two separate, well-shaded campsites here. Both sites are close to the creek and have fire pits, but only one of them has a picnic table. There is abundant shade under the towering trees that line the creek. A hundred or so yards up the hill and away from the creek there is a primitive outhouse on the edge of a flower strewn meadow which may be picturesque but is no longer maintained. Pack in your own toilet facilities.

Getting there: From US 26, take OR 35 (Hood River Highway) 2.6 miles north to Barlow Pass. Turn right (south) on FS3531 toward the Pioneer Woman's Grave and Barlow Road. At 0.2 mile, turn left by the historical marker and sign for Barlow Road. Follow Barlow Road downhill 1 mile, passing campsite #1 at 0.9 mile, to a rough, dirt track going uphill to the left 0.2 mile to site. MVUM F5

Loc: Barlow Road, near Devil's Half Acre Campground	**Road:** Dirt, primitive (see warning above)
L/L: N45 16 315/W121 40 840	**Access:** Park and carry, short distance
Cell: US 26, Government Camp	**Tents:** 5-8
	El: 3768
Lndmk: Devil's Half Acre Campground	**RV:** Road too rough

Description: This cool, shady, prime campsite in the trees sits across the road from a large, sunny meadow that will be full of wildflowers and birds during the summer. It is a good site for a large and/or extended family gathering. Barlow Creek bubbles peacefully along the edge of camp to provide a convenient source of water.

Getting there: See instructions for Site #1. MVUM F5

Loc: Barlow Rd, 1.4 miles south of FS 3531/Barlow Rd Junction	**Road:** Primitive. (see warning above)
L/L: N45 15 973/W121 40 360	**Access:** Drive to campsite
Cell: US 26, Government Camp	**Tents:** 3-4
	El: 3431
Lndmk: Barlow Creek	**RV:** Road too difficult

Description: Find this camp in a clearing to the east of Barlow Road and just south of an old log bridge crossing the creek. An abundance of tall fir trees provide summer shade, and the nearby creek is a dependable source of water. This camp would make an ideal summertime getaway for up to dozen people. As always, pack out what you pack in, and then some.

Getting there: From US 26, drive 2.5 miles to Barlow Pass. Take FS3531 south 0.2 mile to Barlow Road (look for the historical marker sign). Go south on Barlow Road 1.4 miles. Camp will be on the left after crossing the old wooden bridge.
Coming from the south on Barlow Road, go 5.5 to 5.7 miles north of FS43 to site, on right, just before the bridge. MVUM F5

Camp Free in the Mount Hood National Forest | 51

Loc: Barlow Rd.	**Road:** Primitive (See warning above)
L/L: N45 15 337/W121 39 890	**Access:** Park and carry, 200 yards
Cell: US26, Government Camp	**Tents:** 1
	El: 3520
Lndmk: Barlow Creek, Grindstone Campground, Palmateer Meadows	**RV:** Road too rough

Description: Though there is a fire ring here and only one level tent site to boast of, this site takes the prize for seclusion and privacy. Access to Barlow Creek is through thick brush and may be difficult, *making this the only site in this book for which I will feel obliged to warn readers to be especially careful to watch out for bears.*

Getting there: From US 26, take the Hood River Highway 2.5 miles to Barlow Pass. Then turn right (south) at the sign for Barlow Road and the "pioneer woman's grave" (FS3531). Go 0.2 miles and turn left onto Barlow Road. At 2.6 very slow miles and in the vicinity of the preternaturally quiet Palmateer Meadows, turn right (west) on a narrow dirt road. Park and carry gear the remaining two hundred yards to camp. The road to this site was blocked by a small downed log about a hundred yards off of Barlow Road in 2010
If approaching from FS43 to the south, drive 4.8 miles north on Barlow Rd to this camp. MVUM F5
Turn your car around before you turn in for the night. *You never know what might come up after dark. When seconds count you don't want to contend with having to turn a car around on a narrow, tree-lined road in the dark. Actually, this is a good policy any time you are car camping in the wild country.*

GRINDSTONE CAMPGROUND

Loc: Barlow Rd., three miles south of FS3531, 3.9 miles north of FS43	**Road:** Primitive. (See warning above)
L/L: N45 14 812/W121 39 401	**Access:** Drive to sites
Cell: US 26 near Gov't camp	**Tents:** 7-9, maybe more
	El: 3298
Lndmk: Grindstone Campground	**RV:** Road too rough

Description: Another of the prime sites to be found along Barlow Road, this recently decommissioned Forest Service campground offers almost all the amenities of an official campground, except for the friendly camp host to collect your dues at dinnertime. There are three campsites here, each with a surprisingly sturdy picnic table and a Forest Service fire pit and grate. In addition, this classy camp boasts an outhouse in good condition. Grindstone is roughly half-way between paved FS3531 on the north and paved FS43on the south. And Barlow Road, as I have been stressing, is one of the most primitive Roads in the entire National Forest, so if solitude and privacy is your wish, it will most likely be granted here. There is plentiful firewood if the weather turns cool during your visit, and Barlow Creek is within easy walking distance (about 150 yards to the west) if it's hot and a cooling soak is on your mind. If you have company coming, there is plenty of room for extra tents in the surrounding woods, with privacy for all.

Getting there: From US 26, drive 5.3 miles on FS43 to Barlow Road (FS 3530), then go north on Barlow Road 3.9 miles to Grindstone Campground, on left.
Or, coming from OR 35, follow FS3531 two-tenths mile to Barlow Road, then follow Barlow Road 3 miles south to site, on right. Watch for the sign announcing the turn-off to "Grindstone". MVUM F5

Loc: Unnamed Rd. near the confluence of Red Creek and the White R.	**Road:** Gravel
L/L: N45 15 436/W121 36 818	**Access:** Check MVUM
Cell: Gov't Camp and US 26	**Tents:** 4-5
	El: 3300
Lndmk: White River, FS48	**RV:** Check MVUM

Description: This comfortable camp is located in the White River valley in a grove of widely spaced and towering conifers that provide shade while allowing the cool breeze to flow down the valley. For comfort, you will find a hand-crafted log bench situated in front of an elaborate stone fire ring. Water is available from Red Creek, which, in spite of its mud bottom, runs sparklingly clear through a patch of skunk cabbage. Approach it carefully so as not to stir up any undue silt, especially if there are other campers in the vicinity.

Getting there: If coming from US 26 on FS43, drive 5.7 miles. Shortly after crossing the White River, continue another few tenths of a mile to where FS43 T's into FS48. Go left (north) 3.6 miles on FS48 to unnamed road to the left.
Alternatively, drive five miles on the Hood River Highway to FS48. From there go south 5.3 miles to the unnamed road leading downhill on the right to the White River.
The road widens out at the bottom, about a half-mile down the hill. Campsites are to the left of the wide spot. MVUM G5

Loc: Spur Road 220, north of FS43 (Cedar Burn Rd.)	**Road:** Dirt, primitive. Not as bad as Barlow Rd.
L/L: N45 14 104/W121 37 817	**Access:** Drive to camp
Cell: Government Camp on US26	**Tents:** 5-6
	El: 3130
Lndmk: Barlow Creek	**RV:** Smaller MH

Description: Camp on the wild side of Barlow Creek. Except for the noise of Barlow Creek gurgling along just below camp, your peace and quiet is guaranteed. This camp is located just off sparsely traveled spur 220 where an abandoned road leads to the foot of what used to be a bridge crossing Barlow Creek.
*Two and one half-mile-long Trail #471 goes through camp and climbs southwest to Catalpa Lake, which sits in a bowl at an altitude of about 4100 feet. Look for this trail on the west side of spur 220.

(Site 7) Getting there: From US26 about two miles past the US26/FS42 junction, take FS43 (Cedar Burn Road) five miles N/NE. Go left (north) 1.6 miles on Spur 220, which parallels the eastern side of Barlow Creek, watching for a short road to the right leading to the remains of the old bridge and the site. MVUM G5

Loc: Barlow Rd, 1.7 miles north of FS43	**Road:** Dirt but serviceable
L/L: N45 14 026/W121 37 656	**Access:** Drive close to camp
Cell: Gov't camp on FS 26	**Tents:** 3-4
	El: 3135
Lndmk: Barlow Crossing Cg.	**RV:** MH and TT

Description: Situated about a hundred feet from Barlow Creek in a grove of tall conifers, this prime site is cool and inviting, especially toward evening. It also features a sturdy, split-log picnic table.

Getting there: From US 26, go 5.3 miles NE on FS43 (Cedar Burn Road), then go north 1.7 miles on Barlow Road (FS3530) and take a dirt track to the left about 100 yards to camp. MVUM G5
Note: This section of Barlow Road, from FS43 north about two miles and south about a mile, can be easily driven by almost any vehicle with normal ground clearance. Even so, conditions on these primitive roads can change from one season to the next, due to flooding, washouts, and blowdowns.

Loc: Barlow Rd., 1.6 miles north of FS43	**Road:** Dirt, but serviceable
L/L: N45 13 979/W121 37 618	**Access:** Drive to camp
Cell: Government Camp area on US 26	**Tents:** 5-6
	El: 3070
Lndmk: Barlow Crossing Campground	**RV:** MH and TT

Description: Despite having no amenities to boast of beyond a simple rock fire ring, this is nevertheless a delightful site with ample room for many tents in a clearing surrounded by Douglas fir trees.

Getting there: From US 26, go 5.3 miles NE on FS43 (Cedar Burn Road), then another 1.6 miles north on Barlow Road (FS3530) to camp, on left. MVUM G5

Loc: Barlow Rd., 1.5 miles north of FS43	**Road:** Dirt, serviceable
L/L: N45 13 947/W121 37 585	**Access:** Drive close to camp
Cell: US 26 near Gov't Camp	**Tents:** 3-4
	El: 3065
Lndmk: Barlow Crossing Campground	**RV:** MH and TT

Description: A prime site, with a picnic table, fire grate, shade and the music of the creek.

Getting there: From US 26, go 5.3 miles NE on FS43 (Cedar Burn Road), then 1.5 miles north on Barlow Road (FS3530). Turn left and park. Camp is 100 yards from Barlow Road on a sandy track. MVUM G5

Loc: Barlow Road, 1.1 miles north of FS43	**Road:** Dirt, serviceable
L/L: N45 13 639/W121 37 235	**Access:** Park on road, carry gear to camp
Cell: US 26 near Government Camp	**Tents:** 5-6
	El: 3060
Lndmk: Barlow Crossing Campground	**RV:** Beside road only

Description: Hidden from the Road in a grove of dense trees on a bench above the creek, this prime site is easily passed by. In addition to the usual fire ring, it features a sturdy hand-made table about 36" high and a foot bridge across the creek.

Getting there: From US 26, go 5.3 miles NE on FS43 (Cedar Burn Road), then 1.1 miles north on Barlow Road (FS3530). A path leads 100 yards downhill from the Roadside parking area through the trees to camp. MVUM G5

Loc: Barlow Rd, 1.0 mile north of FS43	**Road:** Dirt, serviceable
L/L: N45 13 606/W121 37 236	**Access:** Park and carry gear short distance
Cell: US 26 near Government Camp	**Tents:** 2-3
	El: 3025
Lndmk: Barlow Crossing Campground	**RV:** Parking area only

Description: It would be quite easy to put your tent or RV on the bluff that overlooks the tempting little pool in Barlow Creek at this spot, but the real jewel here is the campsite lying just 40 feet downstream at the end of a sandy incline. It is cooler and shadier because of its proximity to the creek, and definitely offers more privacy from the nearby road.

Getting there: From US 26, go 5.3 miles NE on FS43 (Cedar Burn Road), then drive 1 mile north on Barlow Road (FS3530) to site, on left. MVUM G5

Loc: Barlow Rd., 0.6 mile north of FS43	Road: Dirt, serviceable
L/L: N45 13 355/W121 37 041	Access: Drive to camp
Cell: US 26, near Government Camp	Tents: 3-6
	El: 3045
Lndmk: Junction Barlow RD and FS43	RV: MH and TT

Description: Another prime site: shaded, and cool, with a fire ring and picnic table.

Getting there: From US 26, go 5.3 miles NE on FS43 (Cedar Burn Road), then 0.6 mile north on Barlow Road (FS3530) to site, on left. MVUM G5

Loc: Barlow Rd., 0.4 mile north of FS43	Road: Dirt, good
L/L: N45 13 192/W121 36 883	Access: Drive to camp
Cell: Government Camp area of US 26	Tents: 4-5
	El: 3015
Lndmk: Barlow Crossing Campground	RV: MH and TT

Description: A comfortable, sun-dappled camp in tall trees near Barlow Creek that is suitable for a group.

Getting there: From US 26, go 5.3 miles NE on FS43 (Cedar Burn Road), then 0.4 mile north on Barlow Road (FS3530) to site, on the left and just north of Barlow Crossing Campground. MVUM G5-G6

Loc: Barlow Rd., 0.2 miles north of FS43	Road: Dirt, decent
L/L: N45 13 025/W121 36 810	Access: Drive to camp
Cell: US 26 near Government Camp	Tents: 5-6
	El: 2990
Lndmk: Barlow Crossing Campground	RV: MH and TT

Description: A prime site where sandy-shored Barlow Creek runs close to camp and has pools deep enough for a cooling soak on a hot day.

Getting there: From US 26, go 5.3 miles northeast on FS43 (Cedar Burn Road), then north on Barlow Road (FS3530) 0.2 mile to site, on right, just before crossing the bridge to Barlow Crossing Campground. MVUM G5-G6

Loc: Barlow Rd., 0.5 miles south of FS43	**Road:** Dirt, serviceable
L/L: N45 12 691/W121 36 324	**Access:** Park and carry, 200 yards or more
Cell: US 26 near Government Camp	**Tents:** 5-10
	El: 2940
Lndmk: Barlow Rd./FS43 junction and White River Station Cg.	**RV:** Small MH only

Description: Some might prefer to pass this site by. The environment in this area is noticeably dryer than the Clackamas and Zigzag areas, both of which are firmly on the western slope of the Cascades. Sites off Barlow Road are generally more open and sandy, thanks to the silt-laden White River, which runs nearby and has covered the entire valley floor with sand eroded from Mount Hood, which looms to the north. Here, scrub pine dominates on the valley floor until one gets very close to the river. This site offers no sun-dappled beach. It lacks the deep shade of a solid canopy of conifers overhead, and access to the river is difficult. Nevertheless, it would make a decent early-in-the-year retreat, with enough the trees to slow cold winds while allowing maximum sun to reach into camp.

Getting there: From US 26, go 5.3 miles NE on FS43 (Cedar Burn Road), then south on Barlow Road (FS3530) 0.5 mile. From here, park and follow a very rough and sometimes indistinct dirt track meandering through the trees to camp. Look for the fire ring located at the base of a giant yellow pine tree which forks about twenty feet off the ground. Be sure to check the tree for any weak or dead branches before camping near it, especially in windy conditions. MVUM G5-G6
* *Warning: Barlow Road deteriorates just south of White River Station Campground. From there on, deep cross-ditches abound and intensely strategic driving becomes necessary if one is to avoid the oil pan-piercing rocks and ruts. Pick-up or better recommended.*
When taking water from the White River, be sure to let it sit long enough for the silt to settle out before using it, especially if you intend to filter it with a mechanical device.

Loc: Barlow Rd., 2.4 miles south of FS43	**Road:** Dirt, difficult. Pick-up or better
L/L: N45 11 171/W121 35 310	**Access:** See warning below about berm
Cell: US 26, vicinity of Government Camp	**Tents:** 3-4
	El: 2840
Lndmk: White River Station Campground	**RV:** No

Description: A prime site surrounded by shade-giving conifers, it features a cobble and sand beach on the river. The White River is silt-laden for much of the summer and was probably so named only because the name "Sandy River" was already taken.

Getting there: From US 26, go 5.3 miles NE on FS43 (Cedar Burn Road), then south on Barlow Road (FS3530) 2.4 miles to site, on left. MVUM G6
Vehicles built for low-clearance highway driving are likely to bottom out crossing the berm above this camp, and then have trouble getting back over it again. Park on the road and carry gear to camp.

Camp Free in the Mount Hood National Forest

Loc: Barlow Rd., 2.5 miles south of FS 43 and 0.2 mile from bridge across the White River		**Road:** Dirt, difficult (see warning above)
L/L: N45 11 151/W121 35 218		**Access:** Drive to camp
Cell: US 26 in vicinity of Government Camp		**Tents:** 3-4
		El: 2825
Lndmk: Bridge over White River		**RV:** Road too rough

Description: A prime site. The view upriver definitely leaves one with the feeling of being on a wild river hundreds of miles from civilization. A beach of cobblestones and sand lies just below camp.

Getting there: From US 26, go 5.3 miles NE on FS43 (Cedar Burn Road), then south on Barlow Road (FS3530) 2.5 miles to site, on left. MVUM G6

This campsite beside the White River inspires a feeling of timelessness

Loc: Barlow Rd., 2.6 miles south of FS43	Road: Dirt, difficult (see warning on pg. 50)
L/L: N45 11 070/W121 35 140	Access: Park and carry, about 200 yards
Cell: Government Camp along US 26	Tents: 10-15
	El: 2750
Lndmk: Bridge crossing White River on Barlow Rd.	RV: Road too rough

Description: A cool location suitable for a large party. Fir trees predominate in the sandy soil along this stretch of the river.

Getting there: From US 26, go 5.3 miles NE on FS43 (Cedar Burn Road), then south on Barlow Road (FS3530) 2.6 miles. After crossing the bridge take a dirt track to the right about 100 yards, and then go another 100 yards to campsites. MVUM G6

Loc: Barlow Rd., 2.9 miles south of FS43	Road: Dirt, primitive
L/L: N45 10 887/W121 34 930	Access: Park and carry
Cell: US 26, Government Camp vicinity	Tents: 5-10
	El: 2603
Lndmk: Bridge on Barlow Rd. over White River	RV: Road too rough

Description: A prime site on a bench covered with yielding forest duff and offering seclusion, ample shade and room for many tents, not to mention a sandy beach on the river that should be exposed to the sun in the afternoon.

Getting there: From US 26, go 5.3 miles northeast on FS 43 (Cedar Burn Road). Turn south (right) on Barlow Road toward White River Station and go 2.9 miles on rough, rutted Barlow Road. At approximately 0.3 mile past the bridge, turn onto a dirt track to the right. Park and carry. MVUM G6

Loc: Barlow Rd., 3.2 miles south of FS43	Road: Dirt, rough (see warning on pg. 50)
L/L: N45 10 786/W121 34 715	Access: Drive to camp
Cell: US 26, vicinity of Government Camp	Tents: 10-15
	El: 2704
Lndmk: Bridge across White River, 0.7 mile north	RV: Road too rough

Description: Suitable for a large party, this site sits in a shaded grove of tall pine and fir trees. Below camp the silt-bearing White River has deposited a bench of sand. Remember, though, that what the White River has given, the White River can take away.

(Site 21) Getting there: From US 26, drive 5.3 miles northeast on FS43 (Cedar Burn Road). Turn right and go south 3.2 miles (0.7 mile past the bridge) on Barlow Rd (3530) to site, on the right, just before Barlow road starts to climb away from the river. MVUM G6

22

Loc: Barlow Rd., 0.4 miles south of Forest Creek Campground	**Road:** Dirt, rough (see warning on pg. 50)
L/L: N 45 10 584/W121 31 051	**Access:** Drive close to camp
Cell: US 26, Government Camp vicinity	**Tents:** 1-2
	El: 2960
Lndmk: Forest Creek Campground	**RV:** Road too rough

Description: This prime site tucked under tall trees at the end of a dirt track a hundred or so yards downstream from the bridge crossing Boulder Creek Creek is so private that you will have to look twice to see the corner of the Forest Service picnic table hidden in the trees along the shore. You'll like this site!

Getting there: From US 26, drive 6 miles northeast on FS43 to the T-junction with FS48. Turn right and go 4.4 miles south to FS4885. Turn right again and drive a little less than one mile to Forest Creek Campground. From there take Barlow Rd (FS3530) southeast 0.4 mile to a bridge crossing Boulder Creek. Site is to the right, 100 yards downstream from the bridge. MVUM H6

23

Loc: FS 4310, just southeast of FS43	**Road:** Paved
L/L: N45 09 904/W121 38 351	**Access:** Drive to camp
Cell: US 26 toward Government Camp	**Tents:** 50+
	El: 3340
Lndmk: US 26/FS43 junction	**RV:** MH and TT

Description: A huge, dry site on flat ground under scattered large conifers. Features one primitive outhouse and one picnic table. This has obviously been used previously as a hunter's camp, possibly during elk season, since a large herd of them seems to reside in the area. The camp occupies both sides of FS4310. Though there isn't a drop of water in sight, water can be found in Frog Creek, which crosses under FS43 about three-quarters of a mile to the northeast.

Getting there: From US26, go 0.7 mile northeast on Cedar Burn Rd. (FS43), then turn south on FS4310 (Camas Prairie Rd.). The camps are on the left and right sides of the road, about 0.1 mile south of the junction. MVUM G6

Loc: FS2130 (Frog Creek Rd.), 3.2 miles south of FS43	**Road:** Gravel, good
L/L: N45 09 195/W121 35 272	**Access:** Drive to camp
Cell: US 26 near Gov't. Camp	**Tents:** 2-3
	El: 3030
Lndmk: Frog Creek/Frog Creek Rd. (FS2130)	**RV:** MH

Description: This site offers a lot. Located a few hundred yards off what looks to be a lightly traveled forest road, it is shaded and has a picturesque creek running nearby with a deep pool for summertime cooling. This is a sandwich camp, in the sense that it is sandwiched between Frog Creek and the road. It is a definite pack-out-your-poop site, though the cows that seemed to have frequented this place earlier in the year apparently were not aware of this requirement. Boil your water well before using it for camp purposes.

Getting there: From US 26, go 2.7 miles northeast on FS43, then turn south on FS2130 to its junction with Frog Creek 3.2 miles to the southeast. Look for the access road to this camp on the left just after crossing the bridge over Frog Creek. Southbound traffic will need to make an acute left turn here to access this camp. Alternatively, from the Clear Creek Campground, go 0.5 miles northeast of the FS4310/2130 junction on FS2130/2131. The site will be about 0.5 mile northeast of Clear Creek Campground. MVUM G6

Loc: FS2130 (or 2640?)	**Road:** Paved
L/L: N45 08 515/W121 35 743	**Access:** Drive to camp
Cell: US 26 near Government Camp	**Tents:** 5-6
	El: 2930
Lndmk: Clear Creek Campground	**RV:** MH ok, TT?

Description: Another prime site with room enough for several tents. Beautiful Clear Creek, flowing by about 100 feet away offers a pool deep enough for soaking on a hot afternoon.

Getting there: From US 26, go northeast on FS43 (Cedar Burn Rd) 0.7 mile. Turn right and go 3.2 miles south on Camas Prairie Road (FS4310), then right 0.6 mile on FS2130 to site, on right, at bend in the road where Clear Creek crosses under the road. Space for turning a travel trailer around is very limited here. MVUM G6
Note: Road signage in this area can be somewhat confusing. Keep your GPS plugged in, if you have one.

*FOR OVERNIGHT OR EMERGENCY USE

Loc: FS2130 near Camas Prairie and south of Clear Creek Cg.	**Road:** Paved
L/L: N45 08 427/W121 34 844	**Access:** Park and carry 100 yards downhill
Cell: Mt Hood area, especially along US 26 near Government Camp	**Tents:** 2-3
	El: 3150
Lndmk: Camas Prairie to east, Clear Creek Cg. to north	**RV:** No

Description: Located on a steep, dirt track just 100 yards off FS2130 (Frog Creek Road), this might not be everybody's cup of tea, especially if there are other sites available nearby. Its best use might therefore be as an overnight or emergency stay. A small, unnamed creek arises out of a nearby spring, though evidence of cattle traffic in the area suggests that it might be advisable to drive a mile east on FS2130 to Clear Creek, where there is more abundant, fast-flowing and, presumably, cleaner water to be obtained. Other than that, this site is shady, pleasant, breezy and secluded.

Getting there: Site is on FS2130 (Frog Creek Road) about 1 mile east of Site 25 on a curvy road. *Care should be taken when pulling off the road here, as the shoulder is unusually abrupt.* MVUM G6

Loc: Clear Creek, on Keeps Mill Rd.	**Road:** Paved
L/L: N45 07 898/W121 32 275	**Access:** Drive to camp
Cell: US 26 in vicinity of Government Camp	**Tents:** 2-3
	El: 3170
Lndmk: Keeps Mill Road	**RV:** MH and TT

Description: A large, pleasant camp close to a slow-moving section of Clear Creek. At this point Clear Creek appears to be deep enough for swimming, but be prepared to see abundant evidence that you are in cow country, so make sure that you boil water from the creek thoroughly and avoid swimming if you have any open cuts or sores on your body.

Getting there: From US 26, go northeast on FS43 (Cedar Burn Road) 0.7 mile. Turn right and go south on Camas Prairie or Frog Creek Road (FS2130) 3.2 miles. At junction with FS4310, go right 2.7 miles on FS2130, watching for junction where it forks off to left and becomes FS2131. Follow FS2131 another 0.2 miles. Just after passing a rest stop on the right you will see Spur 230 taking off to the left. Go 2 miles on 230 spur to FS2120 (which may be labeled 220), then left for 0.2 miles to a wooden bridge across Clear Creek. Campsite is on right in a grove of trees beside the creek just before road crosses the bridge toward Keeps Mill Campground. MVUM G6

Loc: Near junction of FS4860/4813 (Badger Creek and Wamic Mill Roads, respectively)	Road: Primitive but okay (dry weather only)
L/L: N45 12 985/W121 31 218	Access: Park and carry 0.1 mi
Cell: US 26 near Government Camp	Tents: 7-10
	El: 4100
Lndmk: Junction FS 4860/ 4813	RV: MH and TT

Description: This site is the now decommissioned Post Camp. It offers solitude, shade, space and the tranquility of the forest, but, unless you don't mind taking your water from the spring which is boxed in by timbers at the bottom of a declivity in the hillside, you may want to consider driving to one of the nearby creeks that cross FS4813 to the north for water.

Getting there: From US 26, go 6 miles northeast on FS43 to its junction with FS48, then turn right and drive 6.5 miles southeast. Turn left on FS4860 (Badger Lake Rd.) and drive 2.2 miles north to its junction with FS4813. From there, go right 0.3 mile. Park and carry 0.1 mile south on an unmarked dirt road. MVUM H5

---

*FOR OVERNIGHT OR EMERGENCY USE ONLY

Loc: At intersection of Gate Creek and FS4811	Road: Gravel, good
L/L: N45 13 878/W121 29 590	Access: Drive to camp
Cell: FS 26 in vicinity of Government Camp	Tents: 1
	El: 3470
Lndmk: Gate Creek and FS4811	RV: On road nearby

Description: This site might be a delight were it not hard by a dirt road that could be a source of dust in hot weather. On the other hand, the creek here runs clear as a bell and gives every appearance of being classic trout habitat.

Getting there: From the FS43/48 junction, drive 8 miles southeast to FS4811. Go 4.5 miles north on FS4811 to where Gate Creek crosses the road. The site is on left.
Alternatively, the site can be reached from FS4813/4811 junction by going south 1.3 miles on FS4811. MVUM H5

Loc: On FS 4813 (Wamic Mill Rd.), 1.7 miles from FS4860	**Road:** Gravel
L/L: N45 14 082/W121 30 477	**Access:** Park on road and carry (see warning below)
Cell: US 26 in vicinity of Government Camp	**Tents:** 1-2
	El: 3940
Lndmk: Intersection of Gate Creek and Wamic Mill Rd.	**RV:** No

Description: A prime site for a weekend getaway at altitude, this camp features a hand-made table. It has most likely been used as a hunters' camp in the past. The creek is small, clear and flows pleasantly through camp, with a small pool on the edge of camp that will be handy for cooling perishables and soft drinks.

Getting there: From US 26, go 6 miles northeast on FS43 to its junction with FS48, then turn right and drive 6.5 miles southeast. Turn left on FS4860 (Badger Lake Rd.) and drive 2.2 miles north to its junction with FS4813 (Wamic Mill Road). Go right on FS4813 to this camp, off the right side of the road just beyond where Gate Creek crosses the road.
Alternatively, this camp can be reached by driving 1.2 miles south on Wamic Mill Road from the junction of FS4813/4811.
Warning: Entry into this camp for vehicles traveling northeast on Wamic Mill Road requires an acute turn to the right over a berm, which poses the risk of high centering or, at the very least scraping bottom, especially in the case of a heavily-loaded passenger vehicle. Consequently, it is a good idea to consider parking on the road above camp and schlepping your gear the forty feet or so downhill into camp. Another reason for this is that the gravel entry road into camp is both short and steep enough to prevent a car from gaining the traction necessary to climb back to the road. MVUM H5

*FOR OVERNIGHT OR EMERGENCY USE ONLY

Loc: FS4813, 2.1 miles northeast of FS4860	**Road:** Gravel
L/L: N45 14 405/W121 30 223	**Access:** Drive to camp
Cell: US 26 near Government Camp	**Tents:** 1-2
	El: 4150
Lndmk: Junction of FS4813/4811	**RV:** MH and TT

Description: A serviceable but not prime site located on a creek that no doubt has its source in Bell Spring, a few hundred yards up the hill to the northwest. Offering shade and a good fire ring, this site will do in a pinch (such as when you arrive late on a busy summer holiday weekend). The creek, though only about a foot wide, flows clear as crystal and is a decent source of camp water due to the proximity of its source. Nevertheless, boil or purify for camp use, as always.

Getting there: From US 26 go 6 miles northeast on FS43 to its junction with FS48, then turn right and drive 6.5 miles southeast. Turn left on FS4860 (Badger Lake Road) and drive 2.2 miles north to its junction with FS4813 (Wamic Mill Road). Go right here. Watch for the creek and fire ring under the trees to the right at 2.1 miles. MVUM H5

Loc: Spur Road 520, off FS48	**Road:** Gravel
L/L: N45 18 658/W121 39 592	**Access:** Drive to camp
Cell: In camp	**Tents:** 1
	El: 4200
Lndmk: Junction OR 35 (Hood River Highway) and FS48, Iron Creek	**RV:** No

Description: Located about 0.2 mile north of FS48 at the end of spur 520, this unpretentious little site next to Iron Creek offers a bit of shade, the promise of fish and the ability to call home on your cell phone (I was able to do so in 2011 so long as I stayed in the open area near the end of the road). Drawbacks: The afternoon sun can be difficult to escape due to the southwestern exposure of the hillside, though the altitude may compensate for this to some degree. Also, the highway noise from FS48 below seems to be funneled up to the camp with amazing efficiency.

Getting there: From US 26, take the Hood River Highway (OR 35) toward Hood River. At 4.5 miles take FS48 to the right 0.6 mile. Turn left on spur 520 and drive 0.2 mile to camp at end of road. Do not confuse 520 with spur 532, which is a hundred or so yards to the east and on the other side of Iron Creek and was hugely rutted and not negotiable in 2011. MVUM F5

Loc: Camp Windy	**Road:** High clearance vehicles recommended
L/L: N45 17 327/W121 34 903	**Access:** ?
Cell: ?	**Tents:** ?
	El: 5400
Lndmk: Camp Windy	**RV:** ?

Description: Camp Windy is a decommissioned Forest Service camp that I became aware of too late in the season to visit. Consequently, I cannot speak to either the quality or to the character of the campsites here.

Getting there: From US 26 go 6.0 miles northeast on FS43 to FS48. Turn right and drive 2.4 miles. Turn left onto FS4890 (Bonney Meadows Road) and go approximately 1.8 miles north to where FS4891 forks to the right. Drive 5.1 miles on FS4891 to the second fork to the right (Bennett Pass Road). The Forest Service recommends high-clearance vehicles on the road to Camp Windy. *Warning: There may be more than one Bennett Pass Road. Check your map carefully.* MVUM G5

Loc: OR 35, between Sherwood and Polallie Campgrounds	**Road:** Paved
L/L: N45 24 659/W121 34 223	**Access:** Park and carry
Cell: US 26 in vicinity of Government Camp, city of Parkdale	**Tents:** 5-6
	El: 3010
Lndmk: Sherwood Campground	**RV:** Maybe a small MH

Description: This site features a secluded little beach and overlooking a pool on the river where one can spend a few pleasant hours. Be informed about local restrictions on fishing here.

Getting there: From US 26, take the Hood River Highway (SR 35) 15.9 miles toward Hood River to a turn-off just past the bridge across the East Fork of the Hood River. Park near the road and look for the site about a hundred feet to the right. A path leads down to the beach. MVUM G4

Loc: OR 35 (Hood River Highway), about 16.4 miles from US 26	**Road:** Short, dirt road off OR35
L/L: N45 25 020/W121 34 173	**Access:** Park and carry
Cell: US 26 in the vicinity of Government Camp, City of Parkdale	**Tents:** 5-6
	El: 2830
Lndmk: Hood River and Zigzag Trail	**RV:** Use judgment

Description: Formerly known as The Polallie Campground, this campsite now serves as a trailhead for the Zigzag Trail. Featuring a sturdy picnic table and abundant fire wood, it presents us with a beautiful, open but shady campsite by a mountain river that catches the afternoon sun. Peace and tranquility. What more could you ask? Nearby Hood River is Bull Trout habitat and was classified as catch and release in 2011. The Zigzag Trail doglegs its way up the side of the mountain across the river and continues southeast to connect with Brooks Meadow Road near Clinger Spring. Remember to pack out what you pack in. Otherwise, this place could become an eyesore overnight.

Campsite #35, beside the East Fork of the Hood River

Getting there: From US 26 take the Hood River Highway (OR 35) northward 16.4 miles. Follow Forest Service spur Road 720 a short 0.1 mile to campsites, near the river. MVUM G4

Loc: Routson County Park	Road: Dirt (into camp)
L/L: N45 26 914/W121 34 834	Access: Drive to camp
Cell: US 26 near Government Camp, City of Parkdale	Tents: 10-20
	El: 2400
Lndmk: Hood River	RV: MH and TT

Description: In the summer of 2010 when I visited it, Routson County Park in Hood River County was a fee-free campground. It is located where the Hood River flows through a grove of tall conifers, and appeared to be fully maintained without a camp host being present. Amenities consist of fire pits, a pit toilet, picnic tables and potable water from a spigot. Whether or not these will continue to be offered to the public without charge in these troubled economic times is anybody's guess. Given its convenient location along the well-traveled Hood River Highway it's a safe bet that it will attract members of the same loud, disrespectful and beer-swilling crowd that drove you out of public campgrounds in the first place.

Getting there: From US 26 drive 17.9 miles northward on the Hood River Highway (OR 35). The sign for Routson Park is a short distance past the turn-off to Cooper Spur.
Routson County Park is not part of the Mount Hood National Forest

Loc: FS4430, 1.6 miles north of FS44 on the South Fork of Fivemile Creek	Road: Paved
L/L: N45 25 165/W121 27 697	Access: Drive to camp
Cell: City of Parkdale	Tents: 1
	El: 3895
Lndmk: Eightmile Crossing Campground	RV: MH

Description: An altogether pleasant site on a babbling little creek. It is not well screened from the nearby road, but privacy along this sparsely-traveled road should not be a huge issue except for those few who are of the unshakeable opinion that nature is best enjoyed in the buff.

Getting there: From US 26, take the Hood River Highway 13.1 miles northeast. Go right for 10.4 miles on FS44 (Brooks Meadows Road) to FS4430. Turn north by the Eightmile Campground sign and go 1.6 miles to site. MVUM H4

Mount Hood at dusk

Loc: FS4430, near Eightmile Crossing Campground	Road: Paved
L/L: N45 24 404/W121 27 478	Access: Drive to camp
Cell: City of Parkdale	Tents: 2-3
	El: 3810
Lndmk: Eightmile Crossing Campground	RV: MH

Description: Limpid little Eightmile Creek pleasantly flowing past camp here is the star attraction, no doubt about it. Young fir trees growing close together along the edge of camp do a good job of assuring privacy from the nearby road. The small power generating facility located just downstream from this site probably provides the minimum power requirements of nearby Eightmile Crossing Campground. Stay away from it!

Getting there: From US 26, take the Hood River Highway 13.1 miles northeast. Go right 10.4 miles on FS44 (Brooks Meadows Road) to FS4430. Turn north by the Eightmile Crossing Campground sign and go 0.4 miles. Look for the dirt track to the right just after passing the entrance to the campground. MVUM H4

Loc: FS3560-222, 3.1 miles N of US 26/SR 35 junction	Road: Dirt track
L/L: N45 17 447/W121 40 172	Access: Park & carry. Check MVUM
Cell: Near camp or on SR 35	Tents: 3-4
	El: 3990
Lndmk: SR 35/FS3560 junction	RV: At end of road only

Description: Two little-used hunters' camps on the north fork of Mineral Creek.

Getting there: On US 26, go 30.6 miles from the junction with SR 211 in Sandy. Go left 3.1 miles on SR 35 to FS3560, then right 0.2 mile. Go left 0.5 mile on spur 222 to the end of the road, which may be a bit narrow and overgrown for an RV. Park and carry gear about 0.1 mile on a gently sloping but rough and rock-strewn track to sites. The first site sits directly above the creek at the end of a track which forks off to the left. The second is a few hundred feet further down the hill. MVUM F-5

Loc: FS3545, 0.5 mile NW of SR 35	Road: Dirt
L/L: N45 19 467/W121 38 258	Access: Check MVUM
Cell: SR 35, US 26, Parkdale	Tents: 5-6
	El: 4550
Lndmk: Elk Meadows/Sahalie Falls Trailhead	RV: Small MH and TT

Description: Shaded, sub-alpine camping on the edge of a pristine mountain meadow. Water is available off FS3545. Boil well.

Getting there: From US 26, go left 7.7 miles on SR 35. Go left (north) 0.5 mile on FS3545 to the fork in the road. Take the dirt track leading off into the woods between the two larger roads. Find campsites at about 0.1 to 0.2 mile. MVUM G4.

68 | NORTHEAST SECTION: BARLOW PASS SITES

Loc: FS3500-630, on the East Fork of the Hood River	**Road:** Dirt (sandy)
L/L: N45 21 275/W121 34 215	**Access:** Check MVUM
Cell: SR 35, US 26, Parkdale	**Tents:** 10-15 (3 sites)
	El: 3360
Lndmk: Nottingham Cg., 0.6 mile	**RV:** Small MH and TT

Description: Three campsites on the river that provide a feeling of remote wilderness isolation.

Getting there: From US 26, go left (north) 12.3 miles on SR 35, then left 0.1 mile FS3500-630 to sites, on right. MVUM G-4

Loc: FS3540/East Fork Hood River	**Road:** Paved
L/L: N45 19 382/W121 34 789	**Access:** Park and carry, short distance. Check MVUM
Cell: SR 35, US26, Parkdale	**Tents:** 5-6
	El: 3780
Lndmk: Junction FS3540/SR 35	**RV:** Beside road only

Description: Private, shaded, destination campsite on a beautiful section of the river.

Getting there: From US 26, go 9.9 miles on SR 35 to FS3540. Go right (SW) 0.5 miles to site, on left, just past the bridge.

*There is another large, private, but waterless site on the left at about 0.4 miles from SR 35.

Loc: On Clark Creek, about 200 yds. beyond end of FS3540-620	**Road:** Dirt
L/L: N45 19 023/W121 35 691	**Access:** Park and carry, about 200 yds. Check MVUM
Cell: SR 35, US 26, Parkdale	**Tents:** 3-4
	El: 3970
Lndmk: Junction FS3540/SR 35	**RV:** MH and TT, end of road only

Description: Remote, creekside camping at the end of a path through the woods.

Getting there: From US 26, go 9.9 miles on SR 35 to FS3540. Go right 0.4 mile to Spur 620. Follow Spur 620 one mile west to a large clearing. Park and carry gear 200 yards to camp.

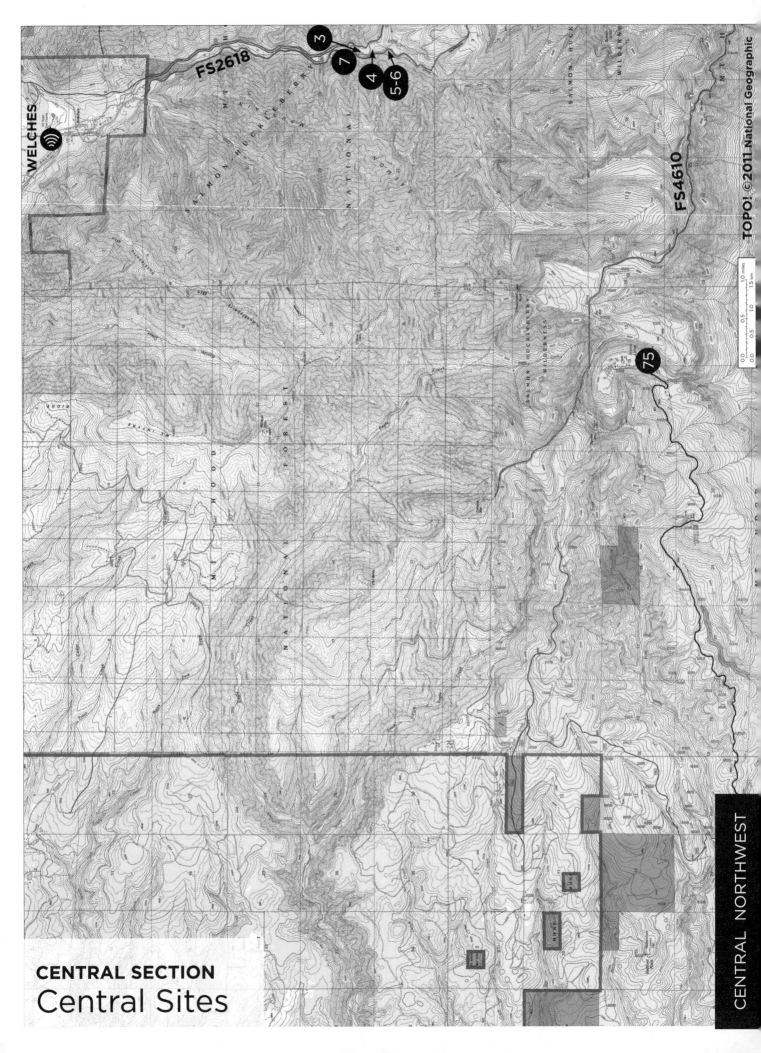

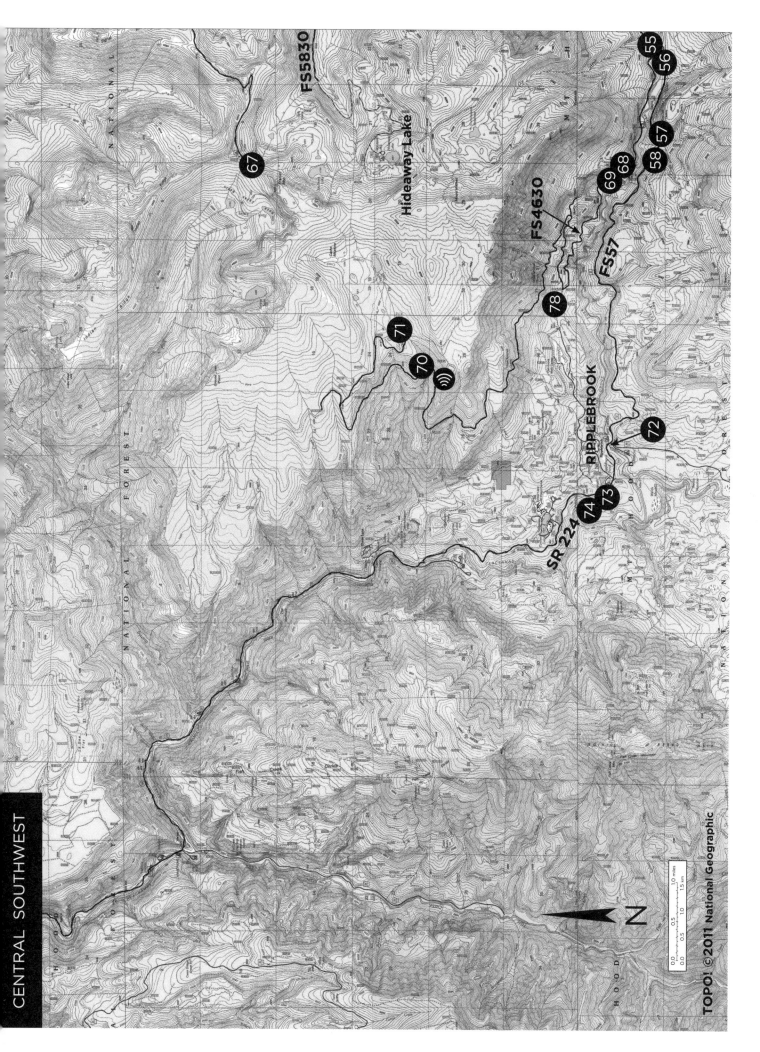

CENTRAL SOUTHWEST

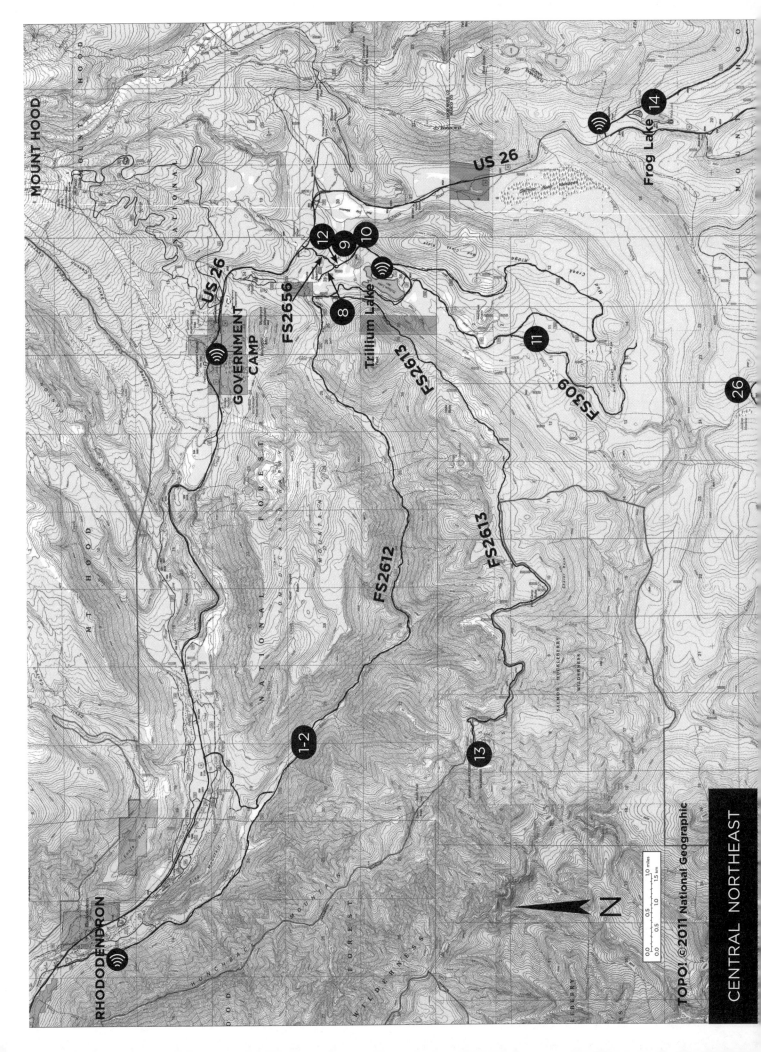

CENTRAL SOUTHEAST

CENTRAL SECTION

Central Sites

US 26 to FS57 and SR 224, Zigzag to Ripplebrook

The Central Section of the Forest has much to offer. Timothy and Clear Lakes, two of the largest lakes in the Forest as well as many smaller ones are located here. While paved roads give smooth access to the heart of this section of the Forest, most of the secondary and even tertiary ones are navigable in a two-wheel drive passenger vehicle. And there are more areas of cell phone receptivity in this area than in any other part of the Forest.

Loc: FS2612 at bridge crossing Still Creek	**Road:** Gravel
L/L: N45 17 205/W121 51 565	**Access:** Drive to camp
Cell: City of Rhododendron	**Tents:** 4-5
	El: 2000
Lndmk: Still Creek Bridge	**RV:** No

Description: Headed east on US 26, this may be the closest campsite to Portland. It is surrounded by both conifers and deciduous trees and offers campsites along a rambunctious mountain creek.

Getting there: From US 26 eastbound and 2.7 miles past the Dairy Queen in Rhododendron (and about 0.1 mile past the Camp Creek Campground), take Road 32 to the right. Go 0.7 mile (staying on paved road where 32 turns east at about 0.2 miles from US 26). At 0.7 mile take unmarked gravel road that forks to left and goes downhill. From here the road will join FS2612 and lead to the bridge in about a mile. Camp is on the right on the opposite side of the bridge. MVUM E5

Loc: At bridge where FS2612 crosses Still Creek	**Road:** Gravel
L/L: N45 17 205/W121 51 565	**Access:** Drive to camp
Cell: City of Rhododendron	**Tents:** 3-5
	El: 2000
Lndmk: Bridge over Still Creek	**RV:** No

Description: More secluded than site #1, this site is located across the bridge and just upstream from it. There are actually two campsites here. The track leading into the first camp goes on another hundred yards to the second site, located on a slower second arm of the creek, where a log in the stream offers a convenient spot to draw water.

Getting there: Follow directions to Site 1. Camp is on the left a hundred yards or so before the bridge. MVUM E5

Loc: FS 2618 (Salmon River Road)	Road: Paved
L/L: N45 16 610/W121 56 433	Access: Park and carry (100')
Cell: Along FS2618 in spots and City of Rhododendron	Tents: 6-10
	El: 1600
Lndmk: Subway Shop in Zigzag	RV: On road only

Description: The location of this site near the end of FS2618 where the Salmon River comes bursting, fresh and pristine from the Salmon-Huckleberry Wilderness, makes it among the most beautiful you will find anywhere in the Forest. Because of its beauty and proximity to Portland, you can expect company here, however. Even so, campsites are far enough apart to satisfy most people's needs for privacy and solitude. These sites overlook a section of the river where it slows and deepens, just upstream from the FS2618 bridge.

Getting there: Driving east on US 26, turn right (south) at the Subway shop in Welches onto FS2618 (The Salmon River Road). Go 4.9 miles. Camp is on left just past the bridge. Park on the side of the road and carry gear into the camping area. MVUM D5

Loc: FS2618 (Salmon River Rd.)	Road: Dirt
L/L: N45 16 334/W121 56 477	Access: Park and carry, steep trail, 200 yards
Cell: Along FS 2618 in spots and City of Rhododendron	Tents: 10-15
	El: 1690
Lndmk: Salmon River	RV: On road only

Camped on the Salmon River

Description: You'll find a number of great tent sites scattered along the river both upstream and downstream at this site. The place is ideal for a small group retreat. A small sand and gravel beach a few hundred yards downstream promises to catch the afternoon sun and may be a pleasant place to wade, soak or fish (catch and release).

Getting there: At the Subway shop in Welches turn south on FS2618 (The Salmon River Road). Go 5.3 miles to site, on left, where you should

Camp Free in the Mount Hood National Forest

find the trail heading down the bank to the river. A fifty-foot section of rope might be handy to help negotiate the initial steep section of the trail from the parking area, especially for the less nimble. A wagon or a backpack would be useful for carrying gear from car to camp and back again. Plan on making more than one trip. MVUM D5

Loc: On the South Fork, beyond the end of Salmon River Rd.	**Road:** Gravel
L/L: N45 16 238/W121 56 433	**Access:** Park and carry gear 0.1 mile
Cell: Along FS 2618 in spots and City of Rhododendron	**Tents:** 2-3
	El: 1646
Lndmk: South Fork Salmon River	**RV:** No RV's

Description: This beautiful and, oh, so private campsite on the South Fork of the Salmon River is located about 0.1 mile from the end of FS2618, but is well worth the walk. Cool, shady and secluded. A prime site!

Getting there: At the Subway shop in Welches turn south on FS2618 (The Salmon River Road). Go 5.4 miles to where the road is blocked, then schlep gear the remaining 0.1 mile to where a bridge crosses the South Fork of the Salmon. Camp is on right and upstream on the South Fork. Watch your step. The ground leading to camp is rough. MVUM D5
*Note: another campsite is to be found just a short distance from where the road is blocked by following the nearby horse trail a short distance upstream.

Loc: On the Salmon River, beyond the end of the Salmon River Rd.	**Road:** Gravel
L/L: N45 16 238/W121 56 433	**Access:** Park and carry, 0.1 mile
Cell: In spots along FS2618, US 26 near Welches, Zigzag	**Tents:** 2-3
	El: 1641
Lndmk: Bridge across South Fork of the Salmon River	**RV:** No

Description: On the opposite side of the road from site #5, but also on the river, this camp shares many of the same advantages of seclusion, shade and beauty, and also has a small stream running through it.

Getting there: Follow directions to Site 5. Camp is on the left, just before the road crosses the bridge over the South Fork of the Salmon. From there it's about one hundred feet to camp on a path which is initially steep, so watch your footing. MVUM D5

Loc: On Old Salmon River Trail #742, a hundred yards east of the road, where FS2618 crosses the Salmon River.)	**Road:** Paved
L/L: N45 16 673/W121 56 410	**Access:** Park and carry gear, 100 yards
Cell: Along FS 2618 in spots and City of Welches	**Tents:** 1
	El: 1654
Lndmk: FS trail 742	**RV:** No

Description: This memorably picturesque little site faces a small waterfall on the opposite side of the Salmon River. Its shaded seclusion and view of the river and falls makes it one of the nicest sites I've seen. Negatives are its small size and the fact that it is located on a popular hiking trail along the river, which means that anyone camping here will have to be resigned to exchanging pleasantries with the occasional hiker or backpacker.

Getting there: From US 26 go right on FS 2618 (Salmon River Road) at the Subway store in Welches. Go 4.8 miles. Trail #742 leading to camp is marked on right about thirty feet before FS2618 crosses the Salmon River. The road here is wide enough to allow ample parking. Carry gear 300 feet to camp. MVUM D5

Loc: Perry Vickers Rd, near Summit Meadow	**Road:** Gravel
L/L: N45 16 832/W121 44 049	**Access:** Drive to camp
Cell: In Camp, along US 26 and Trillium Lake Road	**Tents:** 50-60 in 27 campsites
	El: 3680
Lndmk: Perry Vickers Historical Site	**RV:** Yes

Description: Approximately twenty-seven waterless but spacious campsites within view of Mt. Hood, each accommodating two to four family-size tents.

Getting there: From US 26, go 0.4 mile on FS2656 (Trillium Lake Rd.). Turn right on the road to Summit Meadows and Perry Vickers Historical Site. Campsites start about 200 yards west of FS2656. MVUM F5

Loc: FS2656 Trillium Lake Rd.), 0.8 miles from US 26	**Road:** Paved
L/L: N45 16 619/W121 43 850	**Access:** Park on road, carry gear
Cell: In camp and along Trillium Lake Rd, US 26	**Tents:** 3-4
	El: 3621
Lndmk: Perry Vickers Rd	**RV:** No

(Site 9) Description: A dry, cool, shaded camp about a hundred feet off Trillium Lake Road that is attractive primarily for its proximity to Trillium Lake and other recreational possibilities in the area. There is a fire ring and room for 3-4 family-size tents. Trillium Lake Road will be busy on weekends, but traffic should taper off at night. Try the public rest stop at Government Camp for potable water.

Getting there: From US 26 near Government Camp ski areas, take FS 2656 (Trillium Lake Rd.) 0.8 mile. Camp is on left and may be difficult to spot from the road. MVUM F5

Loc: Trillium Lake Rd. (FS 2656), one mile from US 26	**Road:** Dirt
L/L: N45 16 483/W 121 43 682	**Access:** Park and carry
Cell: In camp	**Tents:** 5-6
	El: 3680
Lndmk: Trillium Lake and Cg., about half a mile away	**RV:** MH under 24' only

Description: Another dry, shaded, cool and secluded camp just off Trillium Lake Road that is attractive because of its proximity to the lake. Trillium Lake Campground is about half a mile away.

Getting there: From US 26, take Trillium Lake Rd. (FS2656) 1.0 mile to a bend in the road. There a short, narrow dirt road turns sharply to the left and leads through the trees to the camping area on a shelf about 100 yards from the road. This is a popular site, so get there early and come prepared to spend about half an hour cleaning up your camp and environs, just in case the previous tenants were the kind of people you'd prefer to see camping somewhere else, such as in another state. MVUM F5

Loc: FS 2656-309	**Road:** Gravel
L/L: N45 14 526/121 45 240	**Access:** Drive to camp
Cell: Trillium Lake area	**Tents:** 1-2
	El: 3300
Lndmk: Trillium Lake	**RV:** No

Description: This dry site provides good access to Trillium Lake and might provide more solitude and privacy than the sites along paved Trillium Lake Rd. For potable water try the public rest area in Government Camp.

Getting there: From Us 26 take the road to Trillium Lake (FS 2656) 1.8 miles south. Turn left at the second turn-off onto the 2656 loop road (about 0.4 miles past the Trillium Lake Campground Road. Go approximately 2 miles south on 2656, then take FS 2656-309 (spur 309), which forks off to the right. Go another 0.4 miles to camp on left. MVUM F5

Loc: Trillium Lake Rd. (FS2656)	Road: Paved
L/L: N45 16 777/W 121 43 970	Access: Drive to camp
Cell: Along Trillium Lake Road and along Perry Vickers Rd.	Tents: 2-3
	El: 3680
Lndmk: Perry Vickers Rd., Summit Meadows	RV: Yes

Description: A dry camp in the trees beside Trillium Lake Road opposite Perry Vickers Rd, this site might provide more actual privacy than the larger camping area across the road. Traffic on the Trillium Lake Road, which is paved, might be a problem on busy weekend days. Trillium Lake day use area is just a short distance away. *Be very careful about riding bicycles on Trillium Lake Road. Vehicles move very fast here, and there are no shoulders, even on the curves.*

Getting there: From US 26, take Trillium Lake Road (FS 2656) 0.4 mile to camp, on the left, almost directly across from Perry Vickers Road and Spur 131. MVUM F5

Loc: Kinzel Lake	Road: Dirt, poor and difficult to drive
L/L: N45 15 239/W121 51 627	Access: Drive to camp
Cell: US 26 in the vicinity of Trillium Lake	Tents: 12-15
	El: 4200
Lndmk: Kinzel Lake	RV: Road too rough

Description: Stand by this lake at sunset and you will feel that you have found the very center of tranquility itself. Spang on the northwest edge of the Salmon-Huckleberry Wilderness, Kinzel Lake is a decommissioned campground that sits in a bowl at the end of a short spur road, 0.3 miles south of and below FS2613. Surrounded by rhododendrons and seldom used, this site should be a Mecca for those who seek solitude and drive high-clearance vehicles. The road into the lake is as much boulder and rut as it is road and is consequently difficult and nerve-wracking to drive.

Late afternoon sun on Kinzel Lake

Kinzel Lake is a lake in transition, on its way to becoming a meadow. It is quite shallow and choked with marsh grass around its edges. Only one difficult boardwalk gives access to the lake, which has a muddy bottom that is not inviting for either swimming or wading. Nevertheless, if careful, it should be possible to collect sufficient water for camp use. There are fire rings and one or more picnic tables. One caveat for those who seek peace and quiet: Dirt bikers love the road into Kinzel Lake.

(Site 13) Getting there: From US 26, take the Trillium Lake Road (FS2656), which curves to the right around the south end of Trillium Lake and becomes FS2612 heading northeast. At approximately 3.1 miles from US 26 go left on Kinzel Lake Rd. (FS 2613) for 8.3 miles
Warning: FS2613 is rough and difficult to drive in a low-clearance vehicle). MVUM E5

Loc: FS 2610 (Frog Creek Rd.)	**Road:** Gravel
L/L: N45 13 161/W 121 41 504	**Access:** Park and carry
Cell: Nearby, if not in camp	**Tents:** 3-5
	El: 3772
Lndmk: Frog Lake Sno-Park	**RV:** Beside road only

Description: A waterless site in a shady grove of fir trees just off of Frog Creek road and so close to the lake that paths must exist that give access to it (though I did not have the liberty to explore them, since there were several parties occupying the site when I came upon it. This site is far enough from Frog Lake Campground (0.4 mile) to provide privacy and solitude for those lucky enough to get there first, even on a busy holiday weekend. When the weather has been hot and dry it would be a good idea to seek a campsite well away from the dusty road.

Getting there: On US 26, at 4.3 miles past the Hood River Highway (OR 35), turn left into the Frog Lake Sno-Park. Go 0.8 miles south on Frog Creek Road. Site is on the right about 0.4 miles past Frog Lake Campground. MVUM F5

Loc: FS 2630 (Clear Lake Rd.)	**Road:** Paved
L/L: N45 11 103/W121 41 688	**Access:** Drive to camp
Cell: In camp, US 26 near Gov't Camp, many places around Clear Lake	**Tents:** 4
	El: 3652
Lndmk: Clear Lake Campground Road/ FS 2630 (Clear Lake Rd.)	**RV:** Small MH, TT?

Description: From the road this site holds more promise than it delivers. At first glance the many towering conifer trees here appear to offer an abundance of shady camp sites, but closer inspection reveals only about four fairly level tent sites. Indeed, this might be one of those rare sites that can actually accommodate more RVs than tents, since RVs can be leveled out relatively easily.

Getting there: Heading east on US 26, turn right on Clear Lake Road (FS 2630) 6.8 miles past Hood River Highway (OR 35) and 1.2 miles past Blue Box Pass. Go 0.7 miles to junction of FS 2630 and the road to Clear Lake Campground. Site is on the right, where FS2630 T's off to the west. MVUM F6

Loc: Spur 222, near Clear Lake on FS2630	Road: Dirt
L/L: N45 11 023/W121 41 602	Access: Check MVUM
Cell: On FS 2630, many places around Clear Lake	Tents: 3
	El: 3600
Lndmk: Clear Lake Campground Road and FS2630 junction	RV: Check MVUM

Description: Though dry, this is a nice site set among tall conifers with little underbrush beneath them. It is located just 0.6 mile from the boat ramp at Clear Lake.

Getting there: Heading east on US 26, turn right on Clear Lake Road (FS 2630) 6.8 miles past Hood River Highway (OR 35) and 1.2 miles past Blue Box Pass. Go 0.7 miles to junction of FS 2630 and the road to Clear Lake Campground. Go left 0.1 mile on dirt spur road 222, then take a dirt road to the right roughly 200 yards to camp. MVUM F6

Loc: Near junction of Clear Lake Rd. and Clear Lake Campground Rd.	Road: Dirt track
L/L: N45 10 960/W121 41 586	Access: Check MVUM
Cell: Many places around Clear Lake	Tents: 2-3
	El: 3640
Lndmk: Clear Lake	RV: ?

Description: A dry camp located in an open area under the trees. If you don't like the idea of camping on the lake shore in full view of your neighbors, this site may appeal to you, since it is hidden in the trees and more likely to provide privacy and solitude while allowing fairly easy access to Clear Lake.

Getting there: Heading east on US 26, turn right on Clear Lake Road (FS 2630) 6.8 miles past Hood River Highway (OR 35) and 1.2 miles past Blue Box Pass. Go 0.7 miles to junction of FS 2630 and the road to Clear Lake Campground. Go left 0.1 miles on dirt spur road (222). Then take dirt road to right roughly 0.1 mile to camp. This site is just past Site #16. MVUM F6

Loc: Off FS2630, 0.5 mile past FS2630/ Clear Lake Campground Rd. junction	Road: Dirt, primitive, difficult, short
L/L: N45 11 310/W121 41 925	Access: Drive to camps
Cell: In camps (all but a few are directly above the lake)	Tents: 10-20
	El: 3422
Lndmk: Clear Lake	RV: Small MH only

(Site 18) Description: These sites (six or more) are almost all in the trees directly above Clear Lake and about a hundred yards or so away from the shore. Because they feature easy access to the lake, several show signs of having been littered used by previous campers. All of them have fire rings, and one features a picnic table.

Getting there: Heading east on US 26, turn right on Clear Lake Road (FS 2630) 6.8 miles past Hood River Highway (OR 35) and 1.2 miles past Blue Box Pass. Go 0.7 miles to junction of FS2630 and the road to Clear Lake Campground, where FS2630 makes a 90 degree turn to the right. From here go 0.5 miles to Spur 270, which takes off to the left toward the lake. Choose your campsite from among about six strung out along the road, which is rough and follows the contours of the lake. MVUM F6

Loc: FS2630 above Clear Lake	Road: Dirt (through camp)
L/L: N45 11 561/W121 42 912	Access: Drive to camp
Cell: If not in camp, along lake shore	Tents: 5-6
	El: 3538
Lndmk: Clear Lake	RV: No

Description: This could be a prime site because of its lake access and its choice location in the trees above the lake, but several (about half) of the otherwise beautiful sites I found here in the summer of 2011 had been desecrated by its previous users. They were littered with party debris of various kinds, including plastic, glass and aluminum food and drink packaging and a couple of discarded automobile tires. Will somebody please help?

Getting there: Heading east on US 26, turn right on Clear Lake Road (FS2630) 6.8 miles past Hood River Highway (OR 35) and 1.2 miles past Blue Box Pass. Go 0.7 mile to junction of FS 2630 and the road to Clear Lake Campground. Continue right 1.5 miles on FS2630. Watch for a short road leading downhill to the left to the sites, which are visible from the road. MVUM F6

Loc: FS2630, 2.7 miles from US 26	Road: Paved
L/L: N45 11 597/W121 43 286	Access: Drive to camp
Cell: Along lake shore	Tents: 1-2
	El: 3460
Lndmk: Clear Lake	RV: Small MH only

Description: One of the tent sites here is for a small tent only. Camp is in trees fairly close to FS2630. There are two fire rings. The map shows a creek running near camp, but I found no evidence of it during my visit. Access to lake from camp is possible by going through open forest, but there is no clear path, and it would be difficult to haul a canoe or small craft through the trees.

Getting there: Heading east on US 26, turn right on Clear Lake Road (FS 2630) 6.8 miles past Hood River Highway (OR 35) and 1.2 miles past Blue Box Pass. Go 0.7 miles to junction of FS 2630 and the road to Clear Lake Campground. Continue right on FS2630 for 2 miles. The short road on the left that leads downhill to the site is easy to miss. MVUM F6

Loc: North and west arms of Clear Lake	Road: Dirt, primitive and rough
L/L: N45 10 713/W121 42 802	Access: Drive to camp
Cell: In camp	Tents: 50-100
	El: 3600
Lndmk: Clear Lake and FS 2630	RV: Questionable

Description: There are at least 27 campsites spread out along these two arms of the lake. All have lake views and cell phone reception and would be prime destination sites but for the fact that many bear evidence of having been heavily used by a careless public.

Getting there: Heading east on US 26, turn right on Clear Lake Road (FS 2630) 6.8 miles past Hood River Highway (OR 35) and 1.2 miles past Blue Box Pass. The majority of these sites can only be accessed from a primitive spur road that contours along the lake for about a mile and connects to FS2630 at two points. The first of these points is a primitive dirt road going toward the lake at about 1.1 miles beyond Site 19 (2.6 miles from the junction of FS2630/Clear Lake Campground Roads). It leads downhill to the lake before it starts to contour its way through the numerous campsites along the lake. The second point of entry is at 3 miles from the above junction off of spur 240, which connects to FS2630. *The road along the lake is also not for the faint of heart! Those who have a high-clearance vehicle will have a much easier time of it on this road.* MVUM F6

Loc: Clear Creek at junction FS42/4290	Road: Paved
L/L: N45 10 061/W121 41 083	Access: Drive to camp
Cell: Clear Lake and along US 26	Tents: 14-16
	El: 3383
Lndmk: Junction FS42/4290	RV: MH and TT

Description: There are two campsites, each with a fire ring but no other amenities. Both sites have a wilderness feeling to them, despite being just a hundred feet from FS42. They are located in a grove of second-growth conifers on a beautiful stretch of Clear Creek that provides a yielding layer of forest duff upon which to pitch a tent.

Getting there: Heading east on US 26, turn right onto FS42 at 10.1 miles past Hood River Highway (OR 35) and 4.5 miles past Blue Box Pass. Go 0.8 mile south on FS42 to a bridge near FS42/4290 junction. Take turn-off to camp, on left, a hundred yards north of the bridge. MVUM F6

Loc: Clear Creek at junction FS42/4290	Road: Paved
L/L: N45 10 014/W121 41 144	Access: Drive to camp
Cell: Clear Lake and/or along US 26	Tents: 1-2
	El: 3503
Lndmk: Junction FS42/4290	RV: Small MH

(Site 23) Description: Find solitude beside the highway at this site. Its location is far enough from the road to make it difficult to spot. The giveaway is a dirt apron large enough for several cars to pull in and park. This is an ideal road location for late summer camping. It's shady everywhere. Clear Creek, a good-sized creek that drains Clear Lake, 0.3 mile away as the crow flies, bubbles along just below camp, is handy for drawing water and probably even deep enough for a cooling summer soak. The downside is the lack of level tent sites, which makes this place a good choice for a family or a couple with but one tent A small motor home might be able to back up under the shelter of the trees to the campsite.

Getting there: Heading east on US 26, turn right onto FS42 at 10.1 miles past Hood River Highway (OR 35) and 4.5 miles past Blue Box Pass. Go 0.8 miles south on FS42 to the bridge near FS42/4290 junction. Turn left into camp just beyond the bridge. MVUM F6

Loc: 0.6 mile north of FS58 on FS5880	**Road:** Gravel
L/L: N45 11 644/W121 48 470	**Access:** Drive to camp
Cell: South end of Timothy Lake, Clear Lake	**Tents:** 2-3
	El: 3794
Lndmk: Frying Pan Lake	**RV:** MH and TT

Description: An unusually peaceful little campsite surrounded by alpine spruce and fir at altitude. A small creek with a simple plank foot bridge flows along just behind camp. Someone has built a meticulously crafted fire ring near the Forest Service-sturdy picnic table that graces the site - probably the same party responsible for the foot bridge. Whoever it was has taken good care of and repeatedly used this campsite. The ground in the immediate vicinity of camp is not ideal for pitching tents, but there are other suitable spots for tents a hundred or so feet away, which isn't too great a distance to walk for a cup of coffee in the morning.

Getting there: Heading east on US 26, turn right onto FS42 at 10.1 miles past the Hood River Highway (OR35) and 4.9 miles past Blue Box Pass. Go 3.9 miles on FS42. Turn right on FS58 and go 7 miles to FS5880 (on right). Go 0.5 miles north on FS5880 to a point where road is blocked by log. Take the spur road 0.1 mile to the right to camp, on right. MVUM E6

Loc: Frying Pan Lake	**Road:** Dirt, rutted
L/L: N45 11 179/W121 47 570	**Access:** Park and carry, up to 200 yds
Cell: Clear Lake and along US 26	**Tents:** 20-30
	El: 4080
Lndmk: Frying Pan Lake	**RV:** Small MH only

Description: Discover the silence, solitude and beauty of Frying Pan Lake. Walk along its western shore and have your breath taken away at the sight of the mountain rising over its opposite shore. Take your pick of abundant campsites and firewood. Downsides include the possibility of a plethora of mosquitoes and the fact that the ground around the lake seems to have a high water table. The shore around the lake bears testimony to a lot of cow traffic in the past, so boil water conscientiously, or bring your own from somewhere else. This lake is shallow, with a muddy bottom and shoreline, and is on its way to becoming a meadow. Unless you are hard-core, take swimming and boating off the list here.

Getting there: Heading east on US 26, turn right on FS42 at 10.1 miles past the Hood River Highway (OR35) and 4.9 miles past Blue Box Pass. At 3.9 miles, turn right on FS58 and go 7 miles to FS5880 (on right). Go 0.1 miles north on FS5880 and take dirt spur 241 to the right another 0.1 mile. Early in the year, this section of the road may have standing water that can hide deep ruts. Straddle them to keep your wheels on high ground. MVUM E6

Frying Pan Lake

Loc: Between Jackpot Meadow and Dry Meadow	**Road:** Gravel
L/L: N45 11 977/W121 46 143	**Access:** Drive to camp
Cell: US 26 and Clear Lake	**Tents:** 8-10
	El: 3900
Lndmk: Jackpot Meadows and the PCT	**RV:** MH and TT

Description: Set under the trees near a sunny meadow, this dry camp at the junction of spur roads 240 and 241 promises rest and respite in the shade. Trail #492 forks off the PCT a mile or two to the south and crosses the road a few hundred yards east of camp to take you north to Jackpot Meadows. Water is to be had from a small stream that crosses under the road 0.4 mile to the north.

Getting there: Heading east on US 26: at 10.1 miles past the Hood River Highway (OR35) and 4.9 miles past Blue Box Pass turn right on FS42. Go 3.9 miles on FS42. Turn right on FS58 and go 4.5 miles to FS spur 240, then north (right) on 240 two miles to site, on the left, where the 241 splits off to the west. MVUM F6

Loc: FS5855	Road: Dirt
L/L: N45 11 196/W121 50 748	Access: Park and carry
Cell: South end Timothy Lake, High Rock, US 26, Clear Lake	Tents: 4-5
	El: 3975
Lndmk: FS58	RV: Road too rough

Description: Though waterless, this is a delightful and secluded spot in a dense stand of Douglas fir and hemlock trees at altitude. The surrounding understory is dominated by rhododendron bushes, which, in full bloom, can be quite striking. Enjoy the unadulterated sound of the afternoon breeze sighing through the trees as it flows upward from lower elevations. Some previous visitor has left his or her mark on the place in the form of an elaborate fire ring. Haul in plenty of water for your stay.

Section of the road to Jackpot Meadows

Getting there: Heading east on US 26: at 10.1 miles past the Hood River Highway (OR35) and 4.9 miles past Blue Box Pass turn right on FS42. Go 3.9 miles on FS42. Turn right on FS58 and go 9.4 miles to FS5855 (on right). Go 1.8 miles north on FS5855 to a short spur road off to the right as you climb the hill. Camp is about a hundred yards to the right off FS5855, which is blocked a few hundred yards north of camp. MVUM E6
Note: The map has FS 5855 listed as a four-wheel drive road, but, in fact, most of it turned out to be one of the smoother mountain roads I've driven.

Loc: On FS5860, 1.1 miles south of FS58	Road: Gravel, good
L/L: N45 09 916/W121 48 785	Access: Check MVUM
Cell: South end Timothy Lake, High Rock	Tents: 2-3
	El: 4115
Lndmk: FS5860	RV: MH and TT

Description: Perhaps a more appropriate as little hideaway for an RV than a tent, this site, barely visible from the road, guarantees plenty of privacy. It is located where one of the headwaters of Dinger Creek forms a deep pool that may have been the birthplace of all the mosquitoes that greeted me as I got out of the car to inspect the place. Nevertheless, it certainly would suffice for an overnight stay on the way to something more desirable.

Getting there: Heading east on US 26, turn right onto FS42 at 10.1 miles past the Hood River Highway (OR35) and 4.9 miles past Blue Box Pass. Go 3.9 miles on FS42, then turn right onto FS58.

At 7.8 miles turn left (south) on onto FS5860. At 1.1 miles south of FS58 turn right onto spur road 230 and go 0.1 mile to campsite, at the end of the road. MVUM E6

Loc: Spur 240, 0.3 mile from FS5890 and 1.1 miles north of Timothy Lake	**Road:** Gravel
L/L: N45 08 018/W121 49 340	**Access:** Park and carry, 100 yds
Cell: South end Timothy Lake	**Tents:** 2-3
	El: 3480
Lndmk: Junction FS5890/spur240	**RV:** On road only

Description: This secluded little camp near Dinger Creek is sheltered and shaded by a grove tall conifers. Dinger Creek is about 200 yards away through the trees and is audible from camp.

Getting there: This camp is best reached from FS57, which passes along the south shore of Timothy Lake. Drive FS 42 from US 26 south to FS57 and Timothy Lake (about eight miles). Go right 3.7 miles on FS57 to FS5810, which is about 0.1 mile beyond the bridge over the outlet of Timothy Lake. Take FS5810 north. At 0.4 mile continue another 0.5 mile north on 5820, then take 5890 four-tenths mile to spur 240. Turn left and go 0.3 mile to camp, on right. MVUM E6

Loc: Spur 240, 0.6 mile from FS5890 and about 1.3 miles north of Timothy Lk.	**Road:** Gravel
L/L: N45 08 245/W121 49 585	**Access:** Park and carry across stream to camp
Cell: South end of Timothy Lake	**Tents:** 5-6
	El: 3499
Lndmk: Junction, spur 240/FS5890	**RV:** On road only

Description: This spacious, shaded site in a grove of cedar and hemlock trees would be a prime site if it were cleaned up properly. You'll have to park near the road and pack your gear across Dinger Creek on an eight-foot slab bridge that may well be carried off with the next high water. Water for camp use can be drawn from the far arm of Dinger Creek, which is a hundred yards north/northeast of camp.

Getting there: This camp is best reached from FS57, which passes along the south shore of Timothy Lake. Drive FS42 from US 26 south to FS57 and Timothy Lake (about 8 miles). Go right 3.7 miles on FS57 to FS5810, which is about 0.1 miles beyond the bridge over the outlet of Timothy Lake. Take FS5810 north. At 0.4 mile continue another 0.5 mile north on 5820, then take 5890 another 0.4 miles to spur 240. Turn left and go six-tenths of a mile to camp, on right. MVUM E6

Loc: Spur 240, 0.9 mile from FS5890, 1.6 miles north of Timothy Lake	Road: Gravel
L/L: N45 08 412/W121 49 812	Access: Park and carry, 100 ft
Cell: South end Timothy Lake	Tents: 2-3
	El: 3600
Lndmk: Junction, spur 240/FS5890	RV: Near road only

Description: Camp within a hundred yards of the road near a small tributary to Dinger Creek. Find shade near an elaborate fire ring hidden in the trees near the larger arm of Dinger Creek. Downsides: There are mosquitoes in the area and the site near the road has been carelessly littered by previous campers.

Getting there: This camp is best reached from FS57, which passes along the south shore of Timothy Lake. Drive FS42 from US 26 south to FS57 and Timothy Lake (about 8 miles). Go right 3.7 miles on FS57 to FS5810, which is about 0.1 miles beyond the bridge over the outlet of Timothy Lake. Take FS5810 north. At 0.4 mile continue another 0.5 mile north on 5820, then take 5890 another 0.4 miles to spur 240. Turn left and go 0.9 mile to camp at end of road. MVUM E6

Loc: FS5890, near spur 240, about 1.2 miles north of Timothy Lake	Road: Paved
L/L: N45 07 819/W121 49 118	Access: Drive to camp
Cell: South end of Timothy Lake	Tents: 3-4
	El: 3411
Lndmk: Junction, FS5890/spur 240	RV: MH

Description: A very clean and pleasant, though waterless, camp shaded by tall Douglas fir and hemlock trees. Set up camp and enjoy the balm of nature within a hundred yards of a paved road. Get water from nearby Dinger Creek, about 0.1 mile to the north on FS5890.

Getting there: This camp is best reached from FS57, which passes along the south shore of Timothy Lake. Drive FS42 from US 26 south to FS57 and Timothy Lake (about 8 miles). Go right 3.7 miles on FS57 to FS5810, which is about 0.1 miles beyond the bridge over the outlet of Timothy Lake. Take FS5810 north. At 0.4 continue another 0.5 mile north on FS5820, then take FS5890 another 0.3 mile to camp on left, about 0.1 mile south of spur 240. MVUM E6

Loc: Junction FS42/4280	Road: Paved
L/L: N45 06 313/W121 44 549	Access: Drive to camp
Cell: South end Timothy Lake	Tents: 5-6
	El: 3420
Lndmk: Joe Graham Horse Camp	RV: MH and TT

Description: A waterless site set back from the road in the trees. There are more desirable sites with lake access along FS4280, but this site will work if those are all taken when you arrive, since it is also close to all the good stuff that Timothy Lake offers. Another smaller site a hundred yards to the south will accommodate a couple of small tents.

Getting there: From US 26, drive 8 miles south on FS42 to FS4280. Site is on right just past FS4280. MVUM F6

Loc: FS42, 0.1 mile south of FS4280, by Joe Graham Horse Camp	**Road:** Paved
L/L: N45 06 225/W121 44 607	**Access:** Drive to camp
Cell: South end Timothy Lake	**Tents:** 10-15
	El: 3420
Lndmk: Joe Graham Horse Camp	**RV:** MH OK, TT?

Description: The many tent sites here sit well away from the road among the tall conifers to provide privacy for a large party. The Oak Grove Fork of the Clackamas starts as a creek behind camp a few hundred feet from the road.

Getting there: From US 26, go 8.1 miles south on FS42 toward Timothy Lake. Passing FS4280 on right at 8 miles, watch for the site on your left and just north of where the PCT crosses the road in the next tenth of a mile. MVUM F6-7

(A SUB-PRIME SITE)

Loc: FS4280, 0.6 mile from FS42 near Timothy Lake	**Road:** Gravel
L/L: N45 06 594/W121 45 088	**Access:** Park and carry 100 ft.
Cell: South End Timothy Lake	**Tents:** 1-2
	El: 3412
Lndmk: Timothy Lake	**RV:** In parking area only

Description: This is best used as an overnight/emergency site. It offers access to the Timothy Lake recreational area and comes with a fire ring and ample shade. Drawbacks are the fact that it is waterless, has no direct lake access and could use some clean-up. FS4280 is dusty in the summertime but should be far enough from the campsite so as not to be a problem.

Getting there: From US 26, drive 8 miles south on FS42 toward Timothy Lake. Turn right on FS4280 and drive 0.6 miles to site, on left. MVUM F6
Warning: FS4280 carries a lot of recreational traffic and can be jarringly washboardy in a few places. Be ready to slow way down at the first hint of this.

Loc: FS4280, 1.1 miles from FS42	Road: Dirt
L/L: N45 06 863/W121 45 432	Access: Park and carry
Cell: South end Timothy Lake	Tents: 3-4
	El: 3363
Lndmk: Timothy Lake	RV: Use judgment

Description: A large, waterless camp with plenty of space to spread out and be comfortable. A previous camper has done a lot of work on this site, erecting long pole supports attached to a ridge pole to form an A-frame skeleton.

Getting there: From US 26, go 8 miles south FS42 toward Timothy Lake. Turn right on FS4280 and drive 1.1 miles. Then go right about 200 yards on an unmarked dirt road to site, on right. MVUM F6
Note regarding cell phone reception in the Timothy Lake vicinity: Though the author and others have found dependable cell receptivity on the south end of Timothy Lake, it is likely that you will also find receptivity along other parts of the lakeshore as well. Give it a try.

Loc: FS4280, 1.8 miles from FS42	Road: Gravel
L/L: N45 07 319/W121 46 037	Access: Park and carry, 100 yds
Cell: South end Timothy Lake	Tents: 2-3
	El: 3310
Lndmk: Timothy Lake	RV: No

Description: This site, though waterless, does give direct access to Timothy Lake a couple hundred yards down the hill, though you'll have to hold out for the Riviera if you have to have a fabulous, sandy beach. Site was well-policed of litter in 2011.

Getting there: From US 26, drive 8 miles south on FS42 toward Timothy Lake. Turn right onto FS4280 and drive 1.9 miles to site, on left. Park and carry gear down the hill toward the lake. MVUM F6

Loc: FS4280, 2.1 miles from FS42	Road: Gravel
L/L: N45 07 345/W121 46 256	Access: Park and carry, 100 yds
Cell: South end of Timothy Lake	Tents: 3-4
	El: 3280
Lndmk: Junction, FS42/4280	RV: On road only

Description: A dry camp about a hundred yards downhill from the road and overlooking Timothy Lake. This site is popular, so you'll have to stake it one out a day or two early on busy summer weekends. The bank of the lake at this point tends to be muddy, rather than sandy, but the Pacific Crest

Trail, which passes along the lakeshore, can be used to gain access to a more desirable part of the lake. Only horse and foot traffic are allowed on this section of the trail, however. No motorcycles or even bicycles. Carrying water uphill from the lake is possible, but would be a chore.

Getting there: From US 26, go right 8 miles on FS42 to FS4280. Turn right onto FS4280 and drive 2.1 miles to site, on left. Park and carry gear downhill to campsite. MVUM F6

Loc: On unnamed road branching from FS4280 at 2.6 miles from FS42 and 3.1 miles south of FS58	**Road:** Dirt, short, rough
L/L: N45 07 669/W121 46 140	**Access:** Check MVUM
Cell: South end Timothy Lake	**Tents:** 2-3
	El: 3230
Lndmk: Junction FS4280/42, 2.6 miles	**RV:** MH

Description: This waterless, secluded and shady camp on the side of FS4280 doesn't offer a view of the lake because of its location on the opposite side of the road, so it might not be your first choice. But if your heart is bent on spending the weekend enjoying Timothy Lake and you arrive too late to snab one of the more desirable sites around the lake, this will certainly do just fine.

Getting there: This site is just as easily reached by coming down FS4280 from the north, but driving FS4280 from the south will take you past some pretty nice sites that overlook the lake, so I'm going to assume that you'll be coming in from that direction. From US 26, take FS42 to the right for eight miles. Go right on FS4280 for 2.6 miles to an unnamed road teeing off to the right. Camp is 100 yards from FS4280 on the left. Alternatively, From FS58, go south 3.1 miles on FS4280 to site, on left. MVUM F6

Loc: FS4280, 2.8 to 3.1 miles from FS42 and 2.6 miles south of FS58	**Road:** Dirt, short but rough
L/L: N45 07 936/W121 46 122	**Access:** Park and carry
Cell: South end Timothy Lake	**Tents:** 2-3
	El: 3358
Lndmk: Timothy Lake	**RV:** No

Description: Located along the northern arm of the lake, this is one of the few sites along the lake that offers a semi-sandy beach where it is possible to easily wade into the water. And though it may require some clean-up, it has prime site potential. A faint trail leads to a bluff and then to the beach a few hundred yards down the hill.

Getting there: Follow directions to FS4280 from US 26 (sites 35-39 above), then go 2.8 to 3.1 miles to dirt track leading downhill in the direction of the lake to the left. Park and walk 0.1 mile to campsite at the end of the road. There is a second campsite to the left about a hundred yards before you reach the bottom of the hill.

Loc: North arm of Timothy Lake on the PCT Trail	Road: Dirt, up and down
L/L: N45 08 334/W121 46 111	Access: Park and carry to camp
Cell: South end of Timothy Lake and possibly in camp	Tents: 5-10
	El: 3280
Lndmk: North arm of Timothy Lake	RV: No

Description: If you can get to them, these prime sites on the Pacific Crest Trail are some of the most appealing to be found in the entire Forest. All are within a stone's throw of the lake. This means a lot of foot and horse traffic passing close to camp, especially during busy summer weekends. All the campsites here show evidence of having been used respectfully and repeatedly, probably by the same group of people. These sites are all so nice that you'll appreciate the opportunity to enjoy any one of them, but there is one tent site directly on the lake for whoever is lucky enough to get first dibs on it.

Getting there: All sites are located at the end of an unofficial dirt road that is not sanctioned for driving by the Forest Service. Follow directions from US 26 for sites 35-39. From FS42, go right on FS4280 for 3.1 miles, watching for a dirt road leading uphill to the left and flanked by two 4/4 posts with yellow plaques. Alternatively, from FS58, drive 2.6 miles south on FS4280, then turn right onto the dirt road flanked by the two 4x4's with the aforementioned yellow plaques. Park on the road and follow this road on foot 0.4 mile to camp. I hope you can make it. This is a Prime site, with a capital P! MVUM F6

Loc: FS5810, 0.7 mile east of Timothy Lake as the crow flies	Road: Gravel
L/L: N45 07 158/W121 49 104	Access: Park and carry
Cell: South end Timothy Lake	Tents: At least 20
	El: 3350
Lndmk: Timothy Lake Day Use Area	RV: Use judgment

Description: This large, flat, well-treed and shady area is well off the beaten path, but still close to all the recreational possibilities of Timothy Lake to make it attractive. You will have to haul in your own water, however, and some of the sites have been left in a sorry state by the beer-drinking, cigarette-smoking crowd and need to be cleaned up before you occupy them. In most cases this amounts to not much more than picking up paper litter and a few beer cans around the fire pits. The forest understory here tends to be open, and it's hard to find the privacy you'll need for bodily functions without walking a great distance into the surrounding woods, so this is another site where the best kind of toilet would be one that's inside a tent.

Campsite #41 on the north arm of Timothy Lake

Getting there: From OR 224 and Estacada, drive 26 miles to milepost 50 at Ripplebrook Campground and turn left on FS57 (Timothy Lake Rd). Drive 14.7 miles along the Oak Grove Fork of the Clackamas River to Timothy Lake. At 7.3 miles, where the road turns to gravel and FS58 takes off to the left, continue straight on FS57. The turn-off to FS5810 and the campsite is at 14.7 miles and about 0.1 mile before you cross the bridge at the south end of Timothy Lake. Go left on FS5810 for 0.4 mile, then turn left onto FS5810 for 0.2 mile to campsite, on left. RVs may not be able to drive to all the sites here.
From US 26, drive 8.5 miles on FS42 and go right 3.7 miles on FS57. Turn right on FS5810 about a tenth of a mile after crossing the outlet at the south end of Timothy Lake and follow directions from OR 224 (above). MVUM E6

43

Loc: East of Timothy Lake on FS5820, 1.2 miles north of FS57	**Road:** Gravel
L/L: N45 07 450/W121 49 400	**Access:** Drive to camp
Cell: South end of Timothy Lake	**Tents:** 20 or more
	El: 3440
Lndmk: Junction FS5820/5890	**RV:** MH and TT

Description: A waterless site with good shade and space for lots of tents set in a protective grove of conifer trees on the south side of a lightly traveled gravel road.

Getting there: From OR 224 and Estacada, drive 26 miles to milepost 50 at Ripplebrook Campground and turn left on FS57 (Timothy Lake Rd). Drive 14.7 miles along the Oak Grove Fork of the Clackamas River to Timothy Lake. At 7.3 miles the road turns to gravel and FS58 takes off to the left. Make sure you continue straight on FS57. Turn left onto FS5810 at 14.7 miles (0.1 mile before you cross the bridge at the south end of Timothy Lake). At four-tenths of a mile stay to the right on FS5820 for another 0.8 mile, being careful to stay to the left when you come to the junction with 5890 a half-mile further on. From the junction it is another 0.2 mile to camp.
From US 26, drive 8.5 miles on FS42 and go right 3.7 miles on FS57. Turn right on FS5810 about a tenth of a mile after crossing the outlet at the south end of Timothy Lake and follow the directions from OR 224 (above) to camp. MVUM E6

Loc: FS5820, 1.4 miles from FS57	**Road:** Gravel
L/L: N45 07 492/W121 49 476	**Access:** Drive to camp
Cell: South end Timothy Lake	**Tents:** 10-12
	El: 3490
Lndmk: Junction FS5820/5890	**RV:** Not suitable for RVs

Description: Another large, waterless camp with multiple sites, desirable for its proximity to Timothy Lake.

(Site 44) Getting there: From OR 224, drive 26 miles from Estacada to milepost 50 at Ripplebrook Campground and turn left onto FS57 (Timothy Lake Rd). Drive 14.7 miles along the Oak Grove Fork of the Clackamas River to Timothy Lake. At 7.3 miles the road turns to gravel and FS58 takes off to the left. Make sure you continue straight on FS57. Turn left onto FS5810 at 14.7 miles (0.1 mile before crossing the bridge at the south end of Timothy Lake). At 0.4 mile, stay to the right on FS5820 for another 0.8 mile, being careful to stay to the left when you come to the junction with 5890, a half-mile further on. From the junction it is another 0.4 mile to camp.

From US 26, drive 8.5 miles on FS42 and go right 3.7 miles on FS57. Turn right on FS5810 about a tenth of a mile after crossing the outlet at the south end of Timothy Lake and follow the directions from OR 224 (above) to camp. MVUM E6

45

Loc: FS57, south end Timothy Lake, 0.5 mile from FS57/42 junction	**Road:** Paved
L/L: N45 06 342/W 121 45 450	**Access:** Park on road, carry up to 500 feet
Cell: South End Timothy Lake	**Tents:** 10-15
	El: 3465
Lndmk: Junction FS42/57, 0.5 mile	**RV:** No

Description: A large, shaded waterless site that is well-suited to either a large party of up to fifteen tents or several smaller parties. It is also near enough to the recreational possibilities of Timothy Lake to make it attractive as a weekend destination. Bring your own water. The Pacific Crest National Scenic Trail passes through camp and gives access to a boat ramp at the end of Timothy Lake, about a mile away. The Oak Grove Fork of the Clackamas is about 0.1 mile down the hill through the trees and might be a source of water for camp use for those willing to carry it back up the hill. Otherwise, potable water might be found at the day use area near the bridge for those willing to pay the regular day use fee.

Note: Those interested in camping here should check with the Forest Service first. I have seen people camping on this site, but in 2011 there was a sign posted just off FS5740, about three miles to the west of Site 45, indicating that camping within 500 feet of FS57 was prohibited.

Getting there: From US 26, drive 8.5 miles on FS42 and go right half a mile on FS57. Camp is on right through the trees. The road shoulder here is high, so ease off the road at an angle, park and carry your gear to the campsite of your choice. You will find an abundance of fire rings to choose from. MVUM F6

Loc: FS57 on the Oak Grove Fork of the Clackamas, 2.9 miles west of the bridge on the south end Timothy Lake	**Road:** Gravel
L/L: N45 05 029/W121 51 625	**Access:** Park and carry 60 yds
Cell: South end Timothy Lake	**Tents:** 2
	El: 2580
Lndmk: Timothy Lake outlet bridge, 2.9 miles east of site	**RV:** On road only

Description: This is a beautiful, shaded, extremely private site on a fast section of the Oak Grove Fork of the Clackamas River. Dense foliage shields the camp from dust churned up by vehicles passing on FS57 above. The first ten feet of the trail leading to camp is steep but walkable, then drops less steeply to the camp, which is close to the river. If you happen to have a section of rope with you, tie one end to your car to make it easier and safer to carry your gear the initial ten feet downhill. This is another sensitive site, however. So be careful with both your litter and your poop.

Getting there: From US 26, drive 8.5 miles on FS42 to FS57, then go right 3.4 miles to the bridge across the outlet from Timothy Lake. Drive another 2.9 miles from the end of the bridge to camp, on the left Park in the pullout across from an unnamed service road taking off and curving up the hill on the north side of FS57 near two huge boulders at the base of a fir tree.
From OR 224 and Estacada, drive 26 miles and turn left on FS57 at Ripplebrook and Rainbow Campgrounds, then go 10.6 miles to site, on right. MVUM E6-E7

Loc: FS57 on Oak Grove Fork of the Clackamas, 3 miles west of outlet bridge on the south end of Timothy Lake	**Road:** Gravel
L/L: N45 05 032/W121 51 768	**Access:** Park on road, carry 50 ft.
Cell: South end Timothy Lake, 3 miles	**Tents:** 5-6
	El: 2575
Lndmk: Timothy Lake outlet bridge, 3 miles east	**RV:** No

Description: The only drawback to this beautiful site next to the river us the fact that it is not well-shielded from the dust churned up by cars passing on FS57, which is gravel and can be busy on summer weekends. Nevertheless, it appears to be popular and frequently used throughout the summer.

Getting there: From US 26, drive 8.5 miles on FS42 to FS57, then go right 3.4 miles to the bridge across the outlet from Timothy Lake. Drive another 3 miles from the end of the bridge to camp, on the left. Park in the pullout directly in front of camp. From here, access to camp with gear is easy.
From OR 224 and Estacada, drive 26 miles from Estacada and turn left onto FS57 at Ripplebrook and Rainbow Campgrounds, then to 10.5 miles to site, on right. MVUM E6-E7

Loc: FS 57, 3.7 miles west of Timothy Lake outlet bridge	**Road:** Gravel
L/L: N45 05 104/W121 52 576	**Access:** Park and carry about 100 ft
Cell: South end of Timothy Lake	**Tents:** 5-6
	El: 2470
Lndmk: Outlet bridge across Timothy Lake	**RV:** No

(Site 48) Description: A delightful spot just downstream from an island that splits the river into two separate streams. Campsites are within feet of the river, which is fast-flowing and may pose a threat to children, especially at night. Bathroom hygiene would have to be across the road if you are not equipped with your own privacy shelter and toilet facility. The site is not well shielded from the dust from FS57.

Getting there: From US 26, drive 8.5 miles on FS42 to FS57, then go right 3.4 miles to the bridge across the outlet from Timothy Lake. Drive another 3.7 miles from the end of the bridge to camp, on left.
From OR 224 and Estacada, drive 26 miles and turn left onto FS57 at Ripplebrook and Rainbow Campgrounds, then go 9.8 miles to site, on right. Park and carry gear into camp. MVUM E7

Loc: FS 57, 3.9 miles west of the end of Timothy Lake outlet bridge	**Road:** Gravel, then dirt
L/L: N45 04 999/W121 52 850	**Access:** Park and carry
Cell: South end of Timothy Lake	**Tents:** 6-10
	El: 2450
Lndmk: Junction, FS57/58, 2.3 miles to the west, and Stone Creek Hydroelectric Project, about one quarter mile to the west	**RV:** MH and smaller TT

Description: A wonderfully private site, featuring, in addition to a fire ring, a small cooling pond next to camp which can be crossed by a log bridge leading to the river. This site is truly a gem if you can get it. It is well shielded from the road by trees and dense foliage, has river access and privacy, and there is room for multiple guest tents along the road leading to camp.

Getting there: From US 26, drive 8.5 miles on FS42 to FS57, then go right 3.4 miles to the bridge across the outlet from Timothy Lake. Drive another 3.9 miles from the end of the bridge to camp, on left. If you pass the Stone Creek Hydroelectric Project you've gone too far.
From OR 224 and Estacada, drive 26 miles and turn left onto FS57 at Ripplebrook and Rainbow Campgrounds, then go 9.5 miles to dirt track, about 0.4 mile beyond the Stone Creek Hydroelectric Project. MVUM E7

Loc: FS57, 5.5 miles west of Timothy Lake and 2.1 miles from Junction FS57/58	**Road:** Paved, then dirt
L/L: N45 04 904/W121 53 114	**Access:** Drive to w/in short distance of camp
Cell: South end Timothy Lake	**Tents:** 1
	El: 2400
Lndmk: Stone Creek Hydroelectric Project, about 200 yds west	**RV:** No

Description: This highly desirable campsite is located along a fast section of the river at the end of a short, rocky road and features both shade and privacy. In spite of the fact that it is the kind of site you might want to share with your friends, there is essentially room for only one large tent here. In season look for huckleberries near camp and along river. Think of the next camper when you leave.

Getting there: From US 26, drive 8.5 miles on FS42 to FS57, then go right 3.4 miles to the bridge across the outlet from Timothy Lake. Drive another 5.5 miles from the end of the bridge to camp, on the left, just after the road turns to pavement and just before the Stone Creek Hydroelectric Project. From OR 224 and Estacada, drive 26 miles and turn left on FS57 at Ripplebrook and Rainbow Campgrounds, then go 9.1 miles to dirt track just beyond the Stone Creek Hydroelectric Project. Camp is about 100 yards from the road and very close to the river. MVUM E7

51

Loc: At junction FS57/58, 7.3 miles from OR 224	**Road:** Paved
L/L: N45 04 684/W121 55 283	**Access:** Park and carry, 100 yds
Cell: South end Timothy Lake and High Rock via FS58	**Tents:** 3-4
	El: 2205
Lndmk: Junction FS57/58	**RV:** On road only

Description: A pleasantly comfortable and shady camp on the river about a hundred yards downhill from FS57. A wheelbarrow or a good-sized backpack would be handy for schlepping gear to camp.

Getting there: From US 26, drive 8.5 miles on FS42 to FS57, then go right 3.4 miles to the bridge across the outlet from Timothy Lake. Drive another 7.6 miles from the end of the bridge to camp, on the left, where the road turns from gravel to pavement.
From OR 224 and Estacada, drive 26 miles and turn left on FS57 at Ripplebrook and Rainbow Campgrounds, then go 7.3 miles to the junction with FS58. MVUM D7

Loc: On Shellrock Creek, at the Junction of FS57/58	**Road:** Paved
L/L: N45 04 709/W121 55 325	**Access:** Park and schlep gear short distance
Cell: South end Timothy Lake and High Rock area	**Tents:** 1-2
	El: 2244
Lndmk: Junction FS57/58	**RV:** On road only

Description: A smaller site on pristine Shellrock Creek at the FS57/58 junction that appears to be in demand most weekends despite the fact that that a fair amount of traffic uses both roads during the busy summer weekends. This is one of those delicate sites that I'm sure the Forest Service would rather see closed down. It has little privacy and is, for sure, a pack-out-your-poop site.

(Site 52) Getting there: From US 26, drive 8.5 miles on FS42 to FS57, then go right 3.4 miles to the bridge across the outlet from Timothy Lake. Drive another 7.6 miles from the end of the bridge to camp, on the other side of FS 58.
From OR 224 and Estacada, drive 26 miles and turn left onto FS57 at Ripplebrook and Rainbow Campgrounds, then go 7.3 miles to the intersection with FS58. MVUM D7

53

Loc: FS57, 7.1 miles from OR 224	**Road:** Paved
L/L: N45 04 643/W121 55 431	**Access:** Park and carry gear to camp
Cell: High Rock and the south end of Timothy Lake	**Tents:** 4-5
	El: 2220
Lndmk: FS57/58 Junction, 0.8 mile west	**RV:** On road only

Description: This is nice site next to a beautiful but swift section of the Oak Grove Fork of the Clackamas. A section of rope attached to the car might be useful for negotiating the first few feet of the path to camp.

Getting there: From US 26, drive 8.5 miles on FS42 to FS57, then go right 3.4 miles to the bridge across the outlet from Timothy Lake. Drive another 7.8 miles from the end of the bridge to camp, about 0.2 mile past the intersection with FS58.
From OR 224 and Estacada, drive 26 miles and turn left on FS57 at Ripplebrook and Rainbow Campgrounds, then go 7.1 miles to camp, on right. Watch for the opening in trees on the south (right) side of the road. MVUM D7

54

Loc: FS57, 7.1 miles from OR 224	**Road:** Dirt, 4x, taking off from FS57
L/L: N45 04 631/W121 55 455	**Access:** Park and carry, 300 ft
Cell: High Rock and the south end of Timothy Lake	**Tents:** 2-3
	El: 2220
Lndmk: Junction FS 57/58, two-tenths of a mile east	**RV:** On road only

Description: But for the rather large pile of trash I discovered in a clearing beside the road leading into this site, it is one of the most private and charming sites along the river, probably because of the difficulty of access. The road leading down from FS57 into this camp is as forbidding as it is short, and only those with high-clearance, four-wheel drive vehicles should attempt to drive it. All others should park on the paved parking area a hundred yards east and carry their gear the rest of the way to camp. *Unfortunately, the river here might pose a danger to small children, due to its swiftness.*

Getting there: From US 26, drive 8.5 miles on FS42 to FS57, then go right 3.4 miles to the bridge across the outlet from Timothy Lake. Drive another 7.8 miles from the end of the bridge to camp, about 0.2 mile past the intersection with FS58.

(Site 54) **From OR 224 and Estacada**, drive 26 miles and turn left on FS57 at Ripplebrook and Rainbow Campgrounds, then go 7.1 miles to camp, on right. Watch for opening in trees on the south side of the road. MVUM D7

55

Loc: FS 57, about 6.4 miles from OR 224, and 0.9 mile from FS57/58 junction	**Road:** Paved
L/L: N45 04 340/W121 56 205	**Access:** Drive to camp
Cell: High Rock and the south end of Timothy Lake	**Tents:** 10-15
	El: 2100
Lndmk: Road to Harriet Lake, 0.2 mile west	**RV:** Use judgment

Description: An excellent site offering shade, solitude from passing cars and access to the river. Those wishing to use the sites further to the rear of the camp from the road will have to park and carry their gear a short distance.

Getting there: From US 26, drive 8.5 miles on FS42 to FS57, then go right 3.4 miles to the bridge across the outlet from Timothy Lake. Drive another 8.7 miles from the end of the bridge to camp, about 0.9 mile past the FS57/58 intersection.
From OR 224 and Estacada, drive 26 miles and turn left on FS57 at Ripplebrook and Rainbow Campgrounds, then go 6.4 miles to camp, on right. Watch for opening in trees on the south side of the road. The shoulder of the road falls off steeply here, so be careful not to hit high center when you pull off. MVUM D7

Loc: At the turn-off to Harriet Lake, 6.2 miles from OR224	**Road:** Gravel
L/L: N45 04 286/W121 56 514	**Access:** Drive to most camps
Cell: South end Timothy Lake and High Rock area	**Tents:** About 10
	El: 2100
Lndmk: Junction FS57/4630 (Harriet Lake Road)	**RV:** MH and TT

Description: There are actually two or three separate campsites at this location. One is to the right as you turn off onto the road to Harriet Lake. The other two are to the left, nearer the bridge. The Oak Grove Fork of the Clackamas is very swift here.

Getting there: From OR 224 and Estacada, drive 26 miles to milepost 50 and turn left onto FS57 by Ripplebrook and Rainbow Campgrounds. Go 6.2 miles on FS57. Just after crossing the bridge over the Oak Grove Fork of the Clackamas make a sharp left onto the road to Harriet Lake and look for the first campsite immediately to your right. Or, make an immediate second left turn onto the dirt road leading back toward the river. Following this, you will pass a second, more exposed campsite on the right, which can be seen from the road. The real jewel here is all the way back at the end of the road under a huge conifer tree, a large flat area capable of accommodating several tents or an RV. Use judgment here. There's an indimidating dip in the road to this camp. MVUM D7

Loc: FS57, 5.1 miles from OR224	Road: Paved
L/L: N45 04 230/W121 57 713	Access: Drive to camp
Cell: South end Timothy Lake and the High Rock area	Tents: 2-3
	El: 2225
Lndmk: Junction FS57/5730	RV: MH and TT

Description: A large but waterless area that is surprisingly private, considering its location just off sometimes busy FS57. Water can be obtained from nearby creeks.

Getting there: From Estacada on OR 224, drive 26 miles. Turn left at milepost 50 and Ripplebrook and Rainbow Campgrounds onto FS57. Go 5.1 miles. Watch for Forest Service Roads 5720 and 5730, which take off to the right. Camp is on left, 0.1 mile past the junction with FS5730. MVUM D7

Loc: FS57, 4.9 miles from OR 224	Road: Paved
L/L: N45 04 270/W121 57 901	Access: Drive to camp
Cell: South end Timothy Lake and High Rock area	Tents: 3-5
	El: 2240
Lndmk: Junction FS57/5730, one-tenth mile west	RV: MH

Description: A very private little clearing just off FS57. Find water from nearby Streams or the Oak Grove Fork of the Clackamas.

Getting there: From Estacada on OR 224, drive 26 miles. Turn left at milepost 50 at Ripplebrook and Rainbow Campgrounds onto FS57. Go 4.9 miles. Camp is on the left, 0.1 mile past the junction with FS5720, which takes off to the right. MVUM D7

Loc: FS 5830 (road to Hideaway Lake), 0.8 miles north of the FS58/5830 junction	Road: Gravel
L/L: N45 07 808/W121 55 110	Access: Park and carry 20'
Cell: Vicinity of High Rock	Tents: 3-4
	El: 2990
Lndmk: Junction FS5830 and High Black Wolf Meadow Creek	RV: Small MH in camp

Description: Another of the many pleasant surprises to be found in the MHNF: the happy murmuring of nearby High Black Wolf Meadow Creek, off-road privacy and abundant shade on a hot day.

Getting there: From US 26, drive 8.5 miles on FS42 to FS57, then go right 3.4 miles to the bridge across the outlet from Timothy Lake. Continue another 7.6 miles from the end of the bridge on gravel FS57. Turn right onto paved FS58 and go 3 miles, then go left on FS5830 toward Hideaway Lake. Find site on left, 0.8 mile beyond the FS58/5830 junction and immediately after crossing over High Black Wolf Meadow Creek. Travel trailers not recommended for this site.
From OR 224 and Estacada, drive 26 miles from Estacada and turn left on FS57 at Ripplebrook and Rainbow Campgrounds, then go 7.3 miles to the intersection with FS58. Follow directions from US 26 (above) from that point on. MVUM D6

Black Wolf Meadow, on the trail to Anvil Lake

Loc: Spur 120 (unmarked) off FS5830 (Hideaway Lake Road)	**Road:** Gravel
L/L: N45 07 794/W121 55 520	**Access:** Drive to camp
Cell: High Rock Area or south end Timothy Lake	**Tents:** 3-4
	El: 2830
Lndmk: Junction, FS58/5830	**RV:** MH and TT

Description: Prime Site! A large, comfortable camp by Shellrock Creek with level tent spaces around a central fire ring located on a very lightly traveled spur road. Tall fir and cedar trees tower over deciduous alders here. A circuitous trail leads through skunk cabbage and vine maple to a cool, shady spot where the creek widens and slows, revealing an undercut bank that begs for a fishing line. Closer to camp, a fork in the trail leads to what looks like a still serviceable outdoor privy.

Getting there: From US 26, drive 8.5 miles on FS42 to FS57, then go right 3.4 miles to the bridge across the outlet from Timothy Lake. Continue another 7.6 miles from the end of the bridge on gravel FS57. Turn right onto paved FS58 and go 3 miles to where FS 5830 forks left toward Hideaway Lake. Continue another 0.9 miles, then take an unmarked spur road to the left three-tenths of a mile to camp, on left, just before the road crosses over Shellrock Creek.
From OR 224 and Estacada, drive 26 miles from Estacada and turn left on FS57 at Ripplebrook and Rainbow Campgrounds, then go 7.3 miles to the intersection with FS58 and follow directions from US 26. MVUM D6

(A SUB-PRIME SITE)

Loc: Lightning Creek, on FS5810, 0.3 mile from FS58	**Road:** Paved
L/L: N45 05 574/W121 55 220	**Access:** Drive to camp
Cell: Vicinity of High Rock	**Tents:** 1-2
	El: 2635
Lndmk: Junction FS58/5810	**RV:** No

Description: Best for overnight or emergency use only, this site is located on a short grade cut into a bank where Lightning Creek crosses the road. In spite of its location along FS5810, the site offers a modicum of privacy, shade and the pleasant sound of a small mountain creek. Its fire ring is well away from the road, which is paved and lightly traveled at that point. Hike to nearby Buck Lake and go swimming on hot summer days. **Caution**: *Do not allow small children to play around the culvert carrying the creek under the road, especially if the water is running high.*

Getting there: From US 26, drive 8.5 miles on FS42 to FS57, then go right 3.4 miles to the bridge across the outlet from Timothy Lake. Continue another 7.6 miles from the end of the bridge on gravel FS57. Turn right onto paved FS58 and go 1.1 miles, then turn right and go 0.3 mile on FS5810 to camp, on left side of road. **From OR 224 and Estacada**, drive 26 miles from Estacada and turn left on FS57 at Ripplebrook and Rainbow Campgrounds, then go 7.3 miles to the intersection with FS58 and follow directions from US 26. MVUM D7

Buck Lake, at end of Buck Lake Trail off FS5810-210

Loc: Pyramid Lake Road, about one-tenth of a mile from FS58	**Road:** Gravel
L/L: N45 08 479/W121 53 799	**Access:** Drive to camp
Cell: Vicinity of High Rock	**Tents:** 4-5
	El: 3580
Lndmk: Junction FS5/Pyramid Lake Road	**RV:** MH and TT

Description: Just one-tenth of a mile off paved FS58, this may not be everybody's idea of a choice site, but it has all the essentials, including High Black Wolf Meadows Creek , as well as abundant berry picking from about mid-August onward. Water is available across the road and down a short, steep path to the creek. Take the nearby trail to Anvil Lake and the source of the creek in magnificent Black Wolf Meadow.

Getting there: From US 26, drive 8.5 miles on FS42 to FS57, then go right 3.4 miles to the bridge across the outlet from Timothy Lake. Drive another 7.6 miles from the end of the bridge. Go right on FS58, staying to the right at three miles, where it forks away from FS5830. Go another 1.9 miles to Pyramid Lake Road, then left about one-tenth mile to site in a clearing on the left.
From OR 224 and Estacada, drive 26 miles and turn left on FS57 at Ripplebrook and Rainbow Campgrounds, then go 7.3 miles to the intersection with FS58, then follow directions from US 26 (above) from that point on. MVUM D7

Loc: Spur 190, High Rock Spring Campground (decommissioned)	**Road:** Dirt
L/L: N45 09 395/W121 53 746	**Access:** Check MVUM
Cell: Vicinity of High Rock	**Tents:** 2
	El: 4315
Lndmk: High Rock	**RV:** No

Description: This is one of the most secluded sites you're going to find anywhere in a car. There was a fire pit with grates and two picnic tables in fair condition in the summer of 2010. The road to it (spur 190) is primitive but drivable in the dryer months of summer, though it is obviously infrequently driven. Early in the year there may be water on the road in the vicinity of the camp, the source of which is no doubt the nearby spring coming out of a pipe on the of the hill above camp and which gives the place its name. Depending on the time of year, there may be mosquitoes present because of the standing water, so keep the repellant at the ready.

Getting there: From US 26, drive 8.5 miles on FS42 to FS57, then go right 3.4 miles to the bridge across the outlet from Timothy Lake. Drive another 7.6 miles from the end of the bridge to FS 58. Drive 6.9 miles on FS58 to its junction with Abbot Road (FS4610), where you will see Spur 190 taking off to the left about 50 feet short of the stop sign at the FS58/4610 junction. Follow it for 1.3 miles to camp.
From OR 224 and Estacada, drive 26 miles and turn left on FS57 at Ripplebrook and Rainbow Campgrounds, then go 7.3 miles to the intersection with FS58. Follow directions from US 26 (above) from this point. MVUM E6

Loc: Junction FS4610/Spur240/Spur 190, near High Rock	**Road:** Gravel
L/L: N45 09 726/W121 53 969	**Access:** Drive to camp
Cell: In camp and vicinity	**Tents:** 7-10 total
	El: 4674
Lndmk: High Rock	**RV:** MH and TT

(Sites 64 and 65) Description: These two camps are of different sizes, the one to the northeast being the larger of the two. Both are dry (waterless), cool and shady. Due to the geography and elevation of the area, cell phone connectivity is easily available in many places nearby. Bring warm sleeping bags. It can get cold up here at night, even in summer.

Getting there: From US 26, drive 8.5 miles on FS42 to FS57, then go right 3.4 miles to the bridge across the outlet from Timothy Lake. Drive another 7.6 miles from the end of the bridge to FS58, then go right another 6.9 miles(all uphill) to FS 4610 (Abbot Road). Turn left and go 1.3 miles to camps, on right and left.
From OR 224 and Estacada, drive 26 miles and turn left on FS57 at Ripplebrook and Rainbow Campgrounds, then go 7.3 miles to the intersection with FS58. Follow directions from US 26 (above) from this point. MVUM D6

Loc: Unnamed Road just beyond where FS4610 forks off to the northwest	**Road:** Gravel
L/L: N45 10 051/W121 53 687	**Access:** Drive to camp
Cell: In camp	**Tents:** 2-3
	El: 4500
Lndmk: Junction with FS4610, just south of site	**RV:** MH or TT

Description: A dry camp that is ideal spot for a self-contained RV! Camp at this site and you'll wake up to a view of Mount Hood so dramatic and sweeping that you won't need that second cup of coffee in the morning. Call for pizza with your cell phone (good luck!).

Getting there: From US 26, drive 8.5 miles on FS42 to FS57, then go right 3.4 miles to the bridge across the outlet from Timothy Lake. Drive another 7.6 miles from the end of the bridge to FS58, then go right another 6.9 miles to FS4610 (Abbot Road). Turn left onto FS4610 at the stop sign and go 1.8 miles to camp, on right..
From OR 224 and Estacada, drive 26 miles and turn left on FS57 at Ripplebrook and Rainbow Campgrounds, then go 7.3 miles to the intersection with FS58. Follow directions from US 26 from this point. MVUM D6-E6
There is another, more exposed campsite with a view a few hundred yards uphill from this site.

Loc: Frazier Turnaround (decommissioned campground)	**Road:** For high clearance vehicles
L/L: N45 08 924/W121 58 235	**Access:** Drive to camp
Cell: Vicinity of High Rock	**Tents:** 4-8
	El: 4600
Lndmk: Campground and Trailheads to Serene and Rock Lakes	**RV:** No. Road too difficult

Description: If you remember nothing else of your visit to this campground, you will remember the four mile-long road that leads to it. If it's not the most primitive road in the national forest, it has to be at least a runner-up. It took 45 minutes to cover the ground in my two-wheel drive Toyota Pickup, and about the same with a friend's all-wheel drive SUV. You will find picnic tables, fire grates and a place for your tent here, but don't count on enjoying much privacy. Not only does the site serve as a trailhead for popular Trail #512 to Serene and Rock Lakes and Cache Meadow in one direction, but backpackers and hikers coming in from Shellrock Lake are likely to be dropping into your back yard from the other direction.

The fact that there is no convenient source of running water nearby is also something to be considered. The main events here are the Rock Lakes, which are fishable and about a mile away on Trail #512, and Serene Lake, which is about a three-mile hike. The trail to Serene Lake is longer and rougher, but the east end of this lake warms up considerably during the summer, making both fishing and swimming a possibility. In the summer of 2011, I discovered an abandoned canoe with paddles, all in good condition, which had obviously been left there on purpose by someone who had portaged them in over the several miles of rough trail to the lake.

Getting there: From US 26, drive 8.5 miles on FS42 to FS57, then go right 3.4 miles to the bridge across the outlet from Timothy Lake. Drive another 7.6 miles from the end of the bridge to FS58, then go right another 6.9 miles to FS 4610 (Abbot Road). Go left at the stop sign onto FS 4610 1.3 miles. Go left on spur 240 for four miles on very primitive road surface. Camp is at end of road. Allow about 45 minutes for this part of the trip.

From OR 224 and Estacada, drive 26 miles and turn left on FS57 at Ripplebrook and Rainbow Campgrounds, then go 7.3 miles to the intersection with FS58. Follow directions from US 26 (above) from this point. MVUM D6

Loc: FS4630, near west end of Harriet Lake	**Road:** Gravel
L/L: N45 04 672/W121 58 270	**Access:** Drive to camp
Cell: High Rock and south end Timothy Lake	**Tents:** 15-20
	El: 2160
Lndmk: Harriet Lake Campground, 1.1 mile	**RV:** MH and TT

Description: This exceptionally large site near Harriet Lake features many tent sites with a large fire ring capable of accommodating a large number of people.

Getting there: From OR 224 and Estacada, drive 26 miles to milepost 50 and turn left onto FS57 at Ripplebrook and Rainbow Campgrounds. Go 6.2 miles on FS57. Just after crossing the bridge across the Oak Grove Fork of the Clackamas, make a sharp left onto the road to Harriet Lake (FS4630). Go 1.8 miles to campsite on right. MVUM D7

Loc: FS4630 (Oak Grove or Pipeline Rd), 1.9 miles west of FS57	Road: Gravel
L/L: N45 04 772/W121 58 344	Access: Park and carry, 30 ft.
Cell: High Rock and south end Timothy Lake	Tents: 3-4
	El: 2150
Lndmk: Harriet Lake Campground, 1.2 miles	RV: No

Description: Another waterless site near Harriet Lake, this camp has a large fire ring that will accommodate a moderately large group. For water, there are several creeks nearby.

Getting there: From OR 224 and Estacada, drive 26 miles to milepost 50 and turn left onto FS57 at Ripplebrook and Rainbow Campgrounds. Go 6.2 miles on FS57. Just after crossing the bridge over the Oak Grove Fork of the Clackamas, make a sharp left onto the road to Harriet Lake (FS4630). Go 1.9 miles to campsite, down a steep bank to the left. Watch your step while hauling gear down the short, steep bank to camp. Better yet, use a rope. MVUM D7

Loc: FS4635, 6.5 miles from FS4630	Road: Gravel, good
L/L: N45 06 896/W122 01 295	Access: Drive to camp
Cell: Intermittent reception along FS4635, 5.5 to 6.5 miles from FS4630 as well as High Rock and south end Timothy Lake	Tents: 1
	El: 3750
Lndmk: Cripple Creek	RV: Maybe small MH

Description: But for its proximity to graveled FS4635, this is a delightful site next to Cripple Creek, a rambunctious little mountain stream that comes tumbling out of a tree and rock-choked ravine on the outside of a curve in the road. On a summer day the intensely purple and blue penstemons nearby seem to challenge the deep alpine blue of the sky above.

Getting there: From OR 224 and Estacada, drive 26 miles to milepost 50 and turn left onto FS57 at Ripplebrook and Rainbow Campgrounds. Go 6.2 miles on FS57. Just after crossing the bridge across the Oak Grove Fork of the Clackamas, make a sharp left onto the road to Harriet Lake (FS4630, aka Oak Grove or Pipeline Roads). Go 4 miles on FS4630. Turn right onto FS4635. Stay alert, because FS4635 turns sharply to the left (north) after the first mile. Camp is on right 6.5 miles from FS4630 on the outside of a sharp bend in the road. MVUM C6-D6

The bright blues and purples of the wild penstemon growing along FS4635 challenge the brilliance of the sky at higher elevations

Loc: On Cripple Creek and spur 140, 2.5 miles from FS4635	**Road:** Gravel
L/L: N45 07 115/W122 00 873	**Access:** Drive to camp
Cell: FS4635 below Cripple Creek, between 5.5 and 6.5 miles from FS4630, High Rock area	**Tents:** 3-4
	El: 4174
Lndmk: Cripple Creek Quarry and Trail #702 to Cache Meadows	**RV:** MH and TT

Description: This remote site might be your weekend paradise on a hot summer day. It offers shade, solitude and the coolness of higher altitude on mountain roads that, though not perfect, won't be a threat to your oil pan. Cripple Creek offers a pool for a bath or a soak near camp, though the mosquitoes may make you decide to be quick about it. Trail #702 to Cache Meadows and an unnamed lake at the headwaters of Cripple Creek is within a stone's throw of camp. In midsummer you will find rhododendrons and bear grass in bloom everywhere here, and can look for huckleberries later in the season. Make sure you bring your fishing pole.

Getting there: From OR 224 and Estacada, drive 26 miles to milepost 50 and turn left onto FS57 at Ripplebrook and Rainbow Campgrounds. Go 6.2 miles on FS57. Just after crossing the bridge across the Oak Grove Fork of the Clackamas, make a sharp left onto the road to Harriet Lake (FS4630, aka Oak Grove or Pipeline Roads). Go 4 miles on FS4630. Turn right onto FS4635. Stay alert, because 4635 turns sharply north after one mile. At 8.5 miles from FS4630, turn right onto spur 140. Camp is on left at 2.5 miles as you cross Cripple Creek. Keep an eye peeled for a small plaque on a tree, which announces the trail. MVUM C6

Loc: OR 224, at milepost 50, just downstream from bridge	**Road:** Paved
L/L: N45 04 770/W122 02 554	**Access:** Park and carry, 100 ft.
Cell: South end Timothy Lake	**Tents:** 4-5
	El: 1550
Lndmk: Rainbow and Ripplebrook Campgrounds	**RV:** No

Description: A spacious, shady, comfortable camp beside a slower-flowing section of the Oak Grove Fork of the Clackamas. Care should be taken if using this spot, however. It is immediately upstream from popular Rainbow Campground, a fee campground. A lot of summertime campers tend to use it and then leave their litter behind for someone else to clean up. It doesn't take a genius to figure out that this is one of those sensitive sandwich camps (between a river and a road), and because of its proximity to a for-fee Forest Service campground, is likely to be high on the Forest Service's hit list of dispersed camping sites to close down, so, if you're going to pack out your poop anywhere, do it here. During the summer there is a public toilet available at the ranger station, a quarter mile away, and also a small store where sundries and potable water can be obtained.

Getting there: From Estacada, drive 26 miles on OR 224 to milepost 50. Park on the shoulder of the road just after crossing the bridge by Ripplebrook Campground. Camp is a hundred feet from the road down a slight hill. If the first site is taken, there may be more downstream. MVUM C7

Loc: Alder Flat Campground parking area	**Road:** Paved
L/L: N45 04 850/W122 03 280	**Access:** Park and carry short distance
Cell: South end Timothy Lake	**Tents:** 1-2
	El: 1550
Lndmk: Alder Flat Campground	**RV:** MH and TT, in parking area

Description: This waterless site about a hundred feet off OR 224 serves as the parking area for decommissioned Alder Flats Campground. Featuring only one tent site, a picnic table and a serviceable fire ring, it doesn't offer much in the way of camping. Two other strikes against it are its location so near a busy highway and the parking lot for the trail leading to Alder Flats Campground, 0.9 mile away. During the summer there is a public toilet and a small store at the ranger station a quarter of a mile east of camp on OR224 where one can buy sundries and obtain potable water. Hike or ride a mountain bike on the gradually sloping trail to Alder Flats.

Getting there: From OR 224 and Estacada, drive 24.5 miles from Estacada. Alder Flat Campground parking lot is on the right. MVUM C6-C7

Loc: Clackamas River, 0.9 mile by trail below SR 224, near MP 49	**Road:** Foot trail
L/L: N45 05 050/W122 03 676	**Access:** Park and carry 0.9 mile
Cell: South End Timothy Lake	**Tents:** 15-20
	El: 1300
Lndmk: Clackamas River and Alder Flat Campground	**RV:** No

Description: If you're ready to park your car and carry your gear on your back or by wheelbarrow less than a mile downhill on a fairly even grade to this campground, you can experience what it feels like to camp away from the sounds of the internal combustion engine and something akin to the feeling that keeps backpackers coming back for more. At about eight-tenths of a mile the trail flattens out onto the so-named Alder Flats, and you'll get a glimpse of the Clackamas, shining through the trees. From there to the river you will see many level campsites and even the vestiges of a few ancient but still semi-serviceable picnic tables and fire grates left over from a better day when this site was a fully supported Forest Service campground. Swim, fish or lie about reading books in what will seem like an impossibly wild setting for being so close to a major metropolitan area. Remember the next camper. Pack out your garbage and bury your poop well away from the river. Dispose of your toilet paper.

Getting there: From OR 224 and Estacada drive 24.5 miles from Estacada to Alder Flat Campground, on the right. Park and haul your gear nine-tenths of a mile on a gradually-sloping trail to a ten or twenty acre river bottom area covered by well-spaced trees. MVUM C6-C7

Loc: Squaw Meadows on FS4610	**Road:** Gravel
L/L: N45 13 216/W122 01 451	**Access:** Drive to camp
Cell: Along FS4610 at about 1000' elevation and 1.25 miles from OR 224, or where OR 224 crests the hill NW of Promontory Pt.	**Tents:** 3-4
	El: 3541
Lndmk: Intersection of Trail #532 and FS4610, 2.8 miles S/SE of site	**RV:** MH OK, TT?

Description: This is the place to head for when all you want is to sit and soak up the nature around you. Camp here and, absent the sound of the breeze in the trees and the occasional bumble bee or dragon fly on the prowl for mosquitoes, you'll swear that you can hear the individual molecules of air bumping into each other. Dragon flies may have been the reason that I didn't see any mosquitoes during my brief visit to the place, though there were one or two deer flies in evidence Water for camp is another matter, however. You'll have to bring your own or find it from a nearby creek. And, though it's possible to park a travel trailer at this site, getting it there over FS4610 might be a challenge.

Getting there: From Estacada, drive six miles to Promontory Point on OR 224. Go left near Promontory Point on FS4610 (here known as Abbot Road). Continue 7.0 miles to where FS4610 forks sharply to the left. Continue on FS4610 another 9.3 miles. Camp in the clearing where the meadows open out to the left. MVUM C5-D5
Navigation note: Roads aren't always well marked in this area, and it's easy to lose FS4610. This is where your GPS can pay for itself by giving you the assurance that the road you turned onto back there is actually the road you wanted.

Loc: FS4610, 0.5 mile from High Rock	**Road:** Paved
L/L: N45 09 227/W121 53 621	**Access:** Park and carry short distance
Cell: Vicinity of High Rock	**Tents:** 2-3
	El: 4570
Lndmk: High Rock	**RV:** Small MH/TT

Description: This dry site is probably best utilized as an overnight only campsite. Its chief recommendations are not only its proximity to High Rock, with its stunning view of Mt. Hood and excellent cell phone reception, but the promise of much cooler temperatures on days when the mercury is soaring in the city. The trees at this altitude are not so tall or dense as they are down in the river valleys, but this site should be shady toward evening.

Getting there: From US 26, drive 8.5 miles on FS42 to FS57, then go right 3.4 miles to the bridge across the outlet from Timothy Lake. Drive another 7.6 miles from the end of the bridge to FS 58. Drive uphill 6.9 miles on FS58 to its junction with Abbot Road (FS4610). Turn left and go 0.5 mile to site, on left.
From OR 224 and Estacada, drive 26 miles and turn left on FS57 at Ripplebrook and Rainbow Campgrounds, then go 7.3 miles to the intersection with FS58. Follow directions from US 26 (above) from this point. MVUM E6-D6

Loc: High Rock on FS4610	Road: Paved
L/L: N45 09 678/W121 53 647	Access: Park and carry short distance
Cell: In camp	Tents: 6-7
	El: 4613
Lndmk: High Rock	RV: MH/TT

Description: This is another waterless site, but with a view out over the Forest to Mt. Hood so stunning that it will have you reaching for your camera before you get out of the car. This site will accommodate a large party or multiple small parties. Plan on making new friends here. The inviting view encourages people driving by on FS58 to stop and take pictures.

Getting there: From US 26, drive 8.5 miles on FS42 to FS57, then go right 3.4 miles to the bridge across the outlet from Timothy Lake. Drive another 7.6 miles from the end of the bridge to FS 58. Drive uphill 6.9 miles on FS58 to its junction with Abbot Road (FS4610). Turn left and go one mile to site, on right.
From OR 224 and Estacada, drive 26 miles and turn left on FS57 at Ripplebrook and Rainbow Campgrounds, then go 7.3 miles to the intersection with FS58. Follow directions from US 26 (above) from this point. MVUM E6-D6

Loc: FS4630, 0.1 mile east of FS4630/4631 junction	Road: Gravel
L/L: 45 05 375/122 00 499	Access: Drive to camp
Cell: South end Timothy Lake, High Rock area	Tents: 20-30
	El: 2175
Lndmk: Junction FS4630/4631, 0.1 mile	RV: MH/TT

Description: A large waterless site less than three miles from Harriet Lake and a short drive from the little store at the Ripplebrook Guard Station, which has potable water. There is plenty of room to spread out here, and even a flat concrete pad that ought to be ideal for someone with a small RV. Creek water is available in abundance along the road to Harriet Lake. May need some cleaning. MVUM D7

Getting there: From Estacada on SR 224, drive approximately 26 miles to Ripplebrook Guard Station. Turn left onto FS4631 just past the little store located there. Drive a shade over 2 miles uphill to the junction with FS 4630 and turn right. Watch for the gravel turn-off to this large and commodious camp on the right, 0.1 miles east of the junction.

*There are a couple of other smaller camps on the opposite side of the road, both also waterless.

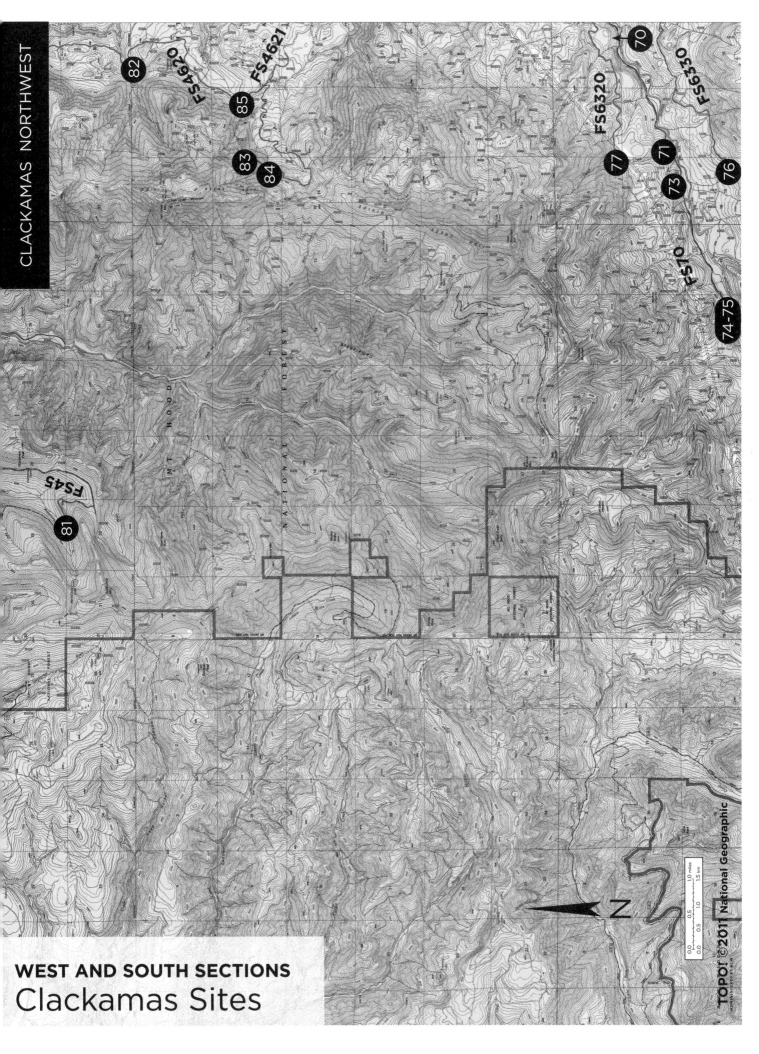

WEST AND SOUTH SECTIONS
Clackamas Sites

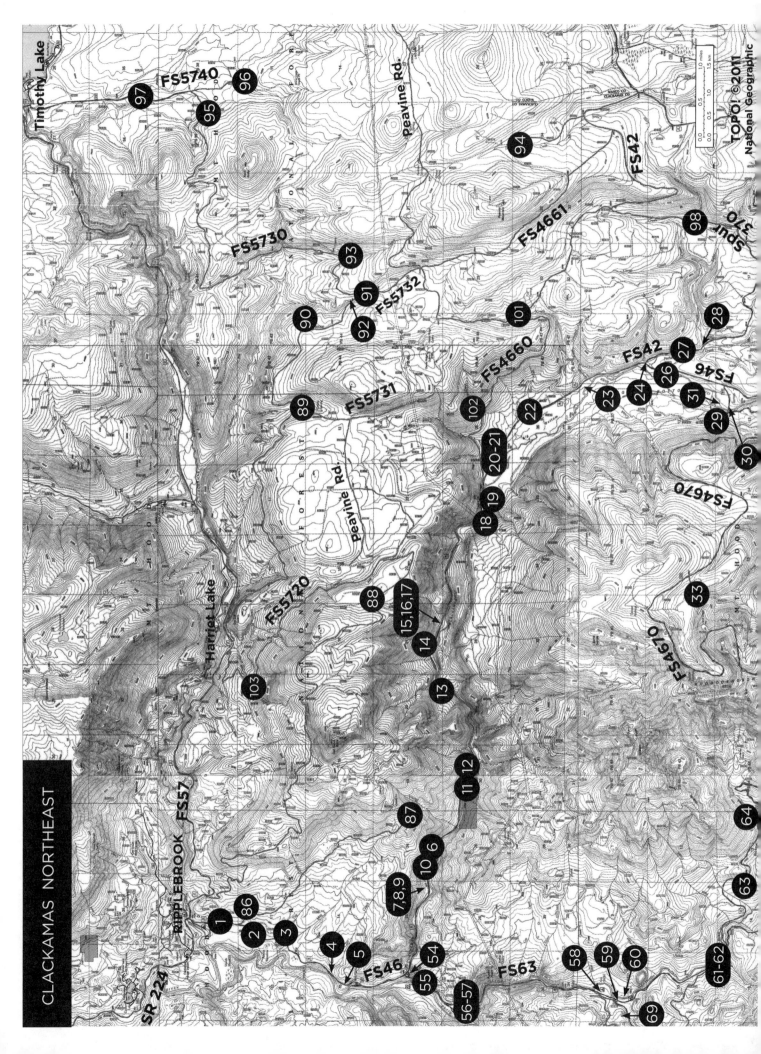

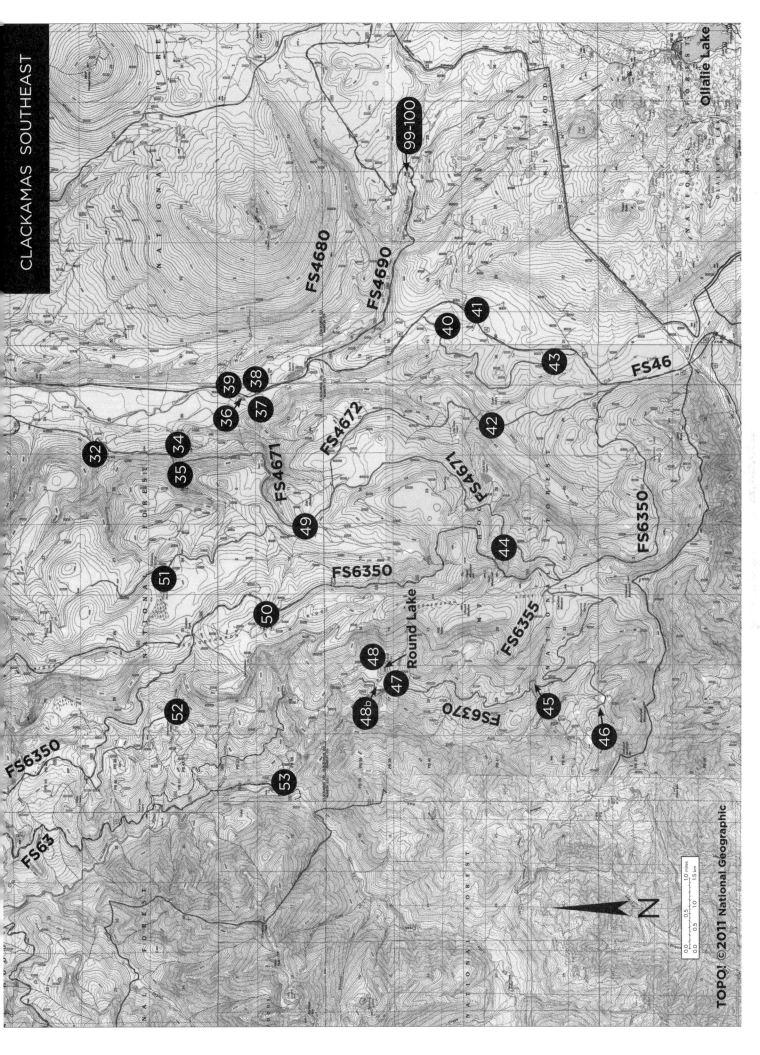

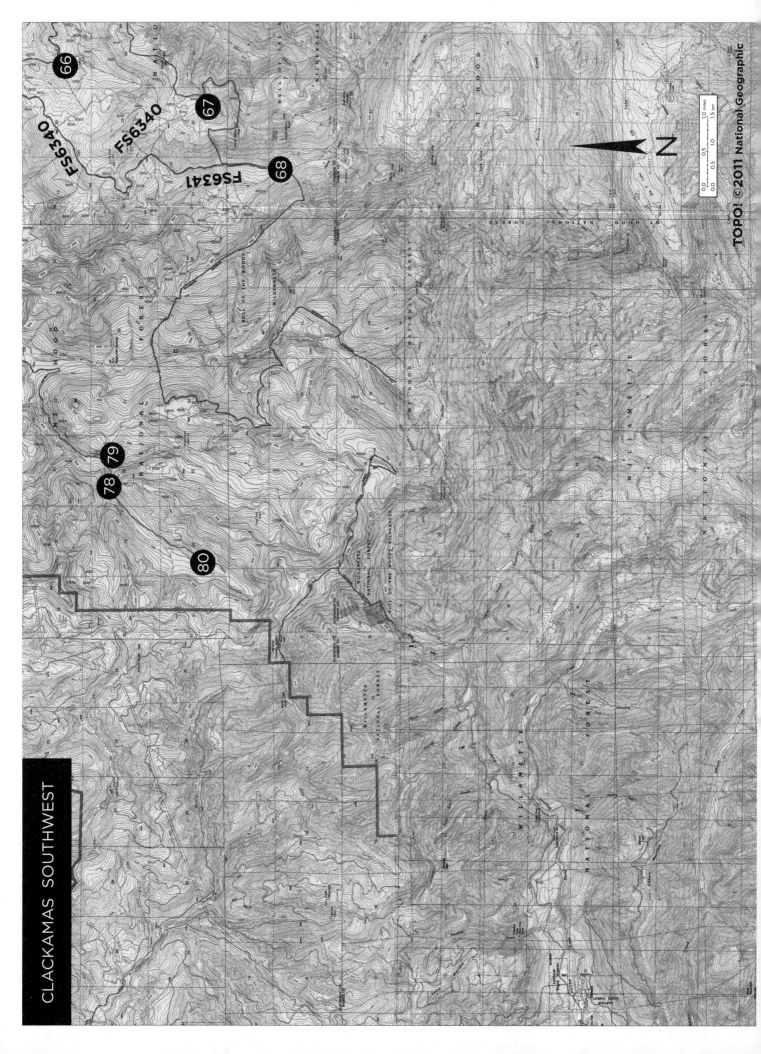

WEST AND SOUTH SECTIONS

Clackamas Sites

Clackamas River, West and South Sites

Many of the campsites directly along the Clackamas River are squeezed into areas of the canyon where the river meanders far enough from the road to create a space for them. These are so popular with Portlanders that they suffer the effects of being trampled by a small herd of humans nine out of the official twelve weekends of summer. The sheer popularity of these sites can lead to the problems of overcrowding and litter. This is especially true of the area immediately around Austin Hot Springs, *which is actually on private property and not under the direct control of the Forest Service.*

A discussion of camping in this section of the Forest has to take into account the Forest Service's new road policy, which does not allow parking and prohibits vehicular traffic within 125 feet of the centerline of virtually all of FSR 46. These restrictions make it all the more difficult for those who would choose to remain in compliance with Forest Service regulations to access the sites along FS46. Be sure to check with your Forest Service district office or consult your MVUM prior to making the decision to camp here.

Another downside to camping along FS46 during the summer is that, even if you are able to claim a relatively unlittered site along the river in the middle of summer, you're going to be sandwiched between the river and the road, with the racket of Harley-Davidson motorcycles frequently jarring your ears as they roar by on the Portland-Detroit-Salem-Portland circuit that is so popular with that crowd.

If your dream is to escape the heat and frenzy of the city on a hot summer weekend, your best bet is to get away from the Forest's main paved roads, where it should be easier to find a site that meets your needs and provides a modicum of solitude as well. That said, you will find listed in this section many of the sites I have found to be in use along the Clackamas River and FS46.

Loc: FS46, near Rainbow Cg.	**Road:** Dirt
L/L: N45 04 376/W122 02 668	**Access:** Park and carry
Cell: South end Timothy Lake or High Rock area	**Tents:** 8-10
	El: 1540
Lndmk: Rainbow Cg.	**RV:** No

Description: A beautiful site that has been loved to death by too many people. The trail to the river leads to a hiking/mountain biking trail that will take you to some of the best and most beautiful parts of the Clackamas, from rocky canyons to wide, deep pools with pebble beaches open to the sun. Potable water is available from a hose bib on the front of one of the buildings at the nearby Ripplebrook Guard Station, where there is also a public toilet and a store that sells sundries. For those who might hunger for fancier fare than can be obtained in camp, the town of Estacada has several restaurants and is just 26 miles away. *Bring your garbage glomper, some rubber gloves and sturdy plastic bags.*

Getting there: From OR 224 and Estacada, go 26 miles to MP50 (milepost 50) and Rainbow Campground, then continue on FS46 another 0.4 mile, where a dirt road leads .02 mile downhill toward the Clackamas to at least three campsites. MVUM C7

Loc: FS46, one mile from MP50	**Road:** Gravel
L/L: N 45 03 980/W122 02 766	**Access:** Park and carry
Cell: South end Timothy Lake and High Rock area	**Tents:** 2-3
	El: 1565
Lndmk: Rainbow Cg.	**RV:** No

Description: At first glance this might seem more appropriate as a one-night stand, but its location in the heart of the Clackamas River District recreational area and the end-of-the- road privacy it offers may make it worth staying longer. Potable water is available 24/7 at the Ripplebrook Guard Station, where sundry camping items may also be purchased during summer business hours through Labor Day weekend.

Getting there: From OR 224 and Estacada, go 26 miles to milepost 50, where OR 224 becomes FS46. Continuing one mile past Rainbow Campground, find a short dirt road leading to camp, a hundred yards to the right. Follow the trail leading out the right rear of the camp to a more secluded campsite and fire ring a little closer to the river. MVUV C7

Loc: FS46, 1.5 mile from MP50	**Road:** Dirt
L/L: N45 03 567/W122 02 958	**Access:** Carry, 0.1 mile
Cell: South end Timothy Lake and High Rock vicinity	**Tents:** 2-3, or many
	El: 1632
Lndmk: Tag Creek and spur 267	**RV:** No

Description: A private, cool and secluded site closer to the river with plenty of level tent sites beneath a sheltering grove of conifer trees. A trail leads from camp toward the river and should connect with the hiking/biking trail between Riverside and Rainbow Campgrounds.

Getting there: From OR 224 and Estacada, go 26 miles to milepost 50, where OR 224 becomes FS46. Continuing 1.5 miles, you will find a paved apron on the right and a short, dirt road that ends at a rock barricade about a hundred feet from FS46. Campsites are located 0.1 mile beyond the rock barricade, across a home-made log bridge. MVUM C7

Loc: FS46, 2.5 miles from MP50	**Road:** Paved
L/L: N45 02 948/W122 03 536	**Access:** Park and carry, 200 yds.
Cell: South end Timothy Lake or High Rock area	**Tents:** 5-6
	El: 1505
Lndmk: Riverside Cg.	**RV:** No

Description: Located along the trail between Riverside and Rainbow Campgrounds, this site offers a tempting beach with places to swim and fish that is also large enough to accommodate several tents. Any highway noise from FS46 is likely to be counterbalanced by the pleasant riffles you will discover just downstream. Access this site by following the trail downstream a few hundred yards from a knoll with a commanding view of the Clackamas. You will be between the road and the river, with no handy place for burying human waste, so, practice POYP (Pack out Your Poop) camping here.

Getting there: From OR 224 and Estacada, go 26 miles to milepost 50, where OR 224 becomes FS46. Continue on FS46 another 2.5 miles to knoll. Follow trail on foot to campsites, 200 yards downstream. MVUM C7

5

Loc: FS46, just north of Riverside Cg.	**Road:** Paved
L/L: N45 02 746/W122 03 739	**Access:** Park and carry, 125'
Cell: South end Timothy Lake or High Rock vicinity	**Tents:** 5-6
	El: 1630
Lndmk: Riverside Cg.	**RV:** No

Description: This site is in the trees on a bluff overlooking the river. A rough trail leads out of camp to connect with the hiking/biking trail along the river between Riverside and Rainbow Campgrounds and a delightfully secluded beach by a slow section of the Clackamas. An ideal campsite for touring cyclists.

Getting there: From OR 224 and Estacada, go 26 miles to milepost 50, where OR 224 becomes FS46. Continue 2.7 miles to site, on right, just two-tenths of a mile north of Riverside Campground. Campsites are beyond the large rocks blocking vehicular entrance to the site. MVUM C7

Loc: FS46, 5.5 miles from Rainbow Cg.	**Road:** Paved
L/L: N45 01 606/W122 01 527	**Access:** Park and carry
Cell: South end Timothy Lake and High Rock area	**Tents:** 1
	El: 1631
Lndmk: FS63 and Collawash River, 3.5 miles	**RV:** No

Description: A one-tent campsite right beside the river that would provide decent privacy, except from the road.

Getting there: From OR 224 and Estacada, go 26 miles to milepost 50, where OR 224 becomes FS46. Continue 5.5 miles on FS46 to site, on right. MVUM C7

Loc: FS46, five miles south of Rainbow Cg.	**Road:** Paved
L/L: N45 01 695/W122 02 019	**Access:** Park and carry gear
Cell: South end Timothy Lake and area of High Rock	**Tents:** 10-20
	El: 1600
Lndmk: Austin Hot Springs, 1,7 miles southeast	**RV:** No

Description: A large open, shaded area near the river and not far from Austin Hot Springs, this site is suitable for multiple families, but is so popular that finding a spot here on a summer weekend may be as difficult as trying to find one in any popular conventional campground. Add in the fact that there are no posted rules of conduct or camp host to provide the illusion of an enforcer and you may conclude that you'll get a better night's sleep somewhere else.

Getting there: From OR 224 and Estacada, go 26 miles to milepost 50, where OR 224 becomes FS46. Continue five miles to site, on right. MVUM C7

Loc: FS46, Five miles from Rainbow Cg.	**Road:** Paved
L/L: N45 01 718/W122 01 932	**Access:** Park and carry
Cell: South end Timothy Lake and vicinity of High Rock	**Tents:** 3-5
	El: 1542
Lndmk: Austin Hot Springs	**RV:** No

Description: Just down and on the other side of the road a bit from the riverside site #7, find a large pull-out giving access to this campsite, located in a grove of fir trees across the road from the Clackamas. Water for camp will have to come from either the Clackamas or one of the tributary creeks up the road, such as Switch Creek, about a mile to the east, near Austin Hot Springs.

Getting there: From OR 224 and Estacada, go 26 miles to milepost 50, where OR 224 becomes FS46. Continue five miles to site, on left. MVUM C7

Loc: FS46, 5.1 miles from Rainbow Cg.	**Road:** Paved
L/L: N45 01 724/W122 01 910	**Access:** Park and carry
Cell: South end Timothy Lake and vicinity of High Rock	**Tents:** 3-4
	El: 1600
Lndmk: Austin Hot Springs	**RV:** No

Description: This site offers more privacy and seclusion than many others in this section of the Forest. There is a small, unnamed stream behind camp to make pleasant sounds for you when there aren't any motorcycles roaring by. Unfortunately, this is one of those delicate areas that the Forest Service is concerned about, so use it lightly, and leave it better than you found it.

Getting there: From OR 224 and Estacada, go 26 miles to milepost 50, where OR 224 becomes FS46. Continue 5.1 miles to site, on left. MVUM C7

Loc: FS46, 5.3 miles from Rainbow Cg.	**Road:** Paved
L/L: N45 01 638/W122 01 661	**Access:** Park and carry
Cell: South end Timothy Lake and vicinity of High Rock	**Tents:** 5-6
	El: 1600
Lndmk: Austin Hot Springs, 1.4 mile	**RV:** No

Description: A beautiful and secluded site giving access to an inviting spot where the Clackamas rolls almost somberly over dark rocks that hold the promise of hiding big trout. Campsites are dispersed along a 200 foot path leading to the river.

Getting there: From OR 224 and Estacada, go 26 miles to milepost 50, where OR 224 becomes FS46. Continue 5.3 miles to site, on right. MVUM C7

(NOT A CAMPSITE!)

Loc: Austin Hot Springs, FS46, 6.7 miles from Rainbow Cg.	**Road:** Paved
L/L: N45 01 166/W122 00 102	**Access:** Do not camp here! Private Property
Cell: End Timothy Lake and High Rock area	**Tents:** None
	El: 1660
Lndmk: Austin Hot Springs	**RV:** No

Description: The only reason for listing this site in this book is to warn you away from it. ***This is private property, and I do not recommend trying to camp here!*** Not only are you likely to find the place trashed from overuse by the people who want to soak in the hot water flowing into the river from the hot springs, but on summer weekends FS46 becomes a busy highway, with a sometimes uninterrupted stream of cars whizzing past, creating a hazard for anyone trying to cross the road. MVUM C7-D7

Loc: FS46, 6.9 miles from Rainbow Cg. and MP50	**Road:** Paved
L/L: N45 01 135/W121 59 888	**Access:** Park and carry
Cell: South end Timothy Lake and vicinity of High Rock	**Tents:** 3-4
	El: 1675
Lndmk: Austin Hot Springs	**RV:** No

(Site 12) Description: You will find several tent sites and good shade along the river at this site.

Getting there: From OR 224 and Estacada, go 26 miles to milepost 50, where OR 224 becomes FS46. Continue 6.9 miles to site, on right. MVUM C7-D7

Loc: FS46, 8.3 miles from Rainbow Cg.	**Road:** Paved
L/L: N45 01 498/W121 58 540	**Access:** Park and carry
Cell: South end Timothy Lake and vicinity of High Rock	**Tents:** 6-10
	El: 1841
Lndmk: Austin Hot Springs	**RV:** No

Description: A beautiful, shaded site on the side of the road opposite the river, but still close enough to hear its soothing sounds at night.

Getting there: From OR 224 and Estacada, go 26 miles to milepost 50, where OR 224 becomes FS46. Continue 8.3 miles to site, on right. MVUM C7-D7

Loc: FS46, 8.9 miles from Rainbow Cg.	**Road:** Paved
L/L: N45 01 654/W121 57 841	**Access:** Carry gear
Cell: South end Timothy Lake and High Rock area	**Tents:** 5-10
	El: 1850
Lndmk: Large open, flat area directly overlooking the river	**RV:** No

Description: An excellent location on the river that might be a little too exposed to the afternoon sun during hot weather to suit some people. In the summer of 2010 this site was left littered and damaged by a single camper who spent the entire summer living here in an RV that was parked about ten feet from the river. There is abundant shade in the trees on the downstream side of camp. The river runs fairly swiftly here.

Getting there: From OR 224 and Estacada, go 26 miles to milepost 50, where OR 224 becomes FS46. Continue 8.9 miles to a gravel road taking off at an acute angle to the right from FS46 to a wide, flat, open area with excellent river access. MVUM C7-D7

Loc: FS46, 9.3 miles from Rainbow Cg.	**Road:** Paved
L/L: N45 01 551/W121 57 461	**Access:** Park and carry
Cell: South end Timothy Lake and High Rock area	**Tents:** 3-4
	El: 1965
Lndmk: Austin Hot Springs, 2.6 miles west	**RV:** No

Description: Because of the proximity of the road here, use discretion before camping on this otherwise delightful, private site near a happy little creek that runs between camp and the river.

Getting there: From OR 224 and Estacada, go 26 miles to milepost 50, where OR 224 becomes FS46. Continue 9.3 miles to camp, on right. MVUM D7

Loc: FS46, 9.4 miles from Rainbow Cg.	**Road:** Paved
L/L: N45 01 544/W121 57 418	**Access:** Park and carry
Cell: South end Timothy Lake and area of High Rock	**Tents:** 1-2
	El: 1960
Lndmk: About 2 miles west of FS46/4650 junction	**RV:** No

Description: This site looked beautiful and private from the road, but was occupied when discovered and could not be inspected at length.

Getting there: From OR 224 and Estacada, go 26 miles to milepost 50, where OR 224 becomes FS46. Continue 9.4 miles to a narrow dirt road on the right. Campsites are located at the end of the dirt road. MVUM D7

(OVERNIGHT/EMERGENCY)

Loc: FS46, 9.8 miles past Rainbow Cg.	**Road:** Paved
L/L: N45 01 543/W121 57 417	**Access:** Park and carry
Cell: South end Timothy Lake and area of High Rock	**Tents:** 2
	El: 2000
Lndmk: A little less than 2 miles west of FS46/4650 junction	**RV:** No

Description: There are two risk factors that should make you think twice before camping at this site: Its location near a pull-off from FS46 may be too close to the road for most people's comfort. Also, the only tent sites are located very close to a swift section of the river. Think before you camp.

(Site 17) Getting there: From OR 224 and Estacada, go 26 miles to milepost 50, where OR 224 becomes FS46. Continue 9.8 miles to site, on right. MVUM D7

(OVERNIGHT/EMERGENCY)

Loc: FS46, 11.4 miles from MP50	**Road:** Paved
L/L: N45 01 037/W121 55 311	**Access:** Park and carry
Cell: South end Timothy Lake and vicinity of High Rock	**Tents:** 1-2
	El: 2080
Lndmk: Just east of FS46/4650 junction	**RV:** No

Description: This location on a pull-out just off the road probably makes it a site of last resort for tent campers. Too bad, because the site otherwise has a lot to offer: the Clackamas deepens and glides grandly by here, with pleasant riffles upstream that invite the camper to cast a fly. Use good judgment.

Getting there: From OR 224 and Estacada, go 26 miles to milepost 50, where OR 224 becomes FS46. Continue 11.4 miles to site, on right. MVUM D7

Loc: FS4650, just past bridge over the Clackamas	**Road:** Paved
L/L: N45 00 970/W121 55 227	**Access:** Park and carry
Cell: South end Timothy Lake and High Rock area	**Tents:** 2-3
	El: 2100
Lndmk: Junction FS46/4650	**RV:** No

Description: Located along a quiet section of June Creek, this beautiful and private site is only about a hundred yards from the south shore of the Clackamas and along lightly-traveled FS4650. The clear water of June Creek meanders slowly through skunk cabbage and dense foliage at this point. I was pleasantly surprised to find only a few mosquitoes when I inspected it.

Getting there: From OR 224 and Estacada, go 26 miles to milepost 50, where OR 224 becomes FS46. Continue another 11.5 miles and go right on FS4650. Camp is on the other side of the Clackamas, just after the bridge. Park on the left hand side of the road and carry gear down the bank to camp. MVUM D7

Loc: FS46, 12.5 miles from Rainbow Cg.	**Road:** Paved
L/L: N45 00 820/W121 54 406	**Access:** Park and carry
Cell: South end Timothy Lake and High Rock area	**Tents:** 30+
	El: 2140
Lndmk: Junction 46/4660, 0.5 mile	**RV:** Check MVUM

Description: This very large site offers many desirable tent sites. It does not offer any visible source of water for camp use, but water is available from a number of nearby creeks, or from the Clackamas River.

Getting there: From Estacada on OR 224, drive approximately 26 miles to Rainbow Campground and milepost 50. Continue ahead on FS46 approximately 12.5 miles to site, on left, on spur 042, 0.5 mile past the FS46/4660 junction. MVUM D7

Loc: FS 46, 0.4 miles past FS 46/4660	**Road:** Paved
L/L: N45 00 869/W121 54 537	**Access:** Park and carry
Cell: Along US 26, South end Timothy Lake and High Rock area	**Tents:** 4-5
	El: 2100
Lndmk: FS46/4660 junction	**RV:** No

Description: This is a spot where the river runs slower and deeper. A small, pebbly beach offers access to the river and may or may not be slow enough for swimming. Use judgment. The path to the river is wide and mostly level.

Getting there: From Estacada on OR 224, drive approximately 26 miles to Rainbow Campground and milepost 50. Continue ahead on FS46 approximately 12.4 miles. At 0.4 miles beyond the junction of FS46/4660 a gravel road leads downhill and to the right to an open field. Camp here or carry gear several hundred yards further on to beautiful sites by river. MVUM D7

Loc: FS46, 13 miles from Rainbow Cg.	**Road:** Paved
L/L: N45 00 428/W121 53 763	**Access:** Park and carry
Cell: Along US 26, South end Timothy Lake and High Rock area	**Tents:** ?
	El: 2130
Lndmk: Junction FS46/4660	**RV:** No

Description: These sites are presumably on the Clackamas River, but have not been explored by the author.

Getting there: From Estacada on OR224, drive approximately 26 miles to Rainbow Campground and milepost 50. Continue ahead on FS46 approximately 13 miles to a single-lane gravel road leading toward the river and campsites. MVUM D7-E7

Loc: FS46, 13.6 miles from Rainbow Cg.	Road: Paved
L/L: N44 59 782/W121 53 248	Access: Park and carry
Cell: Along US 26, South end Timothy Lake and High Rock area	Tents: 2-3
	El: 2300
Lndmk: Junction FS46/42, one mile south	RV: No

Description: A beautiful, secluded, breezy and shady spot. A small, unnamed creek meanders along the edge of camp, though overuse by previous campers might not make it a reliable source of clean water for camp. Boil and/or purify thoroughly. A better bet for water would be the waterfall on the north side of the road about a quarter mile farther on.

Getting there: From Estacada on OR 224, drive approximately 26 miles to Rainbow Campground and milepost 50. Continue ahead on FS46 approximately 13.6 miles to a difficult-to-spot rocky road on the right, leading about 200 feet into the trees to campsite. MVUM D7-E7

Loc: Junction FS46/42, 14 miles from Rainbow Cg.	Road: Paved
L/L: N44 58 978/W121 52 883	Access: Park and carry
Cell: Along US 26, South end Timothy Lake and High Rock area	Tents: 10-12
	El: 2275
Lndmk: Junction FS46/42	RV: MH and TT

Description: Located just off the road at the FS42/46 junction, this site feels secluded and private. Here Bonner Creek flows through a shady grove of alder and cedar trees. There is room for about 3 tents near the creek, which is large and fast-flowing at this point. Another site to the left of the entryway features a large fire ring and space for many tents. It also has a tiny, clear stream trickling through it.

Getting there: From Estacada on OR224, drive approximately 26 miles to Rainbow Campground and milepost 50. Continue ahead 14 miles on FS46 to its junction with FS42. Find your campsite at the end of the gravel driveway to the left of FS46. MVUM E8

Loc: FS46, 0.4 miles south of FS46/42 junction	Road: Paved
L/L: N44 58 699/W121 53 012	Access: Park and carry
Cell: Along US 26, South end Timothy Lake and High Rock area	Tents: 4-6
	El: 2300
Lndmk: Junction FS46/42, 0.4 miles north	RV: No

Description: A pleasant clearing surrounded by thick, tall trees on a bluff above the river. The river below looks to be a good spot for fishing. Follow the path to the river and find another delightful little camp with a small fire ring.

Getting there: From Estacada on OR224, drive approximately 26 miles to Rainbow Campground and milepost 50. Continue ahead 14.4 miles on FS46. Site is located 0.3 mile from FS46 in a clearing located on a primitive road to the right. MVUM E8

Loc: FS42 near confluence of Pinhead and Lost Creeks	**Road:** Paved
L/L: N44 58 404/W121 52 650	**Access:** Park and carry
Cell: US 26, South end Timothy Lake	**Tents:** 5-6
	El: 2425
Lndmk: Confluence of Pinhead and Lost Creeks	**RV:** MH

Description: This site is located on a bluff and just downstream from an island that splits Pinhead Creek, which, in July appeared to be more the size of a small river than a creek. Pinhead Creek is about a hundred and fifty yards from camp via a steep but negotiable path.

Getting there: From Estacada on OR224, drive approximately 26 miles to Rainbow Campground and milepost 50. Continue ahead 14 miles on FS46 to junction with FS42. Go left 0.4 mile on FS42 to site, on right. MVUM E8

Loc: FS42, 0.8 mile from FS46	**Road:** Paved
L/L: N44 58 187/W121 52 576	**Access:** Park and carry, short distance
Cell: US 26	**Tents:** 2-3
	El: 3200
Lndmk: Confluence of Pinhead and Lost Creeks	**RV:** MH and TT

Description: This site on sparsely traveled FS42 puts you a stone's throw from a creek rivaling the Clackamas at its headwaters and whose many pools all seem to hold the promise of a hungry trout lurking beneath the water.

Getting there: From Estacada on OR224, drive approximately 26 miles to Rainbow Campground and milepost 50. Continue ahead 14 miles on FS46 to junction with FS42. Go left 0.8 mile on 42 to site. Find campsite near a narrow bridge crossing Lost Creek upstream of the confluence of the two creeks. MVUM E8

Loc: 0.1 mile from the end of the FS4670 bridge across the Clackamas	**Road:** Dirt
L/L: N44 57 985/W121 53 735	**Access:** Drive to camp
Cell: US 26, south end of Timothy Lake	**Tents:** 10-15
	El: 2250
Lndmk: FS4670 bridge over Clackamas	**RV:** MH yes, TT's?

Camp Free in the Mount Hood National Forest | 125

(Site 29) Description: A prime site on the river that should satisfy all the yearnings of the summertime camper's heart. Get there early. People know about this place. The good news about this site is that it is actually a "two-fer". Take the path upstream a couple hundred yards along the west bank of the river and you will discover another very secluded site suitable for maybe one tent.

Getting there: From Estacada on OR224, drive approximately 26 miles to Rainbow Campground and milepost 50. Continue ahead 15.2 miles on FS46. Go right 0.3 mile at FS4670. Go right after crossing the bridge and look for dirt road #155 leading down to the river about a hundred or so yards from the bridge. Find campsites where the road levels out on the river bottom below. MVUM E8

30

Loc: FS4670, 0.3 mile from FS46	**Road:** Gravel
L/L: N44 57 937/W121 53 667	**Access:** Drive to camp
Cell: South end Timothy Lake, High Rock area and along US 26	**Tents:** 15-20
	El: 3480
Lndmk: Junction FS46/4670	**RV:** On road only

Description: An appealing, shady and open site along a shallower section of the Clackamas. The large and centrally located fire ring makes it ideal for a family or group. Get there early.

Getting there: From Estacada on OR224, drive approximately 26 miles to Rainbow Campground and milepost 50. Continue ahead another 15.2 miles on FS46. Go right 0.3 mile at FS4670. Site is to the left at the end of a short downhill grade just before the bridge across the Clackamas. MVUM E8

31

Loc: FS4670, 0.3 mile from FS46	**Road:** Gravel
L/L: N44 57 937/W121 53 667	**Access:** Park and carry
Cell: South end Timothy Lake, High Rock area, US 26	**Tents:** 4-5
	El: 2310
Lndmk: Junction FS46/4670	**RV:** No

Description: This small park-and-carry site is not to be passed up. It is very private and ringed on all sides with tall trees, and, with its large fire ring, is an ideal retreat for a small party looking for some privacy on the river. Access is near the bridge, down a short steep bank to the right of the road.

Getting there: From Estacada on OR224, drive approximately 26 miles to Rainbow Campground and milepost 50. Continue ahead another 15.2 miles on FS46. Go right 0.3 mile at FS4670. Find camp on right, just across the road from #30. MVUM E8

Loc: FS4671, 2.2 miles from 4670 bridge over the Clackamas	Road: Gravel
L/L: N44 56 166/W121 54 303	Access: Drive to camp, short carry
Cell: South end Timothy Lake, High Rock area, US 26	Tents: 4-5
	El: 2620
Lndmk: FS4670 bridge over the Clackamas, 2.2 miles	RV: Use judgment

Description: Boisterous little Rhododendron Creek comes bouncing out of a cool, shaded ravine and down a series of charming rock terraces in front of this campsite, then passes under FS4671 through a large culvert. A painstakingly constructed reflective fire ring left by some industrious previous party will provide you and yours with heat if the weather turns cool. There is room for only a couple of smaller tents toward the rear of camp, but there's plenty of room for more closer to the road. Use judgment with RV's. The terrain here makes leveling difficult.

Getting there: From Estacada on OR224, drive approximately 26 miles to Rainbow Campground and milepost 50. Continue ahead another 15.2 miles on FS46. Go right 0.3 mile at FS4670 to bridge. Follow FS4670 one mile to junction with FS4671, then go straight on FS4671 for 1.2 miles to camp, on right, where road curves to the left. MVUM D8

Loc: FS4672	Road: Paved
L/L: N44 58 219/W121 56 912	Access: Park and carry, short distance
Cell: South end Timothy Lake, High Rock area, along US 26	Tents: 2-3
	El: 3850
Lndmk: Junction FS4670/4672	RV: Small MH

Description: Lowe Creek sings a pleasant, chuckling tenor as it meanders its leisurely way through camp, in a stand of tall, straight Douglas fir trees.

Getting there: From Estacada on OR224, drive approximately 26 miles to Rainbow Campground and milepost 50. Continue ahead another 15.2 miles on FS46. Go right 0.3 mile at FS4670. After crossing the bridge, continue another 5.2 miles on FS4670, taking care to follow it sharply right at about one mile from the bridge. Go left 0.4 mile on FS4672 to a gravel road on the left. Park and carry gear about 100 yards to camp. MVUM D8

Loc: FS4671-160 (Spur 160 off FS4671), near Fawn Creek	Road: Gravel
L/L: N44 55 118/W121 54 397	Access: Drive to camp
Cell: South end Timothy Lake, High Rock area, US 26	Tents: 5-6
	El: 2740
Lndmk: Junction FS4670/4671, 2.1 miles	RV: MH

Description: This site is located where the road is blocked by a berm near Fawn Creek. It offers the chance to relax and enjoy the sounds of the forest near a peaceful mountain creek that is large enough to look fishable. Bring your mountain bike and ride Spur160 beyond the berm.

Getting there: From Estacada on OR224, drive approximately 26 miles to Rainbow Campground and milepost 50. Continue ahead on FS46 another 15.2 miles. Go right 0.3 mile at FS4670. Follow FS4670 to where it turns to the right at one mile beyond the bridge, then continue 2.1 miles on FS4671 and go left 0.4 mile on spur 160 to the berm and creek. Spur 160 was surprisingly smooth and drivable in the summer of 2010. MVUM D8

Loc: Where Fawn Creek crosses FS4671	Road: Gravel
L/L: N44 55 101/W121 54 759	Access: Park and carry short distance over rough trail
Cell: South end Timothy Lake, High Rock area, US 26	Tents: 1-2
	El: 2940
Lndmk: FS4670/4671	RV: No

Description: Because of the picturesque series of mini-waterfalls and pools formed by Fawn Creek as it works its way through several layers of rocky terraces here, this site is more of a photo-op than a campsite. Though the place fairly begs the camper to set down his or her tent and stay a while, there are scant few tent sites available. The site is located on a wide, newly-graveled section of FS4671. Access to the creek is by a rough and little-used trail. Good luck to those who try camping here. You probably won't have to worry about unexpected company, at least not the two-legged variety.

Getting there: From Estacada on OR224, drive approximately 26 miles to Rainbow Campground and milepost 50. Continue ahead on FS46 another 15.2 miles. Go right 0.3 mile at FS4670. Follow FS4670 to where it turns to the right at one mile beyond the bridge, then continue on FS4671 another 2.8 miles to site, on right, at a sharp bend in the road. MVUM D8

Loc: FS46, 20.5 miles from Rainbow Cg.	Road: Paved
L/L: N44 54 356/W121 53 406	Access: Park and carry
Cell: South end Timothy Lake, High Rock area, US 26	Tents: 3-4
	El: 2520
Lndmk: Bridge over Clackamas, one-tenth mile south	RV: No

Description: While not quite as charming as the site just to the north at 20.3 miles from Rainbow Campground, this site offers the advantages of river access as well as a small, private creek.

Getting there: From Estacada go 26 miles on OR 224 to milepost 50 at Rainbow Campground, then continue straight on FS46. At 20.5 miles look for a gravel driveway to the right. Carry gear a few hundred feet to campsite. A rough path leads about 75 yards down to the creek. MVUM E8

Loc: FS46, 0.1 mile beyond bridge over Clackamas at 20.6 miles from MP50	**Road:** Primitive
L/L: N44 54 217/W121 53 448	**Access:** Park and carry
Cell: South end Timothy Lake, High Rock area, US 26	**Tents:** 5-10
	El: 2640
Lndmk: Bridge over Clackamas at 20.6 miles from MP50	**RV:** No

Description: The dirt track that leads to this camp also leads to a second site nearer the river a few hundred yards beyond the first. *Caution! The river is considerably narrower and swifter here.*

Getting there: From Estacada go 26 miles on OR 224 to milepost 50 at Rainbow Campground, then continue straight on FS46. At 20.7 miles (and 0.1 mile past the bridge), look for a dirt track which curves to the right and leads to the first site, a large, open campsite in the trees. MVUM E8

Loc: FS46, 20.7 miles past Rainbow Cg.	**Road:** Paved
L/L: N44 54 217/W121 53 448	**Access:** Park and carry
Cell: US 26, south end Timothy Lake	**Tents:** 4-5
	El: 2640
Lndmk: Bridge over Clackamas, one-tenth mile north	**RV:** No

Description: This site is on a happy little section of the upper Clackamas, with fir trees, flowers, shade and a breeze from the river. A back eddy of the river forms a pool good for a short soak on a hot day.

Getting there: From Estacada, go 26 miles on OR 224 to milepost 50 at Rainbow Campground, then continue straight on FS46. At 20.7 miles (and 0.1 mile past the bridge) look for a short road leading back toward the river to campsite. MVUM E8

Loc: FS 46, 20.3 miles from Rainbow Cg. and MP50	Road: Paved
L/L: N44 54 404/W121 53 387	Access: Park and carry
Cell: US 26, south end Timothy Lake, High Rock area	Tents: Many
	El: 2520
Lndmk: Bridge across the Clackamas, @ 20.6 miles from Rainbow Cg.	RV: No

Description: This camp gives access to the river by foot only. Large rocks prevent passage of vehicles. The site features a large central fire ring, which might make it a good choice for a large party without children, since the river is swift at this point.

Getting there: From Estacada, go 26 miles on OR 224 to milepost 50 at Rainbow Campground, then continue straight on FS46. At 20.3 miles find a gravel path leading 100 yards into the woods to the right. Follow a wide footpath to an embankment overlooking an outside bend of the river. MVUM E8

Loc: Spur 330, 0.4 mile off FS46	Road: Gravel drive to camp
L/L: N44 51 755/W121 52 230	Access: Drive to camp
Cell: US 26	Tents: 3-4
	El: 3180
Lndmk: Junction FS46/spur330	RV: Use judgment

Description: These two sites on opposite sides of spur 330 are located on an unnamed but rambunctious little creek. In the summer of 2010 I found this site to have been left littered and disrespected, so you might have to break out the garbage glomper and spend a few minutes policing the area before you settle in to enjoy the satisfaction of the righteous for the duration of your stay.

Getting there: From Estacada, go 26 miles on OR 224 to milepost 50 at Rainbow Campground, then continue straight on FS46. At 23.5 miles follow spur 330 to the right 0.4 mile to campsites, where creek crosses under road. MVUM E9

Loc: East side of FS46, 0.7 mile past the north end of spur 330	Road: Dirt
L/L: N44 51 356/W121 511 948	Access: Park and carry, 300 yds +/-
Cell: US 26	Tents: 5-6
	El: 3465
Lndmk: Junction FS46/spur 330	RV: Use judgment

Description: This little-used site is an understated gem set in a grove of tall fir trees that provide shade during the heat of the day without blocking the late evening sunlight. A small, unnamed creek that wasn't supposed to be there was running energetically one hot day in July, when I discovered it and two six packs of beer left there to cool by some previous campers.

Getting there: From Estacada, go 26 miles on OR 224 to milepost 50 at Rainbow Campground, then continue straight on FS46. At 24.2 miles turn left onto spur 350 (which may be unmarked). At 100 yards you will come to another unmarked road running more or less parallel to FS46. Park and carry from this point. Look for a spacious camp in a clearing on the right, about 0.1 mile past the little creek. MVUM E9

Loc: FS4672, 1.9 miles north of junction w/FS6350	**Road:** Gravel
L/L: N44 51 163/W121 53 991	**Access:** Drive to camp. Short carry.
Cell: US 26	**Tents:** 1
	El: 3060
Lndmk: Junction FS 6350/4672	**RV:** Small MH

Description: One would think that this would be one of the most popular campsites around because of its location on Berry Creek, which is large and invitingly pristine, but with nary a fisherperson in sight. One explanation may be that the mostly sloping and rough ground here makes tent sites hard to come by. Where there should have been a well-used trail leading down to the creek, I found what appeared to be impenetrable vegetation.

Getting there: From Estacada, go 26 miles on OR 224 to milepost 50 at Rainbow Campground, then continue straight on FS46. At 27 miles, go right 0.2 mile on FS6350 to FS4672, then right again for 1.9 miles. Site is located on a pull-out near a narrow bridge. MVUM D9-E9

(OVERNIGHT/EMERGENCY)

Loc: Spur 330, 0.3 mile west of southern junction with FS46	**Road:** Dirt
L/L: N44 50 337/W121 52 845	**Access:** Park and carry, short distance
Cell: US 26	**Tents:** 6-7
	El: 3500
Lndmk: FS46/spur 330 junction	**RV:** No

Description: A waterless site with not much more to brag about than its roominess, isolation and privacy. This one is probably better suited to overnight/emergency camping.

Getting there: From Estacada, go 26 miles on OR 224 to milepost 50 at Rainbow Campground, then continue straight on FS46. At 26.1 miles go right on spur 330 (about 2.7 miles from its northern junction with FS46). Just past a gravel pit and at 0.3 mile, find a short dirt road to the left. Park and carry. Camp is 200 yards down the hill, at the end of the road. MVUM E9

Loc: FS4671, 1.2 miles from FS6350	Road: Gravel
L/L: N44 50 974/W121 56 088	Access: Drive to camp
Cell: Some cell receptivity possible along FS6350. Otherwise, US 26	Tents: 2-3
	El: 4166
Lndmk: Junction FS4671/6350	RV: MH and TT

Description: The tent sites here are useable, but a bit too close to dusty FS4671 for my taste. Nevertheless, the road is usually sparsely traveled and the site is otherwise pristine, with abundant wood and a robust little creek (unnamed) dropping through the surrounding understory. There is a beautiful, alpine feel to the place.

Getting there: From Estacada, go 26 miles on OR 224 to milepost 50 at Rainbow Campground, then continue straight on FS46. At 27 miles go right approximately 5 miles on FS6350, then right again 1.2 miles on FS4671 to site, on left. MVUM D9

Loc: FS 6370 near Cachebox Creek	Road: Gravel
L/L: N44 50 587/W121 58 480	Access: Drive to camp
Cell: US 26, and possibly along 6350 at higher altitudes	Tents: 1
	El: 3520
Lndmk: Round Lake	RV: OK MH, TT's?

Description: Though Round Lake, a few miles to the north, is the main recreational magnet of this area, this site is still worth considering as a base camp. Nearby Cachebox Creek is difficult to access, but there is a nice pool visible from near camp that might be worth trying for fish.

Getting there: From Estacada, go 26 miles on OR 224 to milepost 50 at Rainbow Campground, then continue straight on FS46. At 27 miles go right on FS6350. At 5.3 miles you will turn left at the junction with FS6355. Go left again on spur 150 after another quarter mile, then left again (south) 0.8 mile to spur 220, which takes off an a sharp angle downhill to the right. At 2.1 miles go right four-tenths of a mile on FS6370 to site, on right. MVUM D9

Loc: FS6370, 1.3 miles south of spur 220	Road: Paved
L/L: N44 49 727/W121 58 846	Access: Drive to camp
Cell: US 26	Tents: 2-3
	El: 3570
Lndmk: Junction FS6370/spur 220	RV: Use judgment

Description: Coming out of the valley between Scorpion and Mansfield Mountains to the south, the little stream that bubbles happily by near this camp appears to form one of the headwaters of the

Collawash River to the north. It is easily accessible from camp via a short path. Forage for huckleberries along the path that follows the creek upstream in late summer.

Getting there: From Estacada, go 26 miles on OR 224 to milepost 50 at Rainbow Campground, then continue straight on FS46. At 27 miles go right on FS6350. At 5.3 miles go left no more than 0.25 mile at the junction with FS6355 to another junction with spur 150, then left again (south) 0.8 mile to spur 220, which takes off an a sharp angle downhill to the right. At 2.1 miles go left on FS6370. Camp is on the left at 1.3 miles. The shoulder of road is high, so take the turn into camp at an acute angle. MVUM D9

Loc: FS6370, 0.2 mile south of Round Lake Trailhead	**Road:** Gravel
L/L: N44 52 431/W121 58 502	**Access:** Drive to camp
Cell: US 26	**Tents:** 1
	El: 3560
Lndmk: Round Creek's junction with FS6370	**RV:** MH and TT

Description: This site on Round Creek might be used either as either an overnight site or as a base camp for exploring the tempting possibilities of nearby Round Lake. Creek access is via a faint path near the base of a large fir tree to the left of the entrance to camp.

Getting there: From Estacada, go 26 miles on OR 224 to milepost 50 at Rainbow Campground, then continue straight on FS46. At 27 miles go right on FS6350. At 5.3 miles go left at the junction with FS6355 no more than a quarter mile to the junction with spur 150, then left again (south) 0.8 mile to spur 220, which takes off an a sharp angle downhill to the right. At 2.1 miles go right 3.2 miles on FS6370 towards Round Lake. Site is on right, 0.2 mile south of the Round Lake trailhead. MVUM D9

Loc: Round Lake	**Road:** Gravel
L/L: N44 52 624/W121 58 499	**Access:** Park and carry or drive to camp
Cell: US 26	**Tents:** 6-7
	El: 3600
Lndmk: Round Lake	**RV:** MH and TT

Description: On a clear day in July or August Round Lake is an uncut gem shining under the summer sun. This is a place that has been loved and cared for by a few people who have used regularly over the years, most of whom, I am sure, would prefer to keep its location a secret. And it would be a shame to see its sanctity violated by a hoard of disrespectful campers, but, since it is, after all, both a public trust and a public treasure, to be enjoyed and appreciated by all. I therefore offer it to you in good faith that you will visit, enjoy and marvel, then leave nothing behind to mark your passage. There is a decommissioned Forest Service campground here, giving you two possibilities for camping. You can camp near the road by the trailhead and day-hike to the lake, which is an easy ten minutes away (an excellent option for those camping in an RV), or pack your camping gear up the trail and wake up to the lake's beauty in the morning. There are pit toilets and picnic tables still in fair condition, though they have not been maintained since the decommissioning of the campground.

The campsites here are surrounded by rhododendrons, which bloom in July. All overlook the lake and show little evidence of use by campers. The lake is surpassingly beautiful, but there are only one or two places where access to the water is easy, and, due to its coldness, only the hardiest of swimmers will be willing to attempt to do so more than once. The few people I have seen fishing seem to prefer to do so from inner tubes in the center of the lake. Water for camp use is available from a stream which flows into the lake near the camping area. Those who camp near the road and hike to the lake will find water from Round Creek, 0.2 mile south of the trailhead on FS6370.

Summertime at Round Lake

Getting there: From Estacada, go 26 miles on OR 224 to milepost 50 at Rainbow Campground, then continue straight on FS46. At 27 miles go right on FS6350. At 5.3 miles go left no more than 0.25 mile at the junction with FS6355 to another junction with spur 150, then left again (south) 0.8 mile to spur 220, which takes off an a sharp angle downhill to the right. At 2.1 miles go right 3.4 miles on FS6370 to the trailhead, where there is ample parking and even room for a couple of tents or RVs. MVUM D9

Loc: Junction FS4671/4672 on Hunter Creek	**Road:** Gravel
L/L: N44 53 579/W121 55 743	**Access:** Drive to camp
Cell: US 26	**Tents:** 4-5
	El: 3475
Lndmk: Junction FS4671/4672	**RV:** Use judgment

Description: Judging from the name of the slow, clear creek that flows through it, this site probably got its start as a hunters' camp. It is dotted with tall firs that provide seclusion and shade. Its previous users left a bit of a mess behind.

Getting there: From Estacada on OR224, drive approximately 26 miles to Rainbow Campground and milepost 50. Continue ahead on FS46 another 15.2 miles. Go right 0.3 mile at FS4670. After crossing bridge continue 6.6 miles on FS4670 and 4671 to the junction of FS4671 and 4672. Look for the short, rocky road on the left near the junction leading down to the camp. MVUM D8

50

Loc: FS 6350, near Rhododendron Ridge	**Road:** Gravel
L/L: N44 54 005/W121 57 221	**Access:** Drive to camp
Cell: US 26	**Tents:** 5-6
	El: 4450
Lndmk: Rhododendron Ridge	**RV:** Smaller MH only

Description: If you're looking for a comfortable high-altitude camp in the heat of summer, this site on Fawn Creek will fill the bill. Since it is very close to its source in Fawn Meadows, the creek here is but a trickle, with just enough flow to provide water for camp use. Leave the fishing poles in the car.

Getting there: From Estacada, go 26 miles to milepost 50 and Rainbow Campground. Continue ahead on FS46 another 3.5 miles. Turn right and drive 8.9 miles on FS63 to FS6350. Follow 6350 for 8.7 miles (going past Graham Pass and the junction with FS4670). Camp is at the end of a short, rocky road leading down to Fawn Creek. MVUM D8

51

Loc: FS4672, on Rhododendron Creek	**Road:** Gravel
L/L: N44 55 316/W121 56 607	**Access:** Park and short carry
Cell: US 26	**Tents:** 2-3
	El: 4037
Lndmk: Rhododendron Meadows	**RV:** Maybe small MH

Description: Set in a grove of tall fir trees and surrounded on at least two sides by Rhododendron bushes, this site on Rhododendron Creek could be what you're looking for on a hot summer weekend. Following the pattern of most of the creeks to be found at this altitude, Rhododendron Creek is more of a trickle than a roar. But the privacy and seclusion you will find along this sparsely traveled road, coupled with the cool feeling of being close to an immense and silent mountain sky, may be just what the doctor ordered. The size of this location automatically limits it to use by a smaller, more intimate party. Try nearby Fadeway Spring for water.

Getting there: From Estacada on OR224, drive approximately 26 miles to Rainbow Campground and milepost 50. Continue ahead on FS46 another 15.2 miles. Go right 0.3 mile at FS4670. After crossing a bridge, continue on FS4670 another 5.2 miles, taking care to follow it sharply right at about one mile from the bridge. Go left 5.4 miles on FS4672 to Fawn Creek. Park and carry to camp, about 100 yards off the road. MVUM D8

Loc: Jazz Creek, along spur 160	**Road:** Gravel
L/L: N44 55 167/W121 58 983	**Access:** Park and short carry
Cell: US 26	**Tents:** 2-3
	El: 3500
Lndmk: Beaver Dam Quarry	**RV:** Small MH

Description: Whether you are a fisherperson or nature lover, Jazz Creek is a classic mountain riffle that will call you to stop for a visit. If you are looking to stay overnight, however, you might be a bit disappointed by the accommodations. The nearest camp is 200 feet north of Jazz Creek in a shady clearing. There is no fire ring, despite abundant evidence of previous use. You can build one, however. The shores of the creek are brushy downstream and upstream of the road, which might make casting a fly difficult, but there is easy access to the creek near the road.

Getting there: From Estacada go 26 miles to milepost 50 and Rainbow Campground. Continue ahead on FS46 another 3.5 miles. Turn right and follow FS63 8.9 miles to FS6350. Drive 3.2 miles on 6350, then turn right on Spur 160. Stay left where the road splits at two miles. You will see the potential campsite on the right as you approach Jazz Creek, one-tenth of a mile beyond the split. MVUM D8

Loc: On Peat Creek Road	**Road:** Gravel
L/L: N44 53 751/W122 00 283	**Access:** Drive to camp. Do not cross bridge
Cell: US 26, High Rock area, south end Timothy Lake	**Tents:** 10-20
	El: 2354
Lndmk: East Fork, Collawash River	**RV:** Use judgment

Description: Despite the fact that this camp near the Bull of the Woods Wilderness area will accommodate many parties, its location at the end of the road gives it a feeling of remoteness. These sites are located near a steep bank some 50 to 60' above the East Fork of the Collawash and an incomplete bridge just upstream from the bridge where FS6380 crosses the river. Access to the river here is difficult due to the steepness of the bank, but not impossible. There is a wonderful outdoor fireplace in one of the camps.

Getting there: From OR 224 and Estacada, go 26 miles to milepost 50 and Rainbow Campground. Continue 3.5 miles, then go right 12.6 miles on FS63 to its junction with FS6380 (aka Peat Creek Rd.). Follow FS6380 2.3 miles to a dirt road that takes off to the left just before FS6380 crosses the East Fork of the Collawash. Campsites are spread out near the end of this road. *A word to the wise: Peat Creek road has alternating paved and gravel sections. The change from one to the other can jolt a speeding car severely.* MVUM D8

Loc: FS63, on the Clackamas River	Road: Paved
L/L: N45 01 889/W122 03 511	Access: Park and carry, a few hundred yards
Cell: South end Timothy Lake, High Rock area	Tents: 2-3
	El: 1280
Lndmk: Junction FS46/63	RV: On road only

Description: This site is probably the decommissioned Two Rivers Campground. It is on the south shore of the Clackamas and across from the pay-for-use River Ford Campground. The Forest Service has "processed" the ground surface leading into what remains of this campground so as to make it unfit for driving, but it is still possible to walk to the one or two desirable campsites left untouched. One route would be to walk through the Two Rivers Day Use Area for a fee. A more direct, though rougher route could be picked through the vegetation on the east side of FS63 near the foot of the bridge. Either way, you are going to have to schlep your gear a few hundred yards over pretty rough ground. But if you're looking for solitude at a reasonable distance from the city, you'll probably find it here.

Getting there: From OR 224, go 26 miles to milepost 50 and Rainbow Campground. Continue 3.5 miles, then go right on FS63 one-tenth of a mile to its junction with FS6310. Park well off the road, so as not to create a hazard, especially on busy summer weekends. MVUM C7

(OVERNIGHT/EMERGENCY)

Loc: On the Collawash River and FS63, 0.3 mile from FS46	Road: Paved
L/L: N45 01 768/W122 03 739	Access: Drive to camp
Cell: South end Timothy Lake, High Rock area	Tents: 5-6
	El: 1540
Lndmk: Junction FS46/63	RV: MH and TT

Description: This site is probably best as an overnight/emergency site for those wishing to travel on. Watch for an apron on the right giving access to an opening in the woods above the river after you pass the Two Rivers Day Use Area. There is a trail down to the river, but it appears to be a long walk. The river is not visible through the trees.

Getting there: From OR 224, go 26 miles to milepost 50 and Rainbow Campground. Continue 3.5 miles, then go right three-tenths of a mile on FS63 to site, on right. MVUM C7

Loc: FS63, 0.9 mile from FS46	Road: Dirt
L/L: N45 01 278/W122 04 020	Access: Park and carry
Cell: South end Timothy Lake and High Rock area	Tents: 20-30
	El: 1530
Lndmk: Bridge over the Collawash	RV: On road only

(Site 56) Description: A prime site spread out for about a tenth of a mile along the south shore of a bend of the Collawash. It will accommodate many, many tents and several parties. There is easy access to the river for water and recreational purposes and abundant shade from the many tall conifers along the shore. Undoubtedly, this is one of the best sites you are going to find within easy driving distance of the city. The one disadvantage is the distance prospective campers are going to have to carry their gear to find an adequate site along the river.

*Note: this is a sensitive area and subject to degradation from overuse and where POYP is definitely the best policy when it comes to solid body waste, but observe Forest Service recommendations if you're not equipped to pack out your poop. And burn or bury your T.P.

Getting there: From OR 224, go 26 miles to milepost 50 and Rainbow Campground. Continue 3.5 miles, then go right 0.9 mile on FS63. Park on the other side of the bridge and look for the trail leading down the hill. Backpacks and/or a wheeled device will be handy for schlepping your gear. A second road leads about 0.1 mile uphill and away from FS63, which gets a lot of traffic by those headed for Bagby Hot Springs. MVUM C7

(OVERNIGHT/EMERGENCY)

Loc: FS63, above the Collawash, 0.9 mile from FS46	**Road:** Paved
L/L: N45 01 236/W122 03 990	**Access:** Park and carry about 40 ft. to camp
Cell: South end Timothy Lake, High Rock area	**Tents:** 6-10
	El: 1620
Lndmk: Bridge over the Collawash at 0.9 mile from FS46	**RV:** Use judgment

Description: Another overnight/ emergency-only spot. Vehicles are blocked from entering this site, but it is possible to access it on foot. Camp is 15-20 feet above the Collawash just off FS63.

Getting there: From OR 224, go 26 miles to milepost 50 and Rainbow Campground. Continue 3.5 miles, then go right another 0.9 mile on FS63. Find site on the left after crossing the Collawash. MVUM C7

Loc: Fan Creek Cg.	**Road:** Paved
L/L: N44 59 540/W122 03 865	**Access:** Park and carry
Cell: South end Timothy Lake and High Rock area	**Tents:** Around 40
	El: 1650
Lndmk: Junction FS63/Bagby Rd.	**RV:** On road only

Description: Another prime site. Set in a large stand of tall, straight conifers within an easy stroll of a picturesque bend where the Collawash slows and deepens. There are two entrances to this camp, but both are blocked by large rocks to prevent vehicles from accessing them. There is a primitive outhouse, but also ample evidence that it doesn't get much use strewn about in the form of used toilet paper. This is definitely a pack-out-your-poop site. Bring your garbage glomper. A frequent summertime visitor to this place told me that it's generally quiet during the week, but to expect partiers and revelers on weekends.

Getting there: From OR 224, go 26 miles to milepost 50 and Rainbow Campground. Continue 3.5 miles, then go right 3.2 miles on FS63 to site, on left. The first entrance is directly across from FS6320. Park, find your campsite, carry your gear. MVUM C7-C8

59

Loc: A few hundred yards east of FS63, near Little Fan Cg.	**Road:** Paved
L/L: N44 59 289/W122 03 999	**Access:** Park and carry, 200 yds. +/-
Cell: South end Timothy Lake, High Rock area	**Tents:** 6-7
	El: 1660
Lndmk: Fan Creek Cg.	**RV:** On road only

Description: This is a beautiful, shaded and breezy site on a bluff about 40 feet above a deep pool in the Collawash. Its location well away from the road promises seclusion and privacy. River access is another matter, however, since the bluff is steep. Exercise care with small children here.

Getting there: From OR 224, go 26 miles to milepost 50 and Rainbow Campground. Continue 3.5 miles, then go right on FS63 3.4 miles, at which point you should see a dirt road taking off to the left toward the river. Park and carry gear a couple of hundred yards to camp. If you pass Little Fan Campground and cross the bridge, you have gone too far. MVUM C8

60

Loc: Little Fan Campground	**Road:** Paved
L/L: N44 59 167/W122 03 987	**Access:** Park and carry gear a short distance
Cell: South end Timothy Lake, High Rock area	**Tents:** 7-10
	El: 1770
Lndmk: Little Fan Cg.	**RV:** In parking only

Description: There is little doubt that this decommissioned campground is among of the best of the many campsites along the Collawash. Camp near the river, where deep pools present the possibility of effective and quick escape from the summer heat. All of the sites here have a view of the confluence of the two forks of the Collawash, and most of them offer the convenience of picnic tables and fire grates as well. There is an outhouse that still seems to work. And, if that isn't enough, there are still more sites strung out along the Hot Springs Fork of the Collawash hidden from view in the woods across the road, though they have been occupied every time I've passed by the area.

Camping at Little Fan Campground

(Site 60) Getting there: From OR 224, go 26 miles to milepost 50 and Rainbow Campground. Continue 3.5 miles, and then go right on FS63 another 3.6 miles to sites, on left and right. MVUM C8

Loc: FS63 at Van Cleve Creek	Road: Paved
L/L: N44 57 961/W122 03 321	Access: Drive to camp
Cell: South end Timothy Lake, High Rock area	Tents: 7-9 total
	El: 1804
Lndmk: Van Cleve Creek	RV: MH? TT, no

Description: This is actually two sites on opposite sides of Cleve Creek. The first, and smaller of the two, on the north side of the creek under mixed conifers and alders, is wonderfully private with easy creek access. On the opposite side of the creek, the other site will accommodate more tents, but lacks the creekside charm of the first. Few mosquitoes were in evidence in late July. Nearby, the Bull of the Woods Wilderness area provides ample hiking opportunities.

Getting there: Follow directions to Site #60 (Little Fan Cg.), then continue on 1.7 miles to Van Cleve Creek sites. Exercise judgment with motor homes here. MVUM C8

Loc: FS63, 5.7 miles from FS46	Road: Gravel
L/L: N44 57 725/W122 02 353	Access: Park and carry
Cell: South end Timothy Lake, High Rock area	Tents: 2-3
	El: 1940
Lndmk: Toms Meadow	RV: No

Description: A decent, though waterless site near an unnamed creek descending from nearby Granite Peaks. There should be a trail leading from camp to the Collawash River, but I could find no evidence of one. There is a fire ring about 200 yards from the camping area, which would be about the right distance from your sleeping area for cooking and eating, especially if there happen to be bears feeding on the huckleberries in the area.

Getting there: From Estacada on OR 224, go 26 miles to milepost 50 and Rainbow Campground. Continue ahead on FS46 another 3.5 miles. Turn right on FS63, and continue another 5.7 miles (or 1.7 miles beyond sites 61 and 62). Park and carry, following dirt track to right for 100 yards to campsite. MVUM C8

(ANOTHER TWOFER)

Loc: FS63 and Buckeye Creek, 2.9 miles from FS6340	**Road:** Gravel
L/L: N44 57 514/W122 00 833	**Access:** Drive to camps
Cell: South end Timothy Lake, High Rock area	**Tents:** 5-8 total
	El: 2600
Lndmk: Junction FS63/6350, four-tenths mile southwest	**RV:** MH and TT

Description: Buckeye Creek is a happy, chuckling little creek dropping through a stand of mixed alder and cedar trees. It features a small pool for summertime cooling. Look for two good campsites on opposite sides of the creek. Both might be exposed to sun in the afternoon.

Getting there: From Estacada and OR 224, go 26 miles to milepost 50 and Rainbow Campground. Continue ahead on FS46 another 3.5 miles. Turn right on FS63 (Collawash River Rd.) and drive approximately 7 miles to sites, on left at either end of the bridge crossing Buckeye Creek. MVUM C8

Loc: Farm Creek on FS 6340, 4.7 miles from FS63	**Road:** Gravel
L/L: N44 56 776/W122 05 124	**Access:** Drive to camp
Cell: South end Timothy Lake, High Rock area	**Tents:** 6-7
	El: 3400
Lndmk: Where FS6340 crosses Farm Creek	**RV:** MH and TT

Description: A very nice site in an open, circular area roughly 70' in diameter. Farm Creek forms a pool deep enough for swimming here, and there is the possibility of catching a fish among the pools and logs in the creek below camp as well. FS6340 is graveled but gets light traffic. The site's openness to the afternoon sun might not make it a good hot weather choice.

Getting there: From Estacada and OR 224, go 26 miles to milepost 50 and Rainbow Campground. Continue ahead on FS46 another 3.5 miles. Turn right on FS63, and continue another 4.2 miles (or 1.9 miles past Little Fan Creek Cg.). Go right 5.7 miles on FS6340. Site is on right, immediately after crossing the bridge over Farm Creek. MVUM C8

Loc: FS6340, northeast flank of North Dickey Peak	**Road:** Dirt
L/L: N44 54 866/W122 05 861	**Access:** Park and carry, short distance
Cell: Try near camp; otherwise, south end Timothy Lake, High Rock area	**Tents:** 2-3
	El: 4340
Lndmk: North Dickey Peak	**RV:** No

(Site 67) Description: The only summertime sounds you'll hear at this sub-alpine site on the northern edge of the Bull of the Woods Wilderness are the peaceful gurglings of the north fork of Dickey Creek as it descends from the upper flank of North Dickey Peak and the occasional cry of a hawk patrolling the sky for varmints. I can't vouch for the fishing in this small creek, but you may find a few wild strawberries for breakfast if you get there early enough in the year. There is room for two or three medium-sized tents just past where the creek rushes under the road. The three-mile trail to Dickey Peaks and Dickey Lake is about a half mile away.

Getting there: From Estacada on OR 224, go 26 miles to milepost 50 and Rainbow Campground. Continue ahead on FS46 another 3.5 miles. Turn right on FS63, and continue another 5.7 miles to FS 6340. Stay on FS6340 for 7.7 miles to its junction with FS6341, and then stay left for 1.6 miles until you reach a large, open area where a wide gravel road joins with FS6340 from the left. Continue on another 0.3 mile on FS6340, going past the trailhead to Dickey Peaks and Dickey Lake to a dirt road taking off to the right (probably spur 340). Continue another 0.6 mile to the site, on the right, by the creek. MVUM C8

Loc: Pansy Lk. Trailhead, FS6341, 3.5 miles from FS6340/6341 junction	**Road:** Gravel
L/L: N44 54 018/W122 06 965	**Access:** Park and carry, short distance
Cell: South end Timothy Lake, High Rock area	**Tents:** 2-3 small tents
	El: 3580
Lndmk: Pansy Lake	**RV:** MH and TT on road only

Description: A charming grove of tall, straight spruce and fir provides the shade here, while Pansy Creek provides the water. The paucity of tent sites and distance from the road here make this area a better choice for those with a self-contained RV. Popular Pansy Lake Trail #551 takes off just feet from the campsite and climbs a moderate 400 feet to the lake, at 3994 feet elevation in the next 1.2 miles. Or one can cut left after about a mile and hike a third of a mile to smaller Dickey Lake, at 4279 feet elevation. Those with a self-contained RV and an itch to fish might camp in the trailhead parking lot and day hike into the lake with a light pack and a fishing pole.

Getting there: From Estacada, go 26 miles to milepost 50 and Rainbow Campground. Continue ahead on FS46 another 3.5 miles. Turn right on FS63, and continue another 5.7 miles to FS 6340. Stay on FS6340 for 7.7 miles to its junction with 6341, then drive 3.5 miles on FS6341 to the site, located within feet of the Pansy Lake trailhead. MVUM C8

Loc: FS70 (Bagby Road), 0.3 mile from FS63/70 junction	**Road:** Paved
L/L: N44 59 168/W122 04 284	**Access:** Park carry, rough downhill slog
Cell: South end Timothy Lake, High Rock area	**Tents:** 1-2
	El: 1910
Lndmk: Junction FS63/70	**RV:** No

Description: Only those who are in fairly decent physical condition and don't mind leaving their car parked overnight in a spot where it might be vulnerable to car-clouting in an area where such incidents are not uncommon should try for this spot. They will be rewarded with a beautiful, secluded site along a wild and rarely visited section of the Hot Springs Fork of the Collawash. The price of this kind of seclusion and privacy is a quarter-mile-long steep downhill hike over loose soil, which, in some places, would be better accomplished with backpacks and the aid of a rope. This site would work for bicyclists who can take their bikes with them or hide them in the woods above the river. All I can say is, make the hike without your gear, check the place out, and then decide.

Getting there: From OR 224, go 26 miles to milepost 50 and Rainbow Campground. Continue 3.5 miles, then go right 3.5 miles on FS63 to Bagby Rd. Go right 0.3 mile on Bagby Road (FS70) to site, on left. Look for an unmarked trail going downhill toward the river. MVUM C8

Loc: Bagby Road, 0.8 mile from FS63	**Road:** Paved
L/L: N44 58 979/W122 04 711	**Access:** Park and carry, 200 yds.
Cell: South end Timothy Lake, High Rock area	**Tents:** 2
	El: 1880
Lndmk: Junction FS63/70, eight-tenths mile	**RV:** No

Description: Another beautiful and secluded site near the Hot Springs Fork of the Collawash River, one where it is possible to park a car out of sight of Bagby Road. There are wonderful, slow pools just right for swimming.

Getting there: From OR 224, go 26 miles to milepost 50 and Rainbow Campground. Continue 3.5 miles, then go right 3.5 miles on FS63 to Bagby Road (FS70), then drive 0.8 mile to site, on left. Park and carry 100-150 yards to end of the dirt road and down a steep 75-yard trail. Use a rope, if needed. MVUM C8

Loc: Bagby Road, 3.1 miles from FS63	**Road:** Paved
L/L: N44 58 295/W122 06 684	**Access:** Park and carry
Cell: South end Timothy Lake, High Rock area	**Tents:** 7-10
	El: 1890
Lndmk: Thunder Creek, one-tenth mile east	**RV:** MH and small TT

Description: This camp, located on a bench about 20 feet above the river, will accommodate more than a few tents or a few small RVs. It is beautiful, open and partially shaded by tall fir and cedar trees. A second bench near the river will accommodate a single tent for those willing to pack their equipment down the steep slope to set one up. Both sites were fairly clean and uncluttered in the summer of 2010 with the exception of the toilet areas. Haul out your garbage glomper and perform due diligence with the offending trash for the next campers to use the place. Odds are they're going to be good people.

(Site 71) Getting there: From OR 224, go 26 miles to milepost 50 and Rainbow Campground. Continue 3.5 miles, then go right 3.5 miles on FS63 to Bagby Road (FS70). From there, it is 3.1 miles to site, on the left. The entry road into this site is easy to miss from the road, so start looking at around 2.8 miles from FS63, especially if you don't have a GPS. MVUM C8

Loc: On Bagby Road, 3.6 miles from FS63	**Road:** Paved
L/L: N44 58 162/W122 07 324	**Access:** Park and carry several hundred yards
Cell: South end Timothy Lake, High Rock area	**Tents:** 1-3
	El: 1880
Lndmk: Junction FS70/7010	**RV:** No

Description: Located on the Bagby Road almost directly across from the junction of FS70/7010, this site, though hard to reach, will provide an experience similar to that of backpackers in the back country. There is a slow, deep pool nearby for those who can tolerate cold water. This was very clean camp in the summer of 2010.

Getting there: From OR 224, go 26 miles to milepost 50 and Rainbow Campground. Continue 3.5 miles, then go right 3.5 miles on FS63. Go right on Bagby Road (FS70) 3.6 miles. Pull off on an apron directly across from where FS7010 joins the Bagby Road. Follow a dirt trail on foot for about 450 feet to a rocky wash, then go left another 200 feet to site, by the river. Walk it before deciding to haul your gear the distance. *Remove all valuables from your car before leaving it for the night.* MVUM C8

Loc: Bagby Road, 5.7 miles from FS63	**Road:** Paved
L/L: N44 57 495/W122 09 490	**Access:** Drive to first site and park and carry
Cell: South end Timothy Lake, High Rock area	**Tents:** 6-8
	El: 2090
Lndmk: Pegleg Falls	**RV:** Near the road

Description: Another twofer site that gives the choice of camping near the road or parking and carrying down the hill to the river. The higher camp overlooks Blister Creek as it cascades down a steep ravine to join the Hot Springs Fork, but access to the creek is steep and possibly dangerous. The sound of the sing-song of the creek rushing to meet the river combined with that of the wind moving gently through the trees on a warm afternoon, can be golden here, even this close to a paved road. Those willing to undergo the minor rigor of carrying their gear down the steep slope to the more secluded site just below scenic Pegleg Falls will find a beautiful and geologically unique area where the river has worn its way evenly through flat, rocky strata, forming deeper pools and slow spots as it goes.

Getting there: From OR 224, go 26 miles to milepost 50 and Rainbow Campground. Continue 3.5 miles, then go right 3.5 miles on FS63. Go right 5.7 miles on Bagby Road (FS70) to site, on the left on a bench above the Hot Springs Fork of the Collawash. To access the second and lower site, take a steep but negotiable path leading a hundred yards or so down to an even steeper embankment where a rope might be handy. Remember, when in doubt, check it out. Pegleg Falls, 0.1 miles from this site, can be reached via FS70. MVUM C8

76

Loc: FS6330, 4.4 miles from FS63	**Road:** Gravel
L/L: N44 57 495/W122 07 071	**Access:** Drive to camp
Cell: South end Timothy Lake, High Rock area	**Tents:** 5-6
	El: 2290
Lndmk:	**RV:** No

Description: This site is probably a good place to overnight on a busy weekend. There is a small unnamed creek coming out of a steep ravine that is easily accessed from the road and a fire ring that needed some clean-up in 2010. FS6330 is fairly narrow, as mountain roads go. Trees growing very close to the edges of the road along the last half-mile before this campsite make it unsuitable for wider vehicles, such as RVs.

Getting there: FFrom OR 224, go 26 miles to milepost 50 and Rainbow Campground. Continue 3.5 miles, then go right 4.9 miles on FS63. Go right 4.4 miles on FS6330 to site, on unnamed little creek. MVUM C8

Loc: Dutch Creek, on FS6320	**Road:** Gravel
L/L: N44 58 991/W122 06 785	**Access:** Drive to camp
Cell: South end Timothy Lake, High Rock area	**Tents:** 2-3
	El: 2250
Lndmk: Dutch Creek and Power lines, visible through trees	**RV:** Small MH

Description: Camp above Dutch Creek on a pull-out where the road curves downhill toward the power line right-of-way. Dutch Creek is a robust little mountain creek bouncing out of a fairly steep ravine on its way to the Hot Springs Fork of the Collawash. At first glance access to this creek looks more formidable than it really is. Thread your way around a few downed logs and some alder trees, and you're there. Dutch Creek looks fishable, but drops steeply through rough, brushy terrain. Wild strawberries should be waiting for you by mid-July. FS6320 ends several hundred yards down the hill below, so don't expect a lot of company here.

Getting there: From OR 224, go 26 miles to milepost 50 and Rainbow Campground. Continue 3.5 miles, then go right 2.9 miles on FS63 (if you pass the road to Bagby Hot Springs, you've gone too far). Go right 3.4 miles on FS6320 to site, where the road curves sharply left and drops toward the power line right-of-way. *Caution! Like a lot of mountain roads, FS6320 can present unexpected surprises. Keep your speed under control and your eyes open at all times.* MVUM C8

Loc: Junction FS7040/7030	**Road:** Dirt
L/L: N44 56 116/W122 12 265	**Access:** Probably park and carry
Cell: South end Timothy Lake, High Rock area	**Tents:** 1-2
	El: 2540
Lndmk: Junction FS7040/7030	**RV:** Use judgment

Description: Sorry, but this is one of those spots I could not fully inspect, due to the fact that it is quite secluded and was occupied every time I passed by.

Getting there: From OR 224, go 26 miles to milepost 50 and Rainbow Campground. Continue 3.5 miles, then go right 3.5 miles on FS63 to Bagby Road (FS70). Follow Bagby Road 9.2 miles to where it splits into FS7040 and FS7030. Camp is located off a dirt road that leads north to Nohorn Creek, which is about 200 yards away. MVUM B8

Loc: Where Hugh Creek crosses under FS70	**Road:** Gravel
L/L: N44 56 141/W122 12 087	**Access:** Park and carry, short distance
Cell: South end Timothy Lake, High Rock area	**Tents:** 4-5
	El: 2520
Lndmk: Junction FS70/7030/7040, 0.25 mile	**RV:** MH and TT

Description: A lovely destination camp on a ledge just above Hugh Creek. The parking area is about a hundred yards from the camp and appears to have approximately a ten degree slope, which should allow for the leveling out of an RV.

Getting there: From OR 224, go 26 miles to milepost 50 and Rainbow Campground. Continue 3.5 miles, then go right 3.5 miles on FS63 to Bagby Road (FS70). Follow Bagby Road 8.8 miles to site, on left just where FS70 starts curving to the right. Site is about a quarter-mile before the FS70/7030/7040 junction. MVUM B8

Loc: Off FS7040, 1.9 miles from FS7040/7030 junction	**Road:** Gravel
L/L: N44 54 991/W122 13 757	**Access:** Park and carry from FS7040
Cell: South end Timothy Lake, High Rock area	**Tents:** 1-2
	El: 3010
Lndmk: Junction FS7030/7040	**RV:** Use judgment

Description: This site offers abundant shade, the ethereal quiet of the deep woods and access to Nohorn Creek, which is about eight to ten feet wide at this point, and shows some possibility as a trout stream.

Getting there: From OR 224, go 26 miles to milepost 50 and Rainbow Campground. Continue 3.5 miles, then go right 3.5 miles on FS63 to Bagby Road (FS70). Follow Bagby Road 9.2 miles. Turn left onto FS7040 where it splits off to the north. At 1.9 miles take unmarked road to the right. Campsite is located a few hundred yards downhill near a collapsed bridge across Nohorn Creek. Camp on road. MVUM B8
Exercise caution when camping here, especially if there will be children present. Children and collapsed bridges are not a safe combination. If you have children and are determined to camp in this area, you might want to drive to the end of FS7040 (about three-quarters of a mile), where it will be possible to make a dry camp.

Loc: Where FS45 crosses Memaloose Creek	**Road:** Gravel
L/L: N45 06 045/W122 13 263	**Access:** Drive to camp
Cell: Helen Lake and north, along FS45	**Tents:** 2-3
	El: 3390
Lndmk: Memaloose Creek bridge	**RV:** MH

Description: Located in a grove of towering fir trees with an understory of huckleberry bushes, this site is a great weekend destination, especially with Memaloose Creek adding its relaxing murmur of white noise as backdrop. Grab your fishing pole and hit nearby trail #515 to Memaloose Lake, about a mile away and 600 feet higher in altitude.

Getting there: From Estacada on OR 224, drive approximately 9 miles to the Memaloose bridge. Take Memaloose Road (FS45) to the right for approximately 11 miles. Where FS4550 forks off to the left, stay right on FS45 for another nine-tenths mile to site, on right, just past Memaloose Trail sign and bridge. Take the graveled drive to the right down to the site, about a hundred yards from road. MVUM B6

(OVERNIGHT/EMERGENCY)

Loc: Sandstone Creek on FS4620	**Road:** Paved
L/L: N45 05 173/W122 05 149	**Access:** Drive to camp
Cell: South end Timothy Lake, High Rock area, Estacada	**Tents:** 1-3
	El: 1640
Lndmk: Indian Henry Cg., two miles north	**RV:** Small MH or TT

Description: Too close to the Road to be considered as a destination, this would certainly suffice as an overnight site for a small party on a busy weekend, though the swiftness of Sandstone Creek and the steepness of the bank might make it a no-go for people with children. If you do stay here, check out the hike along the Clackamas, starting near Indian Henry Campground.

(Site 82) Getting there: From Estacada on OR 224, drive approximately 21 miles to the turn-off to Indian Henry Campground (FS4620). Drive another 2.5 miles to campsite, on right. MVUM C7

(OVERNIGHT/EMERGENCY)

Loc: FS 4622, 8.9 miles from OR 224	**Road:** Gravel
L/L: N45 03 720/W122 06 800	**Access:** Drive to camp
Cell: South end Timothy Lake, High Rock area, Estacada	**Tents:** 2-3
	El: 3200
Lndmk: Junction FS4620/4622, one mile south	**RV:** Small MH

Description: Not a prime site, but another overnight/emergency site to consider. Here a small rill forms a waterfall near a patch of meadow at a bend in this rarely traveled road. There is good shade in the afternoon, and you will have a clear path to the stream for water. Otherwise, cool and therapeutically quiet.

Getting there: From Estacada on OR 224, drive approximately 21 miles to the turn-off to Indian Henry Campground (FS4620). Drive another 7.9 miles to the junction with FS4622, then follow FS4622 for one mile to site at bend in the road. MVUM C7

Loc: FS4622, 8.4 miles from OR 224	**Road:** Gravel
L/L: N45 03 442/W122 07 029	**Access:** Drive to camp
Cell: South end Timothy Lake, High Rock area, Estacada	**Tents:** 6-7
	El: 1870
Lndmk: Junction FS4620/4622, a half-mile south	**RV:** Small MH only

Description: A cool camp beside a very lightly traveled, one-lane mountain road where Big Creek rushes out of a steep timber-covered ravine. No mosquitoes were noted. Access to water is down a short, steep bank.

Getting there: From Estacada on OR 224, drive approximately 21 miles to the turn-off to Indian Henry Campground (FS4620). Drive another 7.9 miles to the junction with FS4622, then another half-mile to the site, on left. Use judgment with motor homes. MVUM C7

Loc: Where FS4620 crosses Big Creek	**Road:** Gravel
L/L: N45 03 791/W122 05 812	**Access:** Drive to camp
Cell: South end Timothy Lake, High Rock area, Estacada	**Tents:** 6-7
	El: 1880
Lndmk: Junction FS4620/4621	**RV:** Use judgment

Description: Another campsite on a road less traveled, this one within a tenth of a mile of a delightful creek, which is probably a fork of Big Creek. It plunges steeply to form a pool on the east side of the road so picturesque that it will certainly make you want to "set a spell". There were few mosquitoes in evidence in July when I visited the place, but you shouldn't go anywhere in the woods without repellant. Camp is on the east side of the creek, which means that that it is probably exposed to the sun in the afternoon. There is no fire ring.

Getting there: From Estacada on OR 224, drive approximately 21 miles to the turn-off to Indian Henry Campground (FS4620). Drive another 7.9 miles to the junction with FS4622, then follow FS4620 to the right another 2.5 miles to its junction with 4621. From there, go north (on FS4620) a half-mile to site, on left. MVUM C7

Loc: On Tag Creek, off FS4640	**Road:** Gravel
L/L: N45 04 029/W122 02 516	**Access:** Drive to camp
Cell: South end Timothy Lake, High Rock area	**Tents:** 5-10
	El: 1590
Lndmk: Ripplebrook Cg., seven-tenths of a mile	**RV:** Small MH only

Description: This site bears testimony to having been somebody's party site in the past, and, at least in the summer of 2010, was in need of some attention. Otherwise, it's would be a prime weekend site, offering the camper an almost fortress-like seclusion, a convenient source of water from nearby Tag Creek and easy access to the Ripplebrook-Timothy Lake-Austin Hot Springs recreational triangle. Bring your garbage glomper and do something to set this place right.

Getting there: From Estacada on OR 224, drive 26 miles to Rainbow Campground and milepost 50. Then continue straight another 0.7 mile to turn left onto FS4640. Proceed another 0.1 mile on 4640 to a short, dirt lane going downhill to the right. Camp is 100 to 150 yards from road, at the end of the lane. Tag Creek runs in the ravine to the left as you approach camp. MVUM C7

Loc: FS4640, 3.4 miles from FS46	**Road:** Gravel, mountain
L/L: N45 01 976/W122 00 766	**Access:** Drive to camp
Cell: South end Timothy Lake, High Rock area	**Tents:** 5-10
	El: 2800
Lndmk: Curry Gravel Pit, three-tenths mile northeast	**RV:** MH ok, TT?

Description: This dry site on a breezy, tree-covered ridge overlooking Switch Creek and the Clackamas River valley is recommendable because of the view and the cool breeze coming down the river valley in the summertime. The winds here do tend to be stronger than in the valley below, so make sure your tents are firmly staked down.

Getting there: From Estacada on OR 224, drive 26 miles to Rainbow Campground and milepost 50. Then continue straight another seven-tenths mile to turn left onto FS4640. Drive 3.4 miles to site on the ridge to the right. *Warning: the road gains considerable altitude as it climbs. This may make it difficult for a vehicle towing a heavy travel trailer.* MVUM D7

Loc: FS5710, 1.4 miles from FS5720	**Road:** Gravel, mountain
L/L: N45 02 424/W121 57 070	**Access:** Park and carry to most sites
Cell: South end Timothy Lake, High Rock area	**Tents:** 25-30
	El: 3500
Lndmk: Junction FS5710/5720, 1.4 miles	**RV:** MH and TT

Description: This huge, flat, waterless area in the middle of the woods would accommodate a very large party indeed. It is located on the south side of a large curve in FS5710. The trees here provide adequate shade, though not enough to completely block the sun.

Getting there: From Estacada on OR 224, drive 26 miles to Rainbow Campground and milepost 50. Turn left on FS57 and drive six-tenths of a mile before turning right on FS5710 (John Creek Road). Blocked-off spur 180 on right leads to camping area at 7.7 miles. An alternate route would be to continue a little farther on FS57, then take FS5720 to junction with 5710. From that direction the site would be on the left at 1.4 miles. MVUM D7

Loc: FS5730, 4.5 miles from FS57	**Road:** Gravel, mountain
L/L: N45 03 373/W121 53 639	**Access:** Drive to camp
Cell: South end Timothy Lake, High Rock area	**Tents:** 1
	El: 3060
Lndmk: Junction FS5730/5731, 0.25 mile west	**RV:** Doubtful

Description: Devils Spring Creek is a tiny creek arising out of a meadow to the south. This small site is located about 100 yards east of the creek and may need some leveling to accommodate a larger tent. Its location close to this minimally-traveled mountain road may make it more attractive when an emergency/overnight site is needed. You're the decider here.

Getting there: From Estacada on OR 224, drive 26 miles to Rainbow Campground and milepost 50, then go left 5.3 miles on FS57. Go right 4.5 miles on FS5730 to site, on left, about, a hundred yards past Devils Spring Creek and 0.25 mile past the junction with FS5731. MVUM E7

Loc: FS5730, 5.9 miles from FS57	**Road:** Gravel
L/L: N45 03 362/W121 52 275	**Access:** Check MVUM
Cell: South end Timothy Lake, High Rock area	**Tents:** 1-2
	El: 3260
Lndmk: Junction FS5730/5732, 0.7 mile south	**RV:** Check MVUM

Description: A very private, waterless site for a small group.

Getting there: From Estacada on OR 224, drive 26 miles to Rainbow Campground and milepost 50, then go left 5.3 miles on FS57. Go right 5.9 miles on FS5730, then left on a decommissioned road. Park and carry gear to camp, 200 yards off FS5730 near the fire ring. MVUM E7

(OVERNIGHT/EMERGENCY)

Loc: Junction FS5730/5732	**Road:** Gravel, mountain
L/L: N45 02 575/W121 51 715	**Access:** Drive to camp
Cell: South end Timothy Lake, High Rock area	**Tents:** 4-5
	El: 3210
Lndmk: Junction FS5730/5732	**RV:** MH and TT

Description: This site, though pleasant because of the crystal-clear and private little pool formed directly behind camp by Chief Creek is, unfortunately, too close to the road to be considered much more than an emergency/overnight stop.

Getting there: From Estacada on OR 224, drive 26 miles to Rainbow Campground and MP50, then go left 5.3 miles on FS57 to FS5730. Go right 7.2 miles on FS5730. Camp is on the left, at the intersection with FS5732. MVUM E7

Loc: FS5730, 0.1 mile north of Junction FS5730/5732	**Road:** Gravel
L/L: N45 02 706/W121 51 779	**Access:** Drive to camp
Cell: South end Timothy Lake, High Rock area	**Tents:** 8-10
	El: 3190
Lndmk: Junction FS5730/5732	**RV:** MH and TT

Description: Camp near a fire ring a hundred yards east of FS5730. A decommissioned road leads to Chief Creek a few hundred yards beyond a barrier, but access is difficult.

Getting there: From Estacada on OR 224, drive 26 miles to Rainbow Campground and MP50, then go left 5.3 miles on FS57 to FS5730. Go right 7.1 miles on FS5730. Camp is on left about 0.1 mile north of junction with FS5732. MVUM E7

(OVERNIGHT/EMERGENCY)

Loc: Where Snive Creek crosses FS5730	**Road:** Gravel, mountain
L/L: N45 02 763/W121 51 049	**Access:** Drive to camp
Cell: South end Timothy Lake, High Rock area	**Tents:** 2-3
	El: 3100
Lndmk: Junction FS5730/5732	**RV:** Small MH

Description: A surprisingly inviting overnight/emergency site on a lightly traveled road. Snive Creek has a pleasant and private soaking pool.

Getting there: From Estacada on OR 224, drive 26 miles to Rainbow Campground and MP50, then go left 5.3 miles on FS57 to FS5730. Go right 8.1 miles on FS5730. Snive Creek is located where the road bends from southeast to northeast. Camp is on right, about 0.9 mile past the FS5730/5732 junction. MVUM E7

Loc: Off spur 350, on Last Creek	**Road:** Dirt, poor
L/L: N45 00 557/W121 49 082	**Access:** Park and carry, a few hundred yds.
Cell: South end Timothy Lake, High Rock area	**Tents:** 5-6
	El: 4040
Lndmk: FS42/spur 350 junction	**RV:** On road only

Description: Sub-alpine vegetation dominates the landscape here. Trees are neither as tall nor as dense as they are a few miles to the west. That and the altitude mean that a lot of the sky is exposed, making this site a perfect place for stargazing at night. Last Creek is only about a yard wide here, so don't expect to fish or swim.

Getting there: From US 26, turn left onto FS42 about 8 miles past the US 26/OR 35 junction. Go 8.4 miles south on FS42. Continue straight another twelve miles on 42 past the junction with FS57. Go north on spur 350 one mile. Park and carry gear along a primitive dirt road to the left. There are a number of places to put a tent along the way, but the best camping is about a hundred yards past the stream. Note: It is also possible to access this camp via FS4210 from the Clackamas River area, as well. MVUM E7

Loc: FS5730, 0.1 mile from FS5740/5730 junction	**Road:** Dirt
L/L: N45 04 633/W121 48 529	**Access:** Park and carry
Cell: South end Timothy Lake	**Tents:** 2-3
	El: 3418
Lndmk: Junction FS5730/5740	**RV:** MH and TT

Description: Though there is a stream nearby, it is difficult to access, making this a de facto dry camp. Hopefully, the solitude will compensate for the lack of access to water. The most desirable camp is about a hundred yards off FS5730, near a primitive, rocky road. The stream meanders closer to the road about a quarter-mile to the north, but it is very small and difficult to get to through the brush. This area is fairly dry and does not offer the shade of tall conifers.

Getting there: From US 26, turn left onto FS42 about 8 miles past the US 26/OR 35 junction. Go 8.4 miles south on FS42. Turn right on FS57 and go approximately 3.3 miles to the south end of Timothy Lake. Turn left and go 2.5 miles south on FS5740 to FS5730. Turn right and drive another 0.1 mile. Find campsites along spur road 250, on right. Park and carry MVUM E7

Loc: FS5740, on Stone Creek, 3.4 miles south of FS57 and Timothy Lake		**Road:** Gravel
L/L: N45 04 071/W121 47 975		**Access:** Drive to camp
Cell: South end Timothy Lake, High Rock area		**Tents:** 3-4
		El: 3450
Lndmk: FS5730, 0.8 mile north		**RV:** MH and TT

Description: A faded gem of a site: In the summer of 2010 I found that this beautiful and secluded site on picturesque Stone Creek had been left badly littered by a previous user. It may require clean-up before it is fit for use again.

Getting there: From US 26, turn left onto FS42 about 8 miles past the US 26/OR 35 junction. Go 8.4 miles south on FS42. Turn right on FS57 and go approximately 3.3 miles to the south end of Timothy Lake. Turn left and go 3.4 miles south on FS5740. Camp is on left immediately after you cross Stone Creek the second time. Turn left onto an unmarked dirt road, then immediately left again. MVUM E7

Loc: FS5740, 1.6 miles south of FS57 and Timothy Lake		**Road:** Gravel
L/L: N45 05 359/W121 48 206		**Access:** Drive to camp
Cell: South end Timothy Lake, High Rock area		**Tents:** Around 20
		El: 3230
Lndmk: Junction FS5740/spur 240		**RV:** MH and TT

Description: This site has it all, except running water. It is very close to Timothy Lake and is suitable for a large party. There is abundant shade from the Douglas fir trees towering overhead, which are also responsible for a thick layer of forest duff that will be welcome as an extra cushion under your sleeping bag at night. Though there are several other camping areas along the road between this site and Timothy Lake, they are all dry camps which are often exposed to the sun during the heat of the day. *The only caveat is that Stone Creek may be an intermittent Creek at this point, running abundantly during the early part of the year and sinking into the sand later in the summer.*

(Site 97) Getting there: From US 26, turn left onto FS42 about 8 miles past the US 26/OR 35 junction. Go 8.4 miles south on FS42. Turn right on FS57 and go approximately 3.4 miles to the south end of Timothy Lake. Turn left and go 1.6 miles south on FS5740. Site is on left after crossing bridge over Stone Creek. The access road into the camp is steep and rough, which may make entry difficult for motor homes or for any vehicle towing a trailer. Exercise good judgment. Spur 240 takes off to the west along the southern edge of this site. MVUM E7

Loc: Last Creek on spur 370, off FS42 about 3 miles from FS46	**Road:** Gravel
L/L: N44 58 365/W121 50 411	**Access:** Drive to camp
Cell: South end Timothy Lake, High Rock area	**Tents:** 1
	El: 3000
Lndmk: Junction spur 370/FS42	**RV:** MH okay, TT?

Description: A beautiful site on a mountain creek along a lightly traveled spur road that is ideal for a single small motor home, though leveling may be a bit of a problem. The site features a flower-covered terrace above a creek that keeps a tight configuration as it flows past camp and passes under spur 370.

Getting there: From Estacada on OR224, drive approximately 26 miles to Rainbow Campground and milepost 50. Continue ahead on FS46 approximately 14 miles to its junction with FS42. Turn left onto FS42 and go 3.5 miles east to spur 370, then drive 0.9 mile north to site on Last Creek, which may be recognizable by its flowered terrace on the creek during the summer months. MVUM E8
Note: The signage identifying this road was not clear in 2010. It may be either Spur 370 or FS4210.

Loc: FS4690, 4 miles from FS46, on the upper Clackamas	**Road:** Paved
L/L: N44 52 246/W121 49 451	**Access:** Drive to camp
Cell: South end Timothy Lake, High Rock area	**Tents:** 4-5
	El: 3800
Lndmk: FS4690 bridge across the upper Clackamas	**RV:** Small MH

Description: A charming site set in a grove of fir trees. It features a rough turn-around that might be tricky for a small motor home. Water is available from the river below.

Getting there: From Estacada, go 26 miles on OR 224 to milepost 50 at Rainbow Campground, then continue straight on FS46. At 21 miles take FS4690 to the left. Site is on left at 3.9 miles just after a narrow bridge over the Clackamas. MVUM E9

Loc: FS4690, 3.8 miles from FS46, on the upper Clackamas	**Road:** Paved
L/L: N44 52 190/W121 49 465	**Access:** Drive to camp
Cell: South end Timothy Lake, High Rock area	**Tents:** 4-5
	El: 3800
Lndmk: FS4690 bridge across the upper Clackamas	**RV:** MH and TT

Description: This site gives fairly easy access to a delightfully pristine section of the Clackamas where it rushes through a canyon. Expect less privacy from the road at this site. FS4690 seems to carry a lot of traffic for a mountain road, and passersby will have a brief glimpse into your camp. Campsites may need policing before using, so make sure your garbage glomper is handy.

Getting there: From Estacada go 26 miles on OR 224 to milepost 50 at Rainbow Campground, then continue straight on FS46. At 21 miles take FS4690 to the left. Site is on left at 3.8 miles, just before a narrow bridge over the Clackamas. MVUM E9

Loc: On Cabin Creek at the intersection of FS4660/4661	**Road:** Gravel, mountain
L/L: N45 00 544/W121 52 117	**Access:** Drive to camp
Cell: South end Timothy Lake	**Tents:** 10-15
	El: 3000
Lndmk: Junction FS4660/4661	**RV:** MH and TT

Description: A large, clean (in 2011), pristine, and well-shaded site in a grove of tall cedar trees at the junction of these two Forest Service roads. Cabin Creek may be too small or slow here for fishing, but the site is quiet and peaceful enough to make you feel like settling in for a while. Look for a second, smaller site on the other side of 4660.

Getting there: From Estacada on OR224, drive approximately 26 miles to Rainbow Campground and milepost 50. Continue ahead on FS46 approximately 12.1 miles, then go left 3.5 miles on FS4660 to site, at junction with FS4661. MVUM E7

Motor home set up for boondock camping

(OVERNIGHT/EMERGENCY)

Loc: Where Pan Creek intersects FS4660	**Road:** Gravel, mountain
L/L: N45 01 096/W121 53 689	**Access:** Drive to camp
Cell: South end Timothy Lake, High Rock area	**Tents:** 2-3
	El: 2470
Lndmk: Junction FS46/4660, 1.2 miles	**RV:** MH and TT

Description: If it's getting dark and you're in need of a place to camp for the night where you have access to water, this campsite at a wide spot in the road might be your best bet.

Getting there: From Estacada on OR224, drive approximately 26 miles to Rainbow Campground and milepost 50. Continue ahead on FS46 approximately 12.1 miles, then go left 1.2 miles on 4660 to site, where the road intersects Pan Creek. MVUM D7-E7

Loc: Kelley Creek on FS5720, 1.2 miles from FS57	**Road:** Paved
L/L: N45 03 966/W121 58 515	**Access:** Park and carry short distance
Cell: South end Timothy Lake, High Rock area	**Tents:** 2-3
	El: 2650
Lndmk: Junction FS57/5720, 1.2 miles	**RV:** Small MH

Description: Most will consider this an overnight site, but the seclusion and coolness of this camp might tempt others to linger for a second night, especially in view of the proximity of Harriet Lake. Though its waters run clear, mud-bottomed Kelley Creek, meandering slowly through a garden of skunk cabbage, isn't the rushing mountain stream of your dreams. Nevertheless, it does have its charms if you stop to listen and look. Someone has constructed an elaborate reflective fire pit about fifty feet beyond the downed barrier that is supposed to block spur 130. The site is well back from the road, which is paved at this point and will get some traffic on a busy summer weekend.

Getting there: From Estacada on OR224, go 26 miles to Ripplebrook Campground and milepost 50. Go left 2.8 miles on FS57, then turn right onto FS5720, being careful to follow it to the left at around six-tenths of a mile. Site is on right at 1.2 miles from FS57, along blocked-off spur 130. MVUM D7